WOMEN AND DEVIANCE:
ISSUES IN
SOCIAL CONFLICT AND CHANGE

APPLIED SOCIAL SCIENCE BIBLIOGRAPHIES
(General Editor: H. Russell Bernard)
Vol. 1

GARLAND REFERENCE LIBRARY
OF SOCIAL SCIENCE
Vol. 157

Compilers

Melody Hedrick

Sharon Trexler

Catherine Smith

Cora Bute

Mary Osborn

Bob Brown

Dee Thompson

Sarah Young

WOMEN AND DEVIANCE:
ISSUES IN
SOCIAL CONFLICT AND CHANGE
An Annotated Bibliography

Nanette J. Davis, Ph.D.
Jone M. Keith, M.S.W.

GARLAND PUBLISHING, INC. • NEW YORK & LONDON
1984

Library of Congress Cataloging in Publication Data

Davis, Nanette J.
Woman and deviance.

(Applied social science bibliographies ; vol. 1)
(Garland reference library of social science ; vol. 157)
Includes index.
1. Women—United States—Social conditions—Bibliography. 2. Deviant behavior—Bibliography. 3. Social control—Bibliography. 4. Women—Crimes against—United States—Bibliography. I. Keith, Jone M. II. Title. III. Series. IV. Series: Garland reference library of social science ; v. 157.
Z7964.U49D38   1984   [HQ1420]   016.3054'0973   82-49164
ISBN 0-8240-9165-5 (alk. paper)

Cover design by Laurence Walczak

Printed on acid-free, 250-year-life paper
Manufactured in the United States of America

CONTENTS

EDITOR'S PREFACE

There is some confusion about what "applied social science" is. From my perspective, applied social science may show up in three activities: advocacy, management, and research. Social scientists are quite often these days called on to work as advocates for constituent groups: mental health patients, recipients of public housing, ethnic minorities, and so on. Other trained social scientists make their careers in the day-to-day management of programs that deliver public services. Social scientists in advocacy and in management are generally *consumers* of social research, while others are *producers* of research. Applied social research is *the conduct of social research in the context of someone else's need to make a data-based decision (or to justify one) about the distribution of some resources* (day care centers, food stamps, salary raises, etc.). This effort includes such things as "needs assessments," "social impact assessment," and "evaluation research."

Thus, applied social science as I conceive it takes in a wide variety of activities. The "Bibliographies in Applied Social Science" series has been designed to cover all these activities and to meet the needs of new researchers in a particular field. Scholars confronting for the first time such topics as the ones treated in this volume run into thousands of titles very quickly. Where to begin?

The compilers in this series have been selected because they have already gained considerable expertise in their fields of study; they have read through the thousands of titles; and they know "where to begin." There is a major literature on most of the topics covered here, including rape, women's prisons, prostitution, and so on. These topics have been grouped together in a single volume on "Women and Deviance," and Dr. Nanette Davis and Jone M. Keith have conceptualized the literature as dealing with "crimes *by* women" and "crimes *against* women." This is, in itself, a powerful construct, helping the researcher to understand new material as she or he encounters it.

The new researcher on prostitution, then, should not expect to find an exhaustive bibliography but rather a view of *essential* literature on the topic. Researchers will find this annotated work a highly useful starting point. They may work backward from the bibliographies contained in the works that are cited here. Or they may work forward in time by using the Social Science Citation Index to see who has cited, since 1969, any of the works annotated in this volume. In fact, all compilers in this series were asked to keep this last technique in mind as they selected works for their bibliographies. They were asked to "choose works that, for better or for worse, were likely to be cited by other researchers in the field."

H. Russell Bernard
Gainesville, Florida

INTRODUCTION

In traditional social science and applied disciplines, such as sociology, criminology, psychology, anthropology, history, political science, and social work, the penetration of a sex/gender role analysis into these fields' domain assumptions has affected the theory, content, methods, and styles of research. The outpourings from both the new feminist-centered literature and these disciplines provide theories and findings on women's roles that challenge firmly held beliefs about what is "natural" and "normal." Women as a social category may be the last modern population "explained" by scholars and practitioners alike as products of either their biology or of "natural law." The books reviewed here refute these patriarchal assumptions and raise questions about the meanings of deviance and social control for women and society.

This book is a selective, annotated bibliography on women and deviance that includes historical, cross cultural, sociological, psychological, political, legal, philosophical, and social policy perspectives. Limited to works primarily published in the United States, the book is concerned with the origins, change, conflict, and consequences of deviant behavior and "women's adaptation to their changing roles." It encompasses monographs, journal articles, books, and government documents in English. Emphasis is on works published since 1970 although some significant work published in the 1960s or earlier has been included.

Because of the vast number of works that relate directly or tangentially to the issues of women and deviance, we excluded the following subject areas:

(1) works that are predominantly economic or deal with women in the labor force, such as Valerie K. Oppenheimer, *The Female Labor Force in the United States* (Westport, Conn.: Greenwood Press, 1982).

(2) works that are essentially concerned with contemporary feminist politics or are popular versions of women's problems, such as, Kate Millett's *Sexual Politics* (Garden City, New York: Doubleday, 1970), and

Colette Dowling, *The Cinderella Complex: Women's Hidden Fear of Independence* (New York: Pocket Books, 1981).

(3) works that focus on normative sexuality, whether written from the expert's point of view or the feminist perspective. In the latter case, an example is Jeannine Parvati, *Hygieia: a Woman's Herbal* (San Francisco: A Freestone Collective, Peter G. Levison, Associates, distributors, 1978).

(4) literary or biographical works that offer literary criticism of women's scholarly or creative accomplishments. Examples in this genre are Laurie Lisle, *Portrait of an Artist: A Biography of Georgia O'Keefe* (New York: Simon and Schuster, Pocket Books, 1980), and Estelle C. Jelinek (ed.), *Women's Autobiography: Essays in Criticism* (Bloomington: Indiana University Press, 1982).

(5) works that are written from an anti-feminist or traditional control perspective, except where such works have strong redeeming scholarly merit. For example, we left out George Gilder's *Sexual Suicide* (New York: Bantam Books, 1973), which accuses feminism of provoking world destruction, linking this movement to both mindless technology and Nazism! Among neo-conservatives, such attacks against modernism reflect their unquestioned biases for a romanticized nineteenth-century version of the family.

(6) unpublished dissertations, with a few exceptions.

Bibliographic citations were located in the following major sources:

(1) indexes, such as *Psychological Abstracts*, *Sociological Abstracts*, and *Index to International Periodicals*.

(2) annual editions of *Books in Print*.

(3) references from books, journal articles or annotated bibliographies.

(4) review of books through a fairly exhaustive survey of major academic publisher's new listings.

(5) bibliographic materials used in various Women's Studies classes. For example, Professor Susan Armitage, Washington State University, kindly furnished us a list of recommended works in feminist history.

The book has eighteen chapters:

Chapter I, Introduction: Women and change includes three parts: A. Bibliographies, B. Sex roles, and C. The Women's Movement. This chapter provides the context for understanding women's changing roles and the responses of society and women to changing ideologies and social expectations.

Historical and cross-cultural works comprise Chapter II, which also includes a unit on Women's Studies: A Guide To References. These works primarily represent feminists' concerns over the virtual absence of women's experiences in male versions of women's historical roles and anthropological research. Because of the expansive literature in these areas, we aimed essentially to communicate the range of works available rather than providing an intensive coverage of recently published material. The remainder of the chapters, III–XVIII, are organized alphabetically and contain standard topics in the field of deviance and social control as these issues relate to women.

All entries (excluding bibliographies) are annotated; books and major articles are annotated at length. Standard bibliographic information includes author, title, place of publication, publisher, and dates. Page numbers are indicated for journal articles only.

The use of deviance as a central theme provides an opening for addressing the critical, humanistic, and social policy components desirable for an adequate theory of social control for women. Hence, the title, *Women and Deviance: Issues in Social Conflict and Change*, invites us to examine the various topics and concepts usually labeled "misbehavior" or rule breaking and to relate them to a variety of institutional practices.

This approach to the sociology of deviance requires a perspectivist treatment—a multidimensional approach that takes into account cross-cultural, structural, psychological, linguistic, and historical viewpoints.[1] This theoretical trend reflects a range of classic and modern thinkers: Marx, Nietzsche, Durkheim, Weber, Freud, Sartre, Barthes, Foucault, Habermas, and various feminist thinkers as reviewed in these chapters. What these thinkers have in common is their examination of the problematics of meaning in contemporary life. A central issue is the masked nature of social power and its diverse and invisible capacities for shaping symbol systems. Central questions in this mode of inquiry, as these relate to social control of women, take the following form:

(1) What meanings are treated as relevant, necessary and natural in a conflict situation concerning women? For instance, is poverty attributed as a woman's fault when it results from divorce, or are the two viewed as issues of differential legal and political power?

(2) Whose viewpoint (person, group, class, sector, society) is dominant and why? For example, why can middle-class women receiving legal abortions have them paid by health insurance, while women on Medicaid receive no government support if they choose abortion? It is apparent that both class and sex biases operate here.

(3) What control concepts are used for regulating women and how

have they changed? To cite a relevant case from the psychiatric literature, women who have sex with their therapists were once termed "seductive" by members of the helping professions. This justified sexual exploitation while blaming the woman for wrongdoing. Therapists now recognize inherent power differentials between patient and analyst and have strongly attacked professionals involved in such practices.

(4) How are negative social categories constructed for women and how do they become part of everyday discourse? The woman addict, the female criminal, the pornographer's model, and the streetwalker are modern versions of the "fallen woman" who deserve their outcaste status, according to official control agents.

(5) How do knowledge systems foster illusion or conceal fantasies about women's real existence? For example, pornography denies or obliterates altogether women's non-sexual roles; while, traditional legal systems ignore the woman's essential lack of choice in a domestic violence situation. Leaving, she may lose her children and her means of subsistence; staying, she may lose her life.

(6) How are standards employed for abandoning some knowledge systems and technologies and sustaining others? We can illustrate this by pointing to widespread changes in conceptions about rape brought about by the feminist movement which have challenged philosophical, legal, and medical assumptions about the woman's rape experience. New knowledge by scholars, legal systems and social movement partisans resulted in higher prosecution rates for offenders and innovative counseling programs for offenders and victims.

In these questions we adopt a "geneological" strategy, adapted from Michel Foucault,[2] to explore the originating site of control and to see how such constructs take on an objective character. Thus, what is apparently not deviant at all, such as singlehood, divorce, separation, and widowhood, are revealed as behavioral departures from the normal with objective consequences for women's well-being. That women remain tied to and dependent upon men is the dominant social reality. Women without men remain outsiders; a morally suspect category.

Female deviance is often different in form, content, and style than male misbehavior. Categories such as abortion, pornography, prostitution, domestic violence, teenage pregnancy, and most of the self-help treatment are almost entirely women's deviancies or solutions exclusively written about women. For example, while youthful male prostitution is on the rise, most of the published material continues to emphasize female versions only. And while divorce, separation, and death of spouse affect both men and women, it is women who apparently experience more profound economic dislocation and status disruption. Violence perpetuated against women, usually with society's connivance, has emerged as a major research and political issue as a result of the women's movement. Whereas rape and wifebattering immediately come to mind when considering the violence issue, the literature also reveals significantly higher rates of female victims in child abuse and incest. For example, studies show that 95 percent of incest victims are females.

Some of the categories comprise only a few works. In part, this reflects the lack of scholarly attention to an issue (as compared with popular treatments in women's magazines, such as *MS*, *Redbook*, *Cosmopolitan*, and others). Teenage pregnancy provides a difficult topic, not because of the dearth of information, but because much of the material is written from a social control perspective (teenage pregnancy is "bad") or an epidemiological perspective, often in the absence of social or psychological theory.

Expanding our discussion of topics, let us examine some areas of special emphasis, including abortion, alcohol and drugs, women and crime, crimes against women, lesbianism, mental illness, and teenage pregnancy. Both the abundance of literature and the social and scholarly concern generated by these issues persuaded us of their greater importance (as compared with the more limited scholarly literature available in such topics as the older woman and female suicide).

One could argue fairly persuasively that abortion has proven to be the most crucial feature in the women's movement or even the essential element without which social change would be impossible. In its role as political catalyst, the abortion movement pulled together disparate wings of the women's movement and linked this organization to the larger political establishment. And in its overriding ideological importance, abortion reveals itself as a revolutionary act, whereby women for the first time in history choose their own reproductive outcomes. In addition, the abortion issue succeeded in extending the privacy concept, once perceived as a legal nicety having little to do with individual behavior, into the area of personal morality. Moral crusades against women's reproductive rights succeeded in the nineteenth century in outlawing abortion and promoting medicine as the chief gatekeeper over women's bodies. Today, Right-to-Life groups continue to contest permissive abortion on the grounds that the fetus is a person, that there is an ethical connection between abortion and infanticide, and that the failure of the High Court to draw the line beyond which killing is permissible nullifies the current abortion law. Like many other topics covered in this book, abortion (especially late terminations) remains a highly controversial and unresolved public issue.

Alcohol- and drug-addicted women are no longer social pariahs, subjected to silence or scorn by researchers and society. As the literature makes clear, addiction is merely a symptom for a more profound set of socially-induced problems having to do with sex-role conflicts, powerlessness and low self esteem. That alcoholic women express more anxiety and depression than non-alcoholic women, and, moreover, are not responsive to confrontational strategies employed so successfully with men, implies that therapy with this group must take innovative forms to take account of women's greater responsiveness to social and environmental elements. What emerges from this research on the chemically-dependent woman is that women of all ages, races, classes, ethnic, and educational backgrounds are affected, and that a fuller understanding of the psychological effects of addiction requires examining legal, historical and political implications of alcohol and drug use among women located at different points in the social and age structure.

Perhaps no aspect of women's deviant behavior has received more attention by scholars and the popular press than women and crime. Debates over women's "true" crime rates focus on the kind of crimes committed, differences in criminal acts between the sexes, the extent to which women display masculine crime patterns (e.g., violent crime), the treatment of the female offender in the criminal justice system, and the relation of women's alleged increased criminality to the women's movement. The debates often raise more questions than they resolve.

For example, one controversy has raged over the so-called "leniency principle." This stipulates that women have always committed serious crimes, but that they are not prosecuted, because either the true nature of their offense remains hidden or the court refuses to convict. Indeed, the argument goes on, that women have killed husbands, lovers, children, and other household members in such surreptitious ways that prevent their discovery as "crimes." And, if arrested, or more rarely, prosecuted for such acts, the woman receives only a light sentence or is excused entirely. That women have been largely absent from the criminal justice records until recently, lends some support to this thesis.

Other arguments counter the leniency (or chivalry) principle, pointing out that women actually experience heavier sentencing for the same offense, compared to men, and that the heaviest proportion of female crimes remain public order offenses (e.g., prostitution) and property crimes (e.g., shoplifting, check fraud, etc.), not violent crimes. What the increase in sentencing shows, it is argued, is that the social control system has changed—not necessarily women's criminality. But because record keeping has been under the control of men, evidence about women's true criminality probably remains unknown.

Sorting out the issue of teenage crime and prostitution has been equally problematic. Are teenage women committing more serious crimes at higher rates as some observers claim? The statistics suggest that this is the case. Research also shows, though, that the societal bias and negative attitudes toward women have had profound impact on the legal system and on the lives of young women. While there is disagreement in the literature regarding the etiology, rates and social implications of female crime, the research emphasizes that female offenders— whether adult or teenage—are an oppressed group whose involvement in minor crimes has often triggered overly harsh reactions by the legal system.

Whereas, academic criminologists have led in the discussion of opposing points on women's criminal involvement, politically active feminists have stimulated the initial society and scholarly concern about women as victims in domestic violence, pornography and rape. Few observers dispute the findings that the pattern of domestic violence is male offender/female victim. What is disputed is why the woman remains with a battering man. Feminist scholars take exception to police blotter interpretations (which hold that women get what they deserve), emphasizing that women remain with abusive husbands or lovers because of financial and emotional dependence. The "learned helplessness" syndrome that characterizes the battered woman should be understood in the context of normal family life in which women are viewed as responsible for the success or failure of the marriage. In such a context, women perceive no exit from such persistent family ills as economic deprivation, family discord, physical and sexual abuse, and social exclusion. Scholars propose that egalitarian marriages on the one hand and access to jobs and community resources on the other hand would offer women realistic alternatives to staying in an abusive relationship.

Unlike domestic violence which has direct and observable impacts on women's lives, pornography is a more insidious act that makes this crime against women more difficult to control. Because pornography treats women as a mere sexual object to be exploited and manipulated sexually, it negates the woman's need for mutual respect and the recognition of rights and decency towards another human being. Writers point out that it is characteristic of pornography to wipe out women's essential humanity; women are merely anonymous, non-persons. This very anonymity suggests to males that all women are appropriate objects of sexual, especially violent, masculine behavior. Thus, feminists emphasize that pornography violates women's rights; hence, it should not be included under the umbrella of free speech. "Hardcore" pornography, recent studies argue, remains a massive onslaught against the integrity of women's bodies, and in the current political milieu, serves as a socially approved mode of violating the relational, affectionate mode of sexual relating.

These selections on pornography reveal, perhaps more poignantly than for most other topics on women and deviant behavior, the ideological struggle between feminists and the male-dominated commercial interests, wherein pornography is an unregulated multi-billion dollar industry. In sexual matters, it has been said, that what feminists wanted was erotica; what they got was pornography. There is a great deal of anger in much of this literature; some of it undoubtedly inspired by the indifference of the political system to pornography as the systematic degradation of all females.

Unlike pornography, which is overlooked by the legal system as nonserious or "normal" crime, institutional responses to rape reveal some partial successes of the feminist movement: the emergence of rape crisis centers, victim counseling education for police, and revisions of the rape law. Legal discretion in handling rape cases, though, reveals unresolved contradictions. The legal system continues to hold women responsible for rape (on grounds of victim precipitation), and demonstrates suspicion regarding the credibility of female rape complainants.

Lesbianism is both an intricate part of the women's movement—the politics of sexuality—and a recognition of subcultures organized around sexual preferences. Conflicts in the women's movement over the political status of lesbianism revolved around the issue of equal participation versus minority status, or occasionally, exclusion from the movement itself. The discord was resolved when organizational leaders confronted the paradox of a women's movement which followed similar hierarchical principles of excluding deviants as characterized by the larger society. The lesbian struggle alerted the leadership that all women must be accepted regardless of age, race, ethnicity, occupation, education, or sexual preference. Whatever form our womanhood takes should become the organizational norm.

Redefining lesbianism as an alternative life style, not deviant behavior, has been one outcome of movement acceptance. Another feature of lesbianism identified by researchers is that sexual preferences may not be permanent choices: women may move in and out of heterosexual and homosexual relations over time. Lesbianism, thus, constitutes a continuum of sexual choices with exclusive heterosexuality at one end and exclusive homosexuality at the other.

Since the rise of labeling theory in the 1960s as an explanation for deviant behavior, scholars have questioned the effects of stereotyping on mental illness. In recent studies on women and mental illness, some of the same questions are being raised but with special attention to the effects of sexual stereotyping. For instance, is mental illness in women "real," or merely a myth constructed by an insensitive and monopolistic profession to restrain and punish women who stray from conventional roles? The studies discussed in this book certainly emphasize that women experience genuine mental disorder, especially depression, but that blaming the victim is an inappropriate and misplaced diagnostic tool. Scholars castigate the lack of help among the "helping" professions in their contribution to mental health problems among women through their monopolistic control over knowledge and their abuse of the license to define who is ill, needy or deviant, and who is entitled to help as well as by their failure to police their own members. Changing the situation requires altering exploitative institutions and structuring non-aggressive relations and radical policies that move far beyond the boundaries of contemporary psychiatry.

Teenage pregnancy has been popularly termed an "epidemic," a "social disease," a sign of family "breakdown," and a demonstration that society is "out of control." Scholars reject such name calling; instead they identify adolescent pregnancy as the normal outgrowth of sexual permissiveness (itself largely fostered by the media) that leads to high rates of sexual activity, coupled with failure to understand or use contraceptives. Unplanned pregnancies in adolescence have highly negative consequences for teens and their babies that range from the stunting of the adolescent's emotional and social development to premature births, mistreatment of infants, and high mortality rates among these infants. Sex education and sexual counseling for adolescents are among diverse approaches suggested by the research to alleviate this growing social problem.

The purpose of the book is to provide a focused approach to the study of women and the relationship between deviant behavior and social control by bringing together diverse academic fields and scholarly approaches to a new area of concern. This book, however, is not a value-free academic enterprise. Conflict over the meanings and implications of role changes among women has impact for both research and social policy. Denying or avoiding the ideological and critical approaches is to miss the revolution in social thought that is currently underway. Taking sides—interpreting women's deviancies and oppressions from a feminist perspective—both broadens the social reality and provides a more humane and experientially based view of scholarship for constructing social policy.

The book should be useful for teachers, librarians, students, therapists, policymakers, and involved lay persons who seek information about women's roles in this transitional epoch. It should facilitate sociological and psychological research on the broad range of issues surrounding women and their roles in society.

The exclusion of many fine scholarly and research works was unavoidable but deserves mention. The breadth and quantity of the issues required pruning the number of items within each chapter in order to allow for the scope of the issues that, in our judgment, currently represent the field.

We are grateful for the dedicated efforts of the compilers, including the students in Davis' Women and Deviance class as well as the moral support from our other students and colleagues at Portland State University and Western Washington University. Special thanks to Lyle S. Personette, who handled all the word-processing tasks with diligence and humor, and Bruce Brodersen, whose editorial insights and skills were only surpassed by his patience at tracking down citations.

We offer this book as a beginning effort in order to further stimulate research on women's lives and social realities. Women's deviance from social norms, once a puzzle, an object of scorn, or a cause of punishment, can then be understood as an alternative mode of coping.

NOTES

1. This model is further discussed in N.J. Davis and B. Anderson, *Social Control: The Production of Deviance in the Modern State*, New York, Irvington Publishers, Inc., 1983.

2. Michel Foucault, *The Archaelogy of Knowledge and the Discourse on Language*. New York, Pantheon Books, 1976.

Women and Deviance

Women and Change

A. Bibliographies

1. Cardinale, S.

    1982.   ANTHOLOGIES BY AND ABOUT WOMEN: AN ANALYTICAL INDEX. Westport, Connecticut: Greenwood Press.

2. Ireland, N.O.

    1970.   INDEX TO WOMEN OF THE WORLD FROM ANCIENT TO MODERN TIMES: BIOGRAPHIES AND PORTRAITS. Westwood, Mass.: F. W. Faxon Company, Inc.

3. McKee, K.B.

    1977.   WOMEN'S STUDIES: A GUIDE TO REFERENCE SOURCES. University of Connecticut Library: Storrs Bibliography Series, Number 6.

4. Ritchie, M.

    1980.   WOMEN'S STUDIES: A CHECKLIST OF BIBLIOGRAPHIES. London: Mansell.

5. Schlachter, G.A. and D. Belli·

    1977.   MINORITIES AND WOMEN: A GUIDE TO REFERENCE LITERATURE IN THE SOCIAL SCIENCES. Los Angeles: Reference Service Press.

6. Terris, V.

    1980.   WOMAN IN AMERICA: A GUIDE TO INFORMATION SOURCES. Detroit, Mich.: Gale Research Company.

B. Sex Roles

7. Adler, A.

1978.   CO-OPERATION BETWEEN THE SEXES: WRITINGS ON WOMEN, LOVE AND MARRIAGE, SEXUALITY AND ITS DISORDERS. Garden City: Doubleday and Company Inc.

Heinz L. Ansbacher, one of the editors and translators of this work, states in a preface: "The theory of sexuality of Alfred Adler (1870-1937) is best characterized as the opposite of Freud's. Whereas Freud believed a person's sexuality determines his personality, Adler asserted that the total personality, the style of life, determines the sexuality."

This book gathers together Adler's writings on sex and all related matters, such as feminism, love and marriage, and sexual disorders. Ansbacher observes that such a volume seems to be especially called for at this time of heightened interest in sex and growing rejection of Freud's theories, from feminists to psychoanalysts. The contents of this volume include sociological and psychoanalytical writings, including the myth of women's inferiority and masculine protest and critique of Freud; sexuality and the individual, including love and marriage, and finally, sexual disorders, including homosexuality and other deviations (e.g. prostitution).

The volume concludes with a lengthy essay on Adler's sexual theories by Ansbacher. On the whole, the book is rich with information and insight.

8. Andreas, C.

1971.   SEX AND CASTE IN AMERICA. Englewood Cliffs, N.J.: Prentice-Hall, Inc.

In this early feminist study which attacks traditional sex roles, Andreas emphasizes the interplay between agencies of social control and agents of change. Changing old patterns of sexual oppression cannot be accomplished by individual acts. Instead, the book shows the limiting conditions under which women have lived and suggests some possibilities that exist for changing those conditions.

The central idea is that the present division of labor by sex is a caste-like phenomenon that provides a cheap and ready source of labor, thereby preventing the organization of marginal groups to further their common goals. Rationalizations for sexual discrimination in the workplace often mask the true reasons, which are based primarily on needs of the economy, not the capacities of men and women. The nuclear family thrives on sexism, fostering a male chauvinistic culture; a "power pyramid, which is hypocritical and alienating." Political-legislative processes are proposed as essential for bringing about societal change.

9. Babcock, B.A., A.E. Freidman, E.H. Norton, and S.C. Ross.

    1975.   SEX DISCRIMINATION AND THE LAW: CAUSES AND REMEDIES. Boston: Little, Brown, and Company.

In this compendium of women and the law, the authors include five major issues: One is constitutional law and feminist history; the second is employment discrimination; next is sex role discrimination in the law of the family; the fourth section focuses on women and the criminal law; and the fifth considers women's rights to control their reproductive capacities (e.g. abortion), obtain equal education, and gain equal access to places of public accomodation. The material is somewhat uneven, however, inasmuch as some selections emphasize the law by providing large or whole sections of legal decisions (as in the Roe vs. Wade abortion decision). Still other parts of the book include analysis, such as a chapter on a sociological view of divorce. The chapter on rape is well recommended, because it presents not only the problems of the structure and operation of laws designed to punish and prevent rape, but also the court cases themselves. Excerpts from direct testimony are particularly effective for demonstrating the harrowing experience for the victim-witness in a sexual assault case. In one rape case, for example, a psychiatrist testified that the victim could not mentally or physically withstand further testimony. The court subsequently found her "legally unavailable," which resulted in a hung jury. The government did not prosecute the defendent. This is a formidable textbook and guide to basic issues affecting women and the law.

10. Bernard, J.

    1981.   THE FEMALE WORLD. New York: The Free Press.

In this brilliant examination of women's lives and thought, Bernard emphasizes the uniqueness and adaptability of women as they create and recreate social structures and relationships. The notion of a female world "in and of itself, as an entity of its own right, not as a byproduct of the male world," provides the overarching premise. This enables the author to survey a vast interdisciplinary literature (the bibliography is 37 pages) and to report on "women's lives and strategies with depth and appreciation." Although trained as a sociologist, Bernard is clearly a renaissance woman. This is a first rate analysis of women's social condition without being marred by the "sentiment for the underclass" that characterizes much of the analysis of social science when examining women.

3

11.Broverman, I., S. Vogel, D. Broverman, F. Clarkson, and P. Rosenkrantz.

    1972.   "Sex-Role Stereotypes: A Current Appraisal."
             JOURNAL OF SOCIAL ISSUES. 28(2):59-78.

    In "measuring current sex-role perceptions," Broverman et. al. designed their own instrument which included 122 attributes, as listed by three undergraduate psychology classes, for being "all the characteristics, attributes, and behaviors on which they thought men and women differed." Arranged in polar opposites, the items were separated by 60 points; respondents were then asked to indicate the extent to which the item described a male or a female.
    Research revealed that stereotypes are still prevalent in our society with women characterized as "relatively less competent, less independent, less objective, and less logical" than men. Men, on the other hand, were perceived as "lacking interpersonal sensitivity, warmth, and expressiveness in comparison to women."
    Since women's characteristics are deemed less desirable than men's with both sexes incorporating both positive and negative traits into their self-concepts, women develop a more negative self-image than men. In addition, mental health practitioners conceptualize positive mental health for adults as being synonymous with those traits attributed to males. These phenomena result in a double-bind for women. If they choose to adopt the feminine stereotype, their mental health suffers, but if they choose to display male characteristics, they are deemed less feminine.

12. Coles, R. and J.H. Coles.

    1978.   WOMEN OF CRISIS: LIVES OF STRUGGLE AND HOPE.
             Pine Brook, N.J.: Delta.

    In offering portraits of five American women- a migrant worker, an Appalachian, a Chicana, an Eskimo, and a white housekeeper- the authors reflect the stuggles each woman has encountered as a result of her background. Not only sex, but also class differences, shaped these women's lives. The New York Times Book Review stated: "An evocation of five lives neither analyzed or patronized, but recreated with a fullness that is usually achieved only in fiction." Not since Oscar Lewis' portraits of poor families in Mexico, has social science produced such intensity of real lives under conflict and change.

13. Coles, R. and J.H. Coles.

    1982.   WOMEN OF CRISIS II: LIVES OF WORK AND DREAMS.
             Pine Brook, N.J.: Delta.

    This second in-depth documentary by the same authors portrays five American women of diverse backgrounds- an advertising executive, a civil rights activist, a Pueblo girl, a bank teller, and a nurse/housewife- and shows the personal and professional experiences all share in common. As in the first volume, the study is evocative and descriptive in its use of personal materials.

14. Dinnerstein, D.

1977.   THE MERMAID AND THE MINOTAUR: SEXUAL ARRANGEMENTS AND HUMAN MALAISE. New York: Harper and Row.

The author proposes nothing less than to undermine the current organization of male and female roles. She wishes us to grow away from tightly predefined ways of feeling and action in our sexual relationships. The author contends that until we grow strong enough to renounce the pernicious, prevailing forms of collaboration between the sexes, both men and women will remain semi-human, monstrous - like the mermaid and the minotaur.
Subjects covered in this book include: the causes of role conservation; peculiarities of human sexuality; female monopoly of early child care; the muting of female erotic impulsivity; the mother as representative of nature; how our recognition of our mortality colors our attitudes; the relation between our sexual arrangements and our unresolved carnal ambivalence; how child rearing keeps women as idolscapegoat; how all of us fear a woman's will; and the roots of adult male domination.
The author is more Freudian than most other members of the feminist movement, but this fact should not discourage critical readers. Ms. Dinnerstein believes that it is possible to grow away from the effects of an exclusive mother-centered childhood.

15. Duberman, L., et al.

1975.   GENDER AND SEX IN SOCIETY. New York: Praeger Publishers.

In an effort to end gender typecasting, the author has brought together current theory and research on the sociology of sex status and gender roles. Chapter One first gives us a brief historical overview of the roles and statuses of women, while chapter two deals with socialization and sex differentiation among Americans. The third and fourth chapters also specifically examine Americans, looking at, first, the personal interaction of males and females, then, analyzing the inequality of economic and political opportunities for women. Chapter six, on the other hand, examines the topic of sex differentiation from a cross-class, cross-race, and cross-cultural perspective. Chapter seven then addresses the problems of men and their attitudes toward the women's movement. The book concludes with a 16 page bibliography.

16. Edwards, S.

1981.   FEMALE SEXUALITY AND THE LAW. Totowa,N.J.:
         Martin Robertson and Company, Ltd.

The treatment of women by the law, whether as victims or offenders is based on certain stereotypes and attitudes toward female sexuality that have influenced thinking since 1800. The aim of this book is to expose and investigate these underlying attitudes and to show how the law has subtly been inexorably used as an instrument of social control over women and their sexual behavior.

17. Guttentag, M. and P.F. Secord.

1983.   TOO MANY WOMEN? THE SEX RATIO QUESTION.
         Beverly Hills, Ca.: Sage Publications.

Sex ratios are often ignored in thinking about sex roles and social structure. The authors of this controversial volume point out that such theoretical neglect overlooks the causal patterning of sex ratios on sex behavior and mores, patterns of marriage and family breakup, and key elements of the epoch's social structure. The authors argue that when women are scarce, a protective morality surrounds them--one that favors monogamy for women and directs female roles into traditional domestic activities. When men are scarce, however, the protective cocoon around women dissolves, and men become reluctant to commit themselves to one woman for life. Unequal power relationships coupled with demographic pressures have stimulated sexual and family changes throughout history, as witness women's roles in classical Athens and Sparta, and the problem of misogyny in medieval Europe. Arguing from demographics, the authors show the impact of sex ratios on contemporary sex patterning and change.

18. Hammer, S. (ed.)

1975.   WOMEN, BODY, AND CULTURE: ESSAYS ON THE
         SEXUALITY OF WOMEN IN A CHANGING SOCIETY. New
         York: Harper and Row.

These papers present some of the essential feminist issues on women's gender role and sexuality. The range is broad. Representative articles include: Karen Horney's "The Denial of the Vagina", Joyce McDougall's "Homosexuality in Women", John Money's "Psychosexual Differentiation", Helene Deutsch's "Delivery," and Margaret Mead's "A Cultural Anthropologist's Approach to Maternal Deprivation." Hammer takes a cue from Freud and concludes that an inquiry into women's sexuality requires that we consider both women and men because "the two sexes exist in dialectic from the beginning."

19. Horner, M.S. and M. Walsh.

1974. "Psychological Barriers to Success in Women." In WOMEN AND SUCCESS: THE ANATOMY OF ACHIEVEMENT. Edited by Ruth B. Kundsin. New York: William Morrow and Company, Inc. Pp. 138-144.

Discriminatory hiring practices have long received the blame for the low percentage of women in high echelon technical and professional careers. Matina Horner's 1968 study of undergraduate students at a large midwestern university is focused on an alternative answer to women's failure to achieve success. Horner maintains that women have a motive to avoid success. This "fear of success" entails a "disposition to become anxious about achieving success due to negative consequences expected as a result of succeeding." She postulates that when a woman anticipates a high level of success, she becomes anxious.

Horner utilized the Standard Thematic Apperceptive Test (TAT) for measuring achievement motive, coupled with the additional lead question: "After the first term finals, Ann (John) finds herself (himself) at the top of her (his) medical school class." Female students were asked to respond to this cue by describing the future for Ann, while the male students were asked to predict John's future. Her research revealed a "fear of success" imagery dominating the female responses, while being relatively absent from the male responses.

20. Horney, K.

1973. FEMININE PSYCHOLOGY. New York: W. W. Norton and Company, Inc.

This work is a series of previously uncollected early papers by Karen Horney that presents her evolving concepts on feminine psychology, as well as her differences with Sigmund Freud. Dr. Horney's earliest concerns were with Freud's theories of psychosexual development. The essays in this volume contain her confrontation with these theories.

Subjects treated by Dr. Horney in this collection include: the castration complex in women, the flight from womanhood, inhibited femininity, the distrust between the sexes, maternal conflicts, feminine masochism, personality changes in female adolescents and the neurotic need for love.

Dr. Horney spoke for today's feminists. In "inhibited femininity," for example, frigidity in women is due to "supra-individual, cultural factors" and not "the normal sexual attitude of civilized woman." In another paper, "The Denial of the Vagina," she took issue with the whole notion of penis envy as developed by Freud.

In his introduction to this volume, Harold Kelman states: "In reading these early papers of Dr. Horney's, we see a woman of wisdom and experience at work searching for better ways to alleviate human suffering." This classic collection is highly

7

recommended.

21. Kahn-Hut, R., A.K. Daniels and R. Colvard. (eds.)

    1982.   WOMEN AND WORK: PROBLEMS AND PERSPECTIVES.
              New York: Oxford University Press.

    These papers, originally published in SOCIAL PROBLEMS, addresses issues relating to changing roles for women. As the introduction emphasizes, images about women have changed, but the institutions remain unchanged. Occupational hierarchies resist more equitable treatment of women, because it would reduce profits, raise the costs of public services and alter customary relations between men and women, and between superordinates and subordinates. The lack of support structures to help with child care and housework or their scarcity and lack of affordability imply that many women confront almost insurmountable problems in their efforts for occupational equality. Sex harrassment continues to be a pervasive problem and other forms of social pressures from employers, supervisors and peers (both male and female) discourage women from trying to attain the better positions in the labor force. Women's commitment to work, then, should not be interpreted as the individual woman's problem, so much as structural obstacles and systematic sex discrimination. The book includes five major sections: women and division of labor, home work and market work, invisible work, women and the dual economy, and a final section on feminist perspectives. This is a sound sociological overview of an important area of social change.

22. Kanter, R.M.

    1979.   MEN AND WOMEN OF THE CORPORATION. New York:
              Basic Books, Inc.

    Rosabeth Kanter, social psychologist, feminist, and consultant for industry and government, presents in this volume a thorough analysis of the American corporation and how it affects the people who work in these organizations.
    Among the topics that she treats are the growth of masculinization in management and feminization in clerical work. In addition, the author considers the elaborate system of ranks and grades in modern industry; the causes of conformity among managers; how secretaries are rewarded for behavior that keeps their mobility low; the position of wives of management men, how they have "careers" tied to their husband's advancement; how opportunity to get ahead defines the ways people involve themselves in work; certain popular findings about women's activities in the professions, and the dilemmas of token status; how certain models fail to answer the "woman question" and underline the need for a structural approach. Finally, there is a cautionary note about the barriers to change, but an emphasis on the need to go ahead with reforms despite limitations. With great

insight and perception, the author gives a complete guide to the inner workings of the modern corporation. She sees nothing but hope for women once they are given access to power.

23. Lakoff, R.

    1975.   LANGUAGE AND WOMAN'S PLACE. New York: Harper Row.

Women's language expresses subordination and prevents the full development of professional and creative activities. "Talking like a lady" implies that men are in control of all the major institutions and women's speech expresses her subordination. Features of women's language include deference mannerisms, coupled with euphemisms, and hypercorrect and superpolite usage. Women's language avoids the markers of comradeship, backslapping, joke telling, nicknaming, slang, and so forth. Like ethnic stereotypes, sexual stereotypes trivialize women, depicting them as vain, fuzzy-minded, extravagant, imprecise, long-winded, and numerous variants on these themes. The author recommends greater awareness and flexibility in speech styles to offset such linguistic stereotyping.

24. Lee, P.C. and R.S. Stewart. (eds.)

    1976.   SEX DIFFERENCES: CULTURAL AND DEVELOPMENTAL DIMENSIONS. New York: Horizon Books.

This book offers a collection of the key influential twentieth century writings on sex differences. The chapters appear to be chosen not so much for their accuracy of detail, but for their strong influence both in their time and through the present. The editors begin with scholars who laid the foundations of twentieth century thought on sex differences. They then trace such thought forward to the present, drawing on classical works and the most significant and influential writers who have built upon or altered earlier thinking. The first section deals with psychoanalysis and its controversies from the 1920's and 1930's to present reformulations. The second section of the book looks at anthropological and sociological theories with both sections representing excellent pieces of cross-cultural and cross-species work on sex differences.

The final section examines the most influential psychological investigations of sex differences and presents the major theories of sex-role development.

25. Maris, R.W.

1971.   "Deviance as Therapy: The Paradox of the
Self-Destructive Female." JOURNAL OF HEALTH
AND SOCIAL BEHAVIOR. 12(2):113-124.

A change in the conception of the role of deviance in
women's lives led to a research project exploring the theory that
female suicide attempts and other deviant behavior such as drug
abuse, sexual deviation and reactive depression make life
possible rather than expressing a wish to end it. Several
physicians and public health workers have assumed that sexual
deviance, drug abuse and suicide attempts are destructive to the
individual deviant. An extension of Durkheim's, Merton's and
Erikson's theories of deviant adaption to anomie suggests that
deviance is often therapeutic for the individual, as well as
useful in maintaining normative boundaries in the larger,
nondeviant community. This study of deviant females in Baltimore,
Maryland shows that sexual deviance, drug abuse and suicide
attempts are interpreted by the subjects as coping mechanisms
that operate to preserve rather than cripple or end life.

26. Martin, M.K. and B. Voohires.

1975.   FEMALE OF THE SPECIES. New York: Columbia
University Press.

This is an interdisciplinary and cross-cultural look at the
economic roles of women and the biological and psychological
aspects of sex differences. The authors, both anthropologists,
analyze and challenge the androcentric view of cultural
evolution--with its basic assumption of male economic dominance.
They give an excellent overview of the complex interaction
between genetic and environmental factors that influence sex
roles and the status of women over time.

27. Mednick, M.S., S.S. Tangri, and L.W. Hoffman. (eds.)

1975.   WOMEN AND ACHIEVEMENT: SOCIAL AND
MOTIVATIONAL ANALYSES. New York: Halsted
Press.

This basic overview of theories and research in sex roles
focuses on why personality theory has been inadequate to explain
the psychology of women. Articles by Broverman, et al, Safilios-
Rothschild, Haavio-Mannila, Mednick, Hoffman, and Horner, among
others, explore issues of tradition and modernity in sex roles in
a variety of cultures. Obviously, sex-role stereotypes hamper
women from moving into modern roles. Yet their persistence
requires an understanding of how women internalize achievement-
related conflicts. Sex discrimination in the world of education
and jobs clarifies the gaps between feminist ideology and
realistic success patterns for women. Sex discrimination in

academe is a particularly well documented chapter by Astin and
Bayer, and their emphasis on restructuring the system should be
carefully studied. This is a well-recommended book for analysis
of the transitional roles of women: deviant in traditional roles
and marginal in modern ones.

28. Rodgers-Rose, L.F. (ed.)

 1980.   THE BLACK WOMAN. Los Angeles, Ca.: Sage
          Publications.

The contributors to this volume, all of them black women,
analyze the black woman and examine her relationship to the black
man, family, community, political and economic systems, and the
education system. The wide array of topics include: demographic
issues, the black family, political, economic and educational
trends, black professionals, depression in black women, suicide
among black females, and the black woman's understanding of
women's liberation, among others. This book offers a wealth of
information about black women as a growing political force in
American society.

29. Sayers, J.

 1982.   BIOLOGICAL POLITICS: FEMINIST AND ANTI-
          FEMINIST PERSPECTIVES. New York: Tavistock
          Publications.

Biology has played a central role in explanations of sexual
inequality. On closer examination, however, the argument appeals
to archaic attitudes, to nationalism, to class prejudice, and to
sexism. Rather than promoting equality, scientific doctrines,
such as Spencer's conservation of energy, Darwin's selection
theory, Clarke's "race suicide," and Wilson's version of
sociobiology have all been used to justify women's exclusion from
education, higher paid jobs and politics. Opposed to the
unexamined biases of these spurious scientific arguments, Sayers
emphasizes how female biology is essentially a socially
constructed event. Along with Freud and Marx, modern feminists
examine how biology has limited their participation in the world;
but also, how social structures such as capitalism have impeded
the creation of real improvements in the condition of women,
especially among minorities and women of color. This book
includes an extensive bibliography.

30. Schlegel, A. (ed.)

 1977.   SEXUAL STRATIFICATION: A CROSS-CULTURAL VIEW.
          New York: Columbia University Press.

The papers in this book deal with one aspect of the relation
between the sexes: equality and inequality. They have been

arranged with the more male-dominant societies presented first and the more egalitarian societies presented last. Between these types are papers dealing with societies that are neither strongly male-dominant nor notably egalitarian.

First, Morocco, Sicily and India are studied as examples of societies that are sexually stratified. Next, the Sudan, Yoruba and the Ivory Coast are studied as societies in which traditional male dominance is being called into question. The impact of modernization on women's position in Ghana is next examined, followed by a paper on Yugoslavia, a country where women are fully engaged in industrial production. In the remaining societies examined in the book, an ideology of sexual stratification is absent. The societies analyzed here are the Hopi, the Bontoc and the people of Barbados. Finally, the movement towards sexual equality in the Israeli Kibbutz is considered and is contrasted with the Arab village that exists in the same setting.

The concluding chapter discusses the papers in light of the theoretical issues they illuminate and attempts to summarize their findings.

31. Sherman, J.A.

    1976.   "Social Values, Femininity, and the Develop-
                 ment of Female Competence." JOURNAL OF SOCIAL
                 ISSUES. 32(3):181-195.

    This article grapples with the relevance of socialization to competence and femininity. The research shows that roles played by women tend to be expressive roles (giving rewarding responses in order to receive rewarding responses) while males tend to choose the instrumental roles (goal oriented rather than interactional emphasis). Females are expected to be passive and dependent while males are achievement oriented and more independent.

    This article warns that the double bind induced by socializing a girl to be stereotypically feminine may be teaching her to be less mature, healthy and socially competent than her male counterpart. The fact that femininity and positive mental health for females may not necessarily be compatible has important implications for social workers who counsel women experiencing difficulty coping with their life tasks.

32. Stockard, J. and M.M. Johnson.

    1980.   SEX ROLES: SEX INEQUALITY AND SEX ROLE
                 DEVELOPMENT. Englewood Cliffs: Prentice-Hall,
                 Inc.

    The authors of this book have attempted to understand the social and psychological bases for the current inequality between males and females. They contend that sex-differentiated personalities and male motives to dominate are ultimately

12

reproduced by institutional and cultural arrangements that give males access to greater power resources than females.
The work is divided into two parts. Part one explores: (1)sex relations; (2)sex inequality in the American polity, economy, family, and education; (3)sex stratification in modern societies; and (4)a cross-cultural and evolutionary view of sex stratification.
Part two examines: (1)biological influences on sex differences and sex roles; (2)psychological sex differences; (3)becoming sex typed -- theories from psychology; (4)psychoanalytical explanations of sex-role development and male dominance; (5)parents, peers and male dominance; (6)sex roles throughout the life cycle; and finally, (7)the future -- namely, a world without male dominance and one with necessary institutional changes.

33. Stoll, C.S.

   1978.   FEMALE AND MALE: SOCIALIZATION, SOCIAL ROLES,
              AND SOCIAL STRUCTURE. Dubuque: Wm. C. Brown
              Co.

   This book explores the consequences of being female and being male -- the roles, rewards and costs that accompany biological differences.
   At the end of each chapter the author has included provocative questions, such as: (1)What arguments can be made to show that men are biologically inferior to women? (2)How are men and women "naturally" different? (3)What is the relationship between a society's division of labor and its degree of sexism? (4)In what ways are racism and sexism similar in American society? How are they different? (5)What data support the view that girls and boys in our society are raised more alike than different? (6)Which area of socialization -- the family, the peer group or the school -- plays the major role in the development of sexism? (7)To what extent are you a typical male or female? (8)How do the worlds of work and the family interact with regard to sex roles? (9)Why is it simplistic to speak of a male role and a female role? (10)In what areas can one say that women are raised to be victimized? (11)How do women and men differ in the way they cope with stress? (12)How are the actual attitudes of men and women toward love and sexuality at variance with popular notions?
   The author also includes suggested projects for students at the end of each chapter. This book is well researched and thoughtful; informative for both students and the general reader.

34. Sullerot, E.

   1971.   WOMAN, SOCIETY, AND CHANGE. Translated from
              French by M.S. Archer. New York: McGraw-Hill
              Book Company.

This early feminist study emphasizes that only by reference to men's position in society, country, social class, environment, age group, or occupation can one speak of the position of women. This presumes that women have been determined by the partriarchal system, rather than shaped and influenced by male domination. While this is a controversial issue in the field, this approach enables the author to demonstrate the sources and nature of social change. This includes the breakdown of the older patriarchal structure, but with its residue in stereotyped ideas of femininity which restrict women's participation. The study has an international focus, and is enhanced with photographs, copies of artwork, graphs, and statistics.

35. Weitz, S.

1977.   SEX ROLES: BIOLOGICAL, PSYCHOLOGICAL, AND SOCIAL FOUNDATIONS. New York: Oxford University Press.

Using an interdisciplinary approach to the subject of sex roles, Professor Weitz discusses male and female roles in relation to the biological, psychological and social foundations that maintain them.
She begins with the biological maintenance system, including aggression, sexuality and psychosexual abnormalities. Next, she focuses on the psychological maintenance system, considering the effects of parent-child interaction, identification, school, peers, symbolic agents of sex-role socialization, and sex differences in cognitive abilities and in socioeconomic traits.
She considers the social maintenance system from two points of view: the family and symbolism. Under the family she discusses origins and functions of marriage and family, the division of labor according to sex role and male and female career choices. Under symbolism she explores the menstrual taboo, witchcraft and sexual themes in myth and ritual. The author then provides cross-cultural depth through an exploration of attempts at sex-role modification in Russia, China, Israel, and Scandinavia. Finally, she offers an historical view of feminism in America. She sees possibilities for change in the sex-role system, but at a slower pace than many advocates would wish.

36. Williams, F., R. LaRose, and F. Frost.

1981.   CHILDREN, TELEVISION AND SEX-ROLE STEREO-TYPING. New York: Praeger Publishers.

The studies in this book were conducted as part of formative research underlying the development of "Freestyle," a television series designed to combat sex-role stereotyping in nine to twelve year old children in the United States. The editors are concerned with the ways in which children learn about social roles from television, considering the magnitude of information children obtain from the four hours of television the average child

14

watches every day. Examining the content of this information,
these chapters questioned who ought to control television, and,
most importantly, what the impact of television is upon the
developing child. The book also includes an excellent
bibliography on the subject.

C. Women's Movement

37. Daly, M.

1978.   GYN/ECOLOGY: THE METAETHICS OF RADICAL
FEMINISM. Boston: Beacon Press.

The "radical" in this title is well deserved. There is a
need for feminists to transcend or "move beyond" the current
notions of mere reformism. Penetrating language and myth, which
has been totally male dominated in the Judeo-Graeco-Roman-Western
traditions, is the beginning for this re-creation of feminist
values. Daly details the systematic obliteration of women as
having a separate human destiny and identity through examining
the role of religion, medicine, witchburning, and genital
mutilations in Africa and the West. In India, the suttee, in
China, footbinding, and in America, gynecology, are all variants
of the "sado-ritual syndrome," total erasure of male
responsibility for destroying women's reality. While much of this
book is written as reconstructed myth (in the tradition of Levi-
Strauss and Jung), the data on female torture demonstrates the
far reaches to which a social system can go to destroy what Daly
believes is the essential reality of women's experiences as a
unique form of creation and ecstacy. Thus, she brands the women's
movement as a non-movement; a "male-designed, male-orchestrated,
male-legitimated, male-assimilated" enterprise. This is an
uncompromising and brilliant work.

38. Davis, N.J.

1977.   "Feminism, Deviance, and Social Change."
DEVIANCE AND SOCIAL CHANGE. by E. Sagarin
(ed.) Beverly Hills: Sage Publications.

In this overview of the alleged impact of the feminist
movement on women's deviance, Davis maintains that a conception
of deviance is not simply an analytic description, but entails a
variety of moral, political and practical implications. What is
called "deviant" is itself a historical product which results
from historical influences and social movement agitation.
However, women's deviance is not a product of the women's
movement, but rather reflects general trends of increased social
participation. Hence, there is now more autonomy and opportunity
to deviate, and on the other hand, new forms of social control.
As women press for greater equality and participation, deviance
labeling serves as a political weapon for isolating and
stigmatizing change efforts. The article concludes that social
change is the major source for role dislocation among women. The
feminist movement offers a fundamental reconstruction of gender
roles that involves rejecting the notion of deviance as
individual phenomena. Instead, feminism promotes new models that
aim to transform sex, class, race, and status hierarchies.

39. Foreman, A.

1977.   FEMININITY AS ALIENATION: WOMEN AND THE
            FAMILY IN MARXISM AND PSYCHOANALYSIS. London:
            Pluto Press.

        Marx and Engels developed an historical account of the
oppression of women. Freud provided the stress on sexuality
missing from both radical and revolutionary thought. There have
been a number of attempts to fuse the Marxist and Freudian
approaches, but as Ann Foreman shows, they have failed.
Existentialism is unable to deal with three critical problems
related to the liberation of women: the impact of alienation and
reification within capitalist society and its expression within
theory; the theoretical annihilation of individual action; and
the tendency within commodity-producing society to view the
individual in privatized terms.
        The decisive intellectual step needed is to establish the
centrality of women's oppression to the organization of the work
process. Thus, capitalism and the exclusion of workers from
control over the means of production becomes the paradigm model
for developing an analysis of their oppression, for restating the
terms under which women's liberation is possible and for
exploring the strategies required for its achievement.

40. Freeman, J. (ed.)

1979.   WOMEN: A FEMINIST PERSPECTIVE. Palo Alto:
            Mayfield Publishing Company.

        This is a book of essays by various women writers that
provides a new perspective to many areas of women's lives. They
point out the sexist prejudice of older research and show how new
human opportunities can be created by changing outworn
institutions and values.
        The book consists of the following sections: the body and
its control, including the population explosion and women's
changing roles; female sexual alienation, rape and abortion; the
family, including the mother role and the history of day care in
the United States; sex-role socialization; working women--
including myths about women and unemployment, clerical work as
the female occupation and women's labor history; psychological
and social control--including feminism and the law, why witches
were women, sexism and the English language, and women as a
minority group; and, finally, feminism as an ideological system.
Here the book takes up the historical background, the first
feminists, the origins of the organization, and primary ideas of
the women's liberation movement. Feminist consciousness among
black women is also examined. This thoughtful book is highly
recommended.

17

41. Fulenweider, C.K.

1982.   FEMINISM IN AMERICAN POLITICS: A STUDY OF
        IDEOLOGICAL INFLUENCE. New York: Praeger
        Press.

The author investigates the influence of feminism on
political attitudes and behavior, analyzing feminism as a
political ideology and as a social movement. She begins with a
discussion of the concept of ideology as it relates to social and
political behavior. Many aspects of feminism are discussed,
including the ideas of the women's movement, how feminism differs
among white and minority women, and the impact of feminism on the
political attitudes and on the particular behavior of American
women.

42. Kimball, G. (ed.)

1981.   WOMEN'S CULTURE: THE WOMEN'S RENAISSANCE OF
        THE SEVENTIES. Metuchen, N.J.: Scarecrow
        Press, Inc.

An exploration of women's culture reveals themes, images,
and styles vastly different from male culture. The areas explored
include the visual arts, painting, underground comics, film,
theater, goddess imagery, music, literature, religion, fashion,
and the unconscious mind--dreams; feminist therapy and feminist
organizations. The book includes interviews with authors and
other leaders in the women's movement, as well as women scholars
and artists in their attempt to define women's concerns and
values.

43. Krichmar, A., V. Carlson, and A.E. Wiederrecht.

1977.   THE WOMEN'S MOVEMENT IN THE SEVENTIES: AN
        INTERNATIONAL ENGLISH LANGUAGE BIBLIOGRAPHY.
        Metuchen, N.J./London: The Scarecrow Press,
        Inc.

This annotated bibliography lists more than 8600 English
language publications concerning the status of women in nearly
100 countries. The emphasis is on social change and the
continuing problems that confront women. Women's status and roles
are examined from the following perspectives: culture and
literature, economics, education, law and politics, psychology,
religion, philosophy, science and technology, and sociology.
Unfortunately, the criteria for inclusion often appears to be
convenience or availability. Stylistic defects were also
apparent. For example, page numbers in the subject index did not
coincide with the text pagination, the bibliographic annotation
provided too little or inadequate information and popular works
were mingled with serious scholarly material without
differentiation.

44. Reed, E.

1975.   WOMAN'S EVOLUTION: FROM MATRIARCHAL CLAN TO
         PATRIARCHAL FAMILY. New York: Pathfinder
         Press.

Evelyn Reed describes her theory of societal development
from a matriarchal clan system, which she equates with
matriarchy, to the present patriarchal form. She sees the
maternal clan system as the necessary first form of social
organization because women were the chief producers of the
necessities of life. Unlike the present system, this earlier
system was a collectivist order where both sexes were free from
sexual oppression or discrimination. The first two sections of
the book deals with the matriarchal age, the first from the
viewpoint of the mothers and the second from that of the
brothers. The third part of the book delineates the transition
from matriarchy, or the matrifocal family, to patriarchy, or the
father-centered family.

45. Rosenberg, R.

1982.   BEYOND SEPARATE SPHERES: INTELLECTUAL ROOTS
         OF MODERN FEMINISM. New Haven: Yale
         University Press.

Rosenberg relates the issue of women who launched the modern
study of sex differences, and who formulated theories about
intelligence, personality development and sex roles. This not
only altered American thinking about the nature of sex roles, but
also the whole course of American social science has been
affected. It tells the personal as well as the professional story
of these women, caught between the Victorian world of female
domesticity, with its restrictive view of the female role, and
the rapidly expanding commercial world of the late nineteenth and
early twentieth centuries. It examines the dilemmas of women who
went on to college and joined the professions. The author
includes a thirty-page bibliography.

46. Rowbotham, S.

1973.   WOMEN'S CONSCIOUSNESS, MAN'S WORLD.
         Baltimore, Md.: Penguin Books.

In this exploration of feminist consciousness and demands
for human liberation, the author proposes a radical approach.
Sisterhood demands a new woman, a new culture and a new way of
living. For Rowbotham, there are two major oppressions: sex and
class. Women can not hope to liberate themselves and abandon the
exploited working class which suffers under the yoke of

19

capitalism. The book has two parts. The first considers the "problem without a name," or the "feminine mystique." This is the psychology of the women's condition in which dissatisfaction is interpreted as personal failure. The second part emphasizes structure or the nature of female production in advanced capitalism. Here the emphasis is on the sexual division of labor and the role the family plays in maintaining commodity production. Rowbotham calls for a revolutionary socialism in which working class women form the majority in the women's movement.

47. Ruddick, S. and P. Daniels.

     1977.   WORKING IT OUT: 23 WOMEN WRITERS, ARTISTS, SCIENTISTS, AND SCHOLARS TALK ABOUT THEIR LIVES AND WORK. New York: Pantheon Books.

Women have always worked. What is new is that women in growing numbers are choosing to work and that the work they are electing to do is not justified solely by its contribution to their families. The question this book attempts to answer is: What is the place of chosen work in women's lives?

Twenty-three women writers, artists, scientists, and scholars in mid-life and from various parts of the United States and from differing backgrounds, write honestly about this question, relating the problems and rewards that their work has provided them.

Because the editors were concerned with the value of work rather than with its reward, they did not particularly seek well-known women to write for this volume. Nevertheless, the women chosen have been successful. Most have full-time positions with rank and salary appropriate to their age. Some have published, won awards, edited a magazine, or served as a college trustee.

In brief, this beautifully designed volume, which includes a photo essay and pictures of the artists' works, is not about success. It is about the place of work. It should provide both men and women readers with a sense of self-discovery; indeed, elation.

48. Stone, M.

     1976.   WHEN GOD WAS A WOMAN. New York: Harvest/Harcourt, Brace, Janovitch.

The author provides "the story of the most ancient of religions, the religion of the Goddess, and the role this ancient worship played in Judeo-Christian attitudes toward women." The book archeologically documents the existence of the Goddess phenomenon which reigned in the Near and Middle East making for a markedly different position for women from that which has existed under the patriarchal religions. She then documents how the change came about, explaining the historical events and political attitudes which led to the writing of the Judeo-Christian myth of the Fall. This myth attributed all blame to the woman, Eve, an idea which has long served as ideological control over women.

II

HISTORICAL AND CROSS-CULTURAL

A. Women's Studies: A guide to references

49. Agonito, R. (ed.)

1977.   HISTORY OF IDEAS ON WOMEN: A SOURCE BOOK. New
         York: G.P.Putnam's Sons.

This is a collection of readings in the history of ideas on women intended to fill a gap in primary-source studies. The order of the readings is roughly chronological, and each is prefaced by a helpful summary, as well as background information. The particular selections have been chosen for their influence in the developing history of ideas on women and because they reflect representative issues of their various periods.
The writings represented in this volume include selections from Genesis, Plato, Aristotle, Plutarch, St. Paul, Augustine, Thomas Aquinas, Frances Bacon, Thomas Hobbes, John Locke, Jean Jacques Rousseau, David Hume, Immanuel Kant, Mary Wolstonecraft, Georg Hegel, Soren Kierkegaard, Arthur Schopenhauer, Ralph Waldo Emerson, John Stuart Mill, Charles Darwin, Fredrich Nietzsche, Frederich Engels, Bertrand Russell, Sigmund Freud, Karen Horney, Simone de Beauvoir, Ashley Montagu, Betty Friedan, Herbert Marcuse, and the United Nations' "Declaration of Women's Rights."
This book is a must for Women's Studies programs, as well as for courses in history, political theory, philosophy, and psychology that deal with the woman question. For persons doing research in Women's Studies, this volume offers access to much-needed primary sources that have been widely scattered and difficult to locate. This work is highly recommended.

50. Barker-Benfield, G.J.

1977.   THE HORRORS OF THE HALF-KNOWN LIFE: MALE
         ATTITUDES TOWARD WOMEN AND SEXUALITY IN 19TH
         CENTURY AMERICA. New York: Harper and Row.

In this excellent documentation of medical misogyny, Barker-Benfield critically assesses nineteenth-century gynecological techniques as debilitating, hazardous and even life threatening. Long hot baths, enforced bed rest, hysterectomies, and clitoredectomies were all part of the regulatory regime. As an historical note on the early medical treatment of women's reproductive health, it makes chilling reading.

51. Blanchard, P.

    1982.   MARGARET FULLER: FROM TRANSCENDENTALISM TO REVOLUTION. Pine Brook, N.J.: Delta.

A biography of the nineteenth-century woman of letters whose lonely struggle to educate herself and become a writer against a siege of domestic duties, as well as prevailing social dictates, has a renewed significance today. The approach is both historical and critical, and reveals what it meant to be an intellectual woman in a male-centered world of nineteenth-century New England.

52. Bordin, R. and A.F. Davis (eds.)

    1981.   WOMEN AND TEMPERANCE: THE QUEST FOR POWER AND LIBERTY, 1873-1900. Philadelphia: Temple University Press.

This book analyzes the growth, maturity and decline of the WCTU, the largest organization of women in nineteenth-century America. In their accepted role as "guardians of the home," women have been involved with temperance from its beginnings in the late eighteenth century. Lacking political participation in the mainstream, the WCTU became a base for participation in reformist causes, a sophisticated avenue for political action, a support for demanding the vote, and a vehicle for supporting a wide range of charitable activities. Under the guidance of Frances Willard and her radical social philosophy, the temperance movement politicized large numbers of women, exposing them to public activity.

53. Boulding, E.

    1976.   THE UNDERSIDE OF HISTORY: A VIEW OF WOMEN THROUGH TIME. Boulder, Colorado: Westview Press.

In this social macrohistory of women, Boulding attempts to portray the development of sex roles from the paleolithic period to the current feminist benchmarks (e.g. International Women's Year). While lamenting the enormous exploitation and suffering of women, Boulding's focus is on the "underlife" structures and their influence in shaping women's lives and behaviors. As private spaces, the domestic world of women is neither superior nor inferior, but it does represent the forcible exclusion of women from public life. In this formidable scholarly work, Boulding takes us on a "walk through history," showing us the repressed, invisible, private, and officially denied lives of women. And whether as a slave or nun, housewife or politician, aristocrat or serf, the conditions of women are penetratingly and sympathetically described.

54. Bridenthal, R. and C. Koonz. (eds.)

      1977.   BECOMING VISIBLE: WOMEN IN EUROPEAN HISTORY.
                Boston: Houghton Mifflin Company.

    Canons of traditional history provide few guideposts to the
quest for a women's history. Average women of the past have
remained obscure, almost invisible, unless they resembled men or
fulfilled male expectations of the "ideal" woman. This book
restores women to history by exploring the meanings of women's
unique historical experience. The book considers women as a force
in politics; women as producers; women in their family roles; and
women in organized religion, including nuns, witches and pious
wives. Above all, the authors emphasize that women's lives have
been profoundly affected by structural changes, affecting women's
roles and statuses; the most visible evidence of which can be
seen in the family. The book's message clearly articulates the
new feminist history: "We the 'new women' are searching for a new
identity with freer attitudes toward work, sexuality, family,
religion, individual development, and sisterhood." The articles
cover a broad historical front, including preliterate, classical,
medieval, Reformation, and the modern epoch.

55. Cantor, M. and B. Laurie. (eds.)

      1977.   CLASS, SEX AND THE WOMAN WORKER. Westport,
                CT: Greenwood Press.

    The editors have gathered ten recent pieces of scholarship
on the history of American urban working women. They show how
women of the poorer classes experienced social change decades in
advance of most American women. They also discuss such topics as
the formation of class consciousness, the work of immigrant women
and women and the trade unions.

56. Cesara, M.

      1982.   NO HIDING PLACE: REFLECTIONS OF A WOMAN
                ANTHROPOLOGIST. New York: Academic Press.

    This fascinating document, the story of the encounter
between a Canadian woman anthropologist (writing under the
pseudonym of Manda Cesara) and an African people, asserts that
the researcher is affected by her research. The book, part diary,
part letters, part comments, moves the reader to feel and think
through sensitive issues in the life of a social scientist,
especially those dealing with sex, love, freedom, and an all
absorbing immersion into research. The book shows the transition
of the author from girl to woman, from guilt to freedom, from
dependence to responsibility, from blindness to understanding and
shows a thoughtful comprehension of social interaction in the
fieldwork experience.

57. Chafe, W.H.

 1974.   THE AMERICAN WOMAN: HER CHANGING SOCIAL,
          ECONOMIC AND POLITICAL ROLES, 1920-1969.
          London: Oxford University Press.

    Although the author states in his preface that "there is no
single, effective approach to the study of women's history," he
proceeds to give a lively account of a fifty-year period of
women's development that has been largely neglected.
    Mr. Chafe treats the question as to whether women achieved a
general improvement in their position after gaining the
sufferage. He concludes that popular indifference constituted the
chief reason for the decline of feminism after 1920. Another
important factor in the decline was factionalism within the
women's movement.
    This volume emphasizes the economic role of women, and it
gives a detailed account of the changes in women's activities
covering the years prior to 1940, when employment of married
women had been regarded as unseemly; to the war years, when
women's work became a national priority; up to the late 1940's
and 1950's with the debate over women's place; and finally, to
the 1960's and the revival of feminism.
    In his concluding chapter, the author delineates the
obstacles to the realization of feminist goals. He concludes on a
hopeful note: whatever the fate of feminism per se, it seems
clear that history is on the side of continued positive changes
in women's status.

58. Cooper, J.L. and S. Cooper. (eds.)

 1973.   THE ROOTS OF AMERICAN FEMINIST THOUGHT.
          Boston: Allyn and Bacon, Inc.

    To appreciate the rich history of the feminist movement in
the nineteenth century, the authors have gathered together works
of seven major theoreticians and activists of the movement: Mary
Wolstonecraft, Sarah Grimke, Margarette Fuller, John Stuart Mill,
Charlotte Gilman, Margaret Sanger, and Suzanne LaFollette. The
contributors are mostly Americans, although two Britishers were
included who were widely read in the United States. Originally
book-length essays, all of the selections have been edited and
abridged to make them more readily accessible to contemporary
readers. They include essays preceding each selection to provide
biographical information on the author, as well as on the
intellectual, social and historical context. The introductory
material also includes bibliographic references for further
study.

59. Cott, N.F.

1977.   THE BONDS OF WOMANHOOD: 'WOMAN'S SPHERE' IN
          NEW ENGLAND, 1780-1835. New Haven and London:
          Yale University Press.

   This period, from 1780 to 1835, was significant because of
the social transformation from preindustrial work to modern
industrial work patterns. For women, it represented major
discontinuity in roles as single women, especially, left
households and entered the new disciplines of the factory. The
shift from rural, artisan, "task orientation" to "time
discipline" in work organization sharply separated the home and
the workplace. Women became identified with domesticity, a
preindustrial structure, in which there was a blending of
recreation, household activities and work. Men, contrariwise,
were linked into the world of work, which was systematic,
efficient, and hierarchical. The canon of domesticity for women
was often a cherished role; it provided a sense of usefulness and
contribution. But for many adolescent females and young women,
the "marriage trauma" with its attendant separations from family,
multiple, unplanned pregnancies, and death from childbirth
restrained women from marriage. By the latter part of the
nineteenth century, there existed the highest proportion of
never-marrying women in American history. The author discusses
the "women's sphere" as both positive and negative for women.
Because it softened the hierarchy of marriage and created a
common identity that made feminism possible, the author
emphasizes that historians should not focus so exclusively on the
ninteenth-century woman-as-victim theme.

60. Croll, E.

1980.   FEMINISM AND SOCIALISM IN CHINA. New York:
          Schocken Books.

   This book examines the evolving relationship of feminism and
socialism and the contribution of each toward the redefinition of
the role and status of women in twentieth-century China. The
impact of feminism is examined at the village level, in the work
place, in the home, in government, and in the Communist Party.
Croll deals with a wide range of fundamental issues, including
women's and class oppression, the relation of female solidarity
groups to class organization, reproduction and the accomodation
of domestic labor, women in the work process, and the
relationship between women's participation in social production
and their access to and control of political and economic
resources. This study offers the fullest account so far of the
emancipation of Chinese women during the last hundred years.

61. Currie, E.P.

   1968.   "Crimes Without Criminals: Witchcraft And Its
              Control In Renaissance Europe." LAW AND
              SOCIETY REVIEW. 3(1):7-32.

   Medieval Europe followed the "unquestioned" model of law
under which "accusation, detection, prosecution, and judgement
are all in the hands of the official control system." This
implies that women as relatively powerless "already in disfavor
with their neighbors," could be summarily dispatched in secret
trials. Midwives were especially susceptible to witchcraft
labelling, but household servants, poor tenants and other women
of low status were also vulnerable. England with its
"accusational model" was less oppressive, and witchcraft remained
an underdeveloped industry there. In addition, where persecution
was profitable, as in Europe, the scope and extent of attacks on
women were pervasive.

62. Degler, C.N.

   1980.   AT ODDS: WOMEN AND THE FAMILY IN AMERICA FROM
              THE REVOLUTION TO THE PRESENT. New York and
              Oxford: Oxford University Press.

   Drawing on marriage manuals, popular advice books, medical
texts, and feminist writings, Degler argues that repression of
female sexuality represented new forms of social control: the
alliance of physicians and women to enhancing women's "autonomy"
in the home. As proponents of the doctrine of "separate spheres"
-- whereby men ruled the world, while women rocked the cradle --
social reformers of the 1840's and 1850's generated an entirely
new literature on sexual behavior in which women's sexuality was
either played down or virtually ignored. Paradoxically, the new
ideology of sexual denial was not aimed to curb sexual
expression, as much as to enhance women's health through the
reduction of pregnancies. In Degler's analysis, the new
therapeutic regime of sexual purity freed women from male
domination. While the autonomy thesis is original and intriguing,
Degler tends to underestimate the severe isolation of women in
this "new autonomy."

63. Donegan, J.B.

   1978.   WOMEN AND MEN MIDWIVES: MEDICINE, MORALITY,
              AND MISOGYNY IN EARLY AMERICA. Westport,
              Conn.: Greenwood Press.

   Feminists have rediscovered the midwife as an important
feature in traditional childbirth. As late as 1910, as many as 50
percent of all births in the United States were assisted by
midwives. As significant as midwives were in the childbirth
process, they remained a deviant category; suspect because as

"experts" in birth control, they were believed likely to cooperate in abortion and infanticide. The takeover of physicians in obstetrics involved an extended conflict between the idea of female modesty and the need for improved medical training. Since midwives were excluded from medical colleges -- on the misogynist assumption that women lacked the necessary intelligence for learning medicine -- male physicians eventually overcame the modesty obstacle in favor of the safety ethic. By the middle of the nineteenth century, feminist women were gradually admitted into medical colleges and encouraged to administer to a "suffering and abused sex."

64. Douglas, A.

> 1978.   THE FEMINIZATION OF AMERICAN CULTURE. New York: Avon Books.

The main theme of this book is the exploration of the link between Victorian culture and modern mass culture. The author sees the nineteenth century as a period of sentimentalization of theological and secular culture.

She begins by exploring the religion of this period, especially the effects of disestablishment among the Protestant clergy, which represented the formal capitulation of the Protestant churches to the American way of commercialism and competitiveness.

Next, she examines the disestablishment of the nineteenth-century well-bred Northeastern woman from producer to consumer, interested more in the purchase of clothing than in the making of cloth. The author also analyzes the flight from history to the writing of memoirs. Clergy and women both suffered an irrevocable loss of status during this period.

In addition, Ms. Douglas writes movingly on certain nineteenth-century themes: the fascination with death and mourning, the women's magazines and on the bitterness of some intellectual women, for example, Harriet Beecher Stowe. The author concludes with case studies in American Romanticism; namely, Margaret Fuller and Herman Melville.

65. Ehrenreich, B. and D. English.

> 1973.   WITCHES, MIDWIVES, AND NURSES: A HISTORY OF WOMEN HEALERS. Old Westbury, New York: The Feminist Press.

This monograph traces the rise of the nursing profession to the Middle Ages, where it emerges as a strictly subordinate female occupation. Uncovering some of the long-suppressed history of women as lay healers, the authors argue that many of the women who were killed during the witch-hunting era (fourteenth to seventeenth centuries) were actually medical practitioners. Midwives were especially detested by the Church, and may have been a special target for the witch hunters. Once the alliance

between the male medical profession and the Church was
established, women healers were denigrated and persecuted. This
study documents an important chapter in the social control of
women's health care.

66. Fruzzetti, L.M.

    1982.   THE GIFT OF A VIRGIN: WOMEN, MARRIAGE, AND
               RITUAL IN A BENGALI SOCIETY. New Brunswick,
               N.J.: Rutgers University Press.

    Based on observation and participation in the rituals of
daily life in the Bengali town of Vishnupur, this study sheds new
light on Indian society as a whole by focusing on the separate
domain of women's activities, especially their marriage rituals,
from the point of view of the women. A central anthropological
concern entails the characteristics attributed to and the roles
assigned to women in society, and the manner in which these shape
the total culture. This woman anthropologist penetrated the
women's world, but also by taking women as the point of
reference, portrayed and illuminated their activities. As an
ethnographer of Hindu Bengali society, the author focuses on
important facts and details and provides useful interpretations.

67. Gailey, C.W. and M. Etienne. (eds.)

    1982.   WOMEN AND THE STATE IN PRE-INDUSTRIAL
               SOCIETIES: ANTHROPOLOGICAL PERSPECTIVES. New
               York: Praeger Publishers.

    This book specifically examines the impact on women when
their culture moves from tribal to a state formation. It includes
twelve case studies focusing on state formation, either
indigenous or through penetration by pre-capitalist states,
addressing issues related to the origins of gender hierarchy and
its articulation with emerging class and state structures. The
contributors survey cultures in Africa, the Middle East, the
Americas and Europe, including both historical and contemporary
societies.

68. Gilman, C.P.

    1966.   WOMEN AND ECONOMICS. Edited by C.N. Degler.
               New York: Harper Torchbooks.

    A growing number of students of American history have
recognized that the achievement of sufferage did not settle the
question of women's rights. Gilman's work, originally published
in 1898, emphasizes the broad and important question of the place
and destiny of women in a modern industrial society. In viewing
women against the broad perspective of time, this early feminist,
who was a prolific writer and a self-proclaimed "sociologist,"

Gilman raised fundamental questions about the nature and potentialities of the sexes. Aside from its feminist argument, WOMEN AND ECONOMICS is a compendium of the dominant intellectual currents of the late nineteenth century: socialism, democracy, Darwinism, and progress.

69. Gray, O.

1976.   WOMEN OF THE WEST. Millbrae, Ca.: Les Femmes.

Drawing on autobiographies, unpublished letters, diaries, and other documentation on nineteenth-century women, Gray attempts to "break trail" in a new historical analysis into the migrations west as experienced by women. While documenting the hardships of these pioneers, the author emphasizes the courage, creativity and adaptability of women performing on various western frontiers: the cattle frontier, the farm frontier, the professional frontier, the political frontier, and the social frontier.

70. Hartman, M.S.

1976.   VICTORIAN MURDERESSES: A TRUE HISTORY OF THIRTEEN RESPECTABLE FRENCH AND ENGLISH WOMEN ACCUSED OF UNSPEAKABLE CRIMES. New York: Schocken Books.

The subjects of this study of Victorian criminal trials include the independently wealthy wives and daughters of merchants, industrialists and professional men, as well as near-resourceless shopkeepers' wives and one spinster governess. The victims were the women's husbands, lovers, rivals, pupils, siblings, offspring, and grandchildren. These trials reach into some of the private areas of women's experiences in the past which have rarely been explored. In scrutinizing aberrant behavior, Ms. Hartman has pointed to the norm.

71. Hymowitz, C. and M. Weissman.

1978.   A HISTORY OF WOMEN IN AMERICA. New York: A Bantam Book.

In presenting a general history of women in the United States, the authors strike a balance between describing the lives of ordinary women and the lives of extraordinary women. The book also demonstrates the struggle between two poles: on the one hand, women's experience can be interpreted as a document of oppression. On the other hand, women as human beings are far more significant than their exclusion from institutional and economic life would indicate. The merging of these two polar views provides strength to a study which celebrates women, whether as pioneer mothers, migrant farm laborers, immigrant mothers and daughters, flappers, or the new feminists.

72. Jeffrey, J.R.

     1979.   FRONTIER WOMEN: THE TRANS-MISSISSIPPI WEST,
                 1840-1880. New York: Hill and Wang.

     This book traces the emigration of women and their families
to the West drawing on documents by women: journals,
reminiscences and letters. What did it mean for wives and
daughters who were presumably responsible for civilizing the
wilderness? Did the West offer women any special economic and
political opportunities, as scholars have argued it did for men?
Did living on the frontier result in the shattering of familiar
norms or in their strengthening? Did women play a part in the
process of mediating between culture and environment and in
building new communities on the frontier? And what did the
Western experience mean for them? These questions which form the
core of the book enable the author to destroy the myth that women
had more egalitarian status in the West. Women were not equal in
legal, political, economic, or family matters, and most went only
reluctantly into the frontier. Major reasons for emigrating
include economic, health and climate reasons. But women's
hardships more than offset the advantages: loss of friends and
family, chronic fatigue, death of children, loss of female
community, and an ongoing conflict between a feminine culture of
sensibility and a harsh environment. The book suggests that,
sex/gender change may depend upon external changes in social
structure. This will have an impact on later generations of women
in liberating themselves from inequality.

73. Jordan, T.

     1982.   COWGIRLS: WOMEN OF THE AMERICAN WEST. Garden
                 City, New York: Anchor Press, Inc.

     A serious contribution to the oral history of the United
States as well as the history of women, this book presents the
personal stories and experiences of women who worked the ranches,
plains and trails of the American frontier, some since the turn
of the century. The author, herself a cowgirl, employs classic
American literature, folklore and song, as well as photographs
dating from 1890 to the present.

74. Kennedy, S.E.

     1979.   IF ALL WE DID WAS TO WEEP AT HOME: A HISTORY
                 OF WHITE, WORKING-CLASS WOMEN IN AMERICA.
                 Bloomington: Indiana University Press.

     The current class conflict in feminist thought entails two
opposing work ethics. Middle-class women view work as self-

fulfilling in social and psychological terms, while working-class
women see freedom from work as a positive goal. It is important
to gain some understanding of the roots and development of such
different perceptions of women's values and goals. Working-class
women have been largely invisible in America. They have lacked an
apparent or consistent ideology or sense of social, political,
economic, or cultural cohesiveness. As a "hidden minority," white
working-class women were becoming working women by 1900, as their
labor passed from home to factory. But lack of skills, permanence
or organization made them vulnerable to prejudice and
exploitation, often in the form of low wages, long hours and bad
working conditions. At the turn of the century, the typical
working woman was the young, single daughter of immigrants or
economically-marginal native parents. She had only minimal public
education, no trade or craft training, and viewed herself as a
temporary worker until her marriage.
    The book details working conditions for these women, which
included sexual exploitation, back-breaking labor and an almost
total lack of job security. This is an insightful book about the
real history of the working-class woman.

75. Kunzle, D.

    1981.   FASHION AND FETISHISM: A SOCIAL HISTORY OF
                 THE CORSET, TIGHTLACING, AND OTHER FORMS OF
                 BODY SCULPTURE IN THE WEST. Totowa, N.J.:
                 Rowman and Littlefield.

    Is the use of the corset sexually repressive or sexually
expressive? Is it a matter of men forcing women's bodies into the
shapes their fantasies desire? Or is it a matter of women
rejecting their traditional passive, family-centered and
childbearing role?
    In this first fully-documented study of corsetry and tight-
lacing, David Kunzle shows how this neglected and misunderstood
phenomenon is central to the history of female emancipation and
repression. His book delves into fundamental aspects of social
history, the history of costume, and anthropological, sexological
and feminist elements in Western culture.
    Kunzle uses a wealth of previously untapped primary sources,
notably the medical literature and popular magazine articles and
caricature, and relates the historical and literary evidence to
the testimony of tight-lacing fetishists living today. The
practice of tight lacing, it appears, provoked hysterical
clerical and medical censure at times when traditional
conservative morality was both powerful and under attack. The
corset-wearer was seen as a witch who used sexual magic to
threaten traditional social roles.
    The author's canvas stretches from Minoan Crete to modern
California. At its center is that enigmatic figure, usually
female, but sometimes male, whose way of making a statement about
the world is to sculpture the body's bones and sinews. FASHION
AND FETISHISM helps us towards an understanding of that enigma.

76. Lavrin, A. (ed.)

1978.   LATIN AMERICAN WOMEN: HISTORICAL
PERSPECTIVES. Westport, Conn.: Greenwood
Press.

In this broadly-conceived collection, contributors attempt
to move beyond the "great Latin American woman syndrome," whereby
only prominant females are the subjects of history. Instead, they
offer an inquiry into the roles, statuses, thought, and action
that were representative of women's times and societies. Revising
the stereotype of the Latin American woman as a passive element,
the book emphasizes the role of women as doers and agents.
Specific chapters include: colonial women in Mexico, women and
the family in colonial Brazil, sixteenth-century Indian women and
white society in Peru, noble women in Mexico, Indian nuns of
Mexico City, the feminine religious orders in colonial Brazil,
the feminine press, the participation of women in the Columbia
independence movement, education, philanthropy, and feminism as
components of Argentine womanhood and women's rights in Brazil
and Mexico. The final chapter explores trends and issues in Latin
American women's history. Women in politics, work and feminist
activities are examined. An interesting discussion of women's
participation in some women-controlled institutions opens the
possibility that in the future social change will foster women's
needs.

77. Leacock, E.B., (ed.)

1982.   MYTHS OF MALE DOMINANCE: COLLECTED ARTICLES
OF WOMEN CROSS-CULTURALLY. New York: Monthly
Review Press.

This is a collection of articles, some previously published,
others new, on the position of women as perceived by a cultural
anthropologist. The articles fall under three categories: the
author's social, historical and anthropological research on the
egalitarian Montagnais-Naskapi of Canada; reflections on social
evolution and Engel's notions concerning class and women's
oppression; and rebuttals to contemporary arguments that male
domination is universal and, perhaps, inevitable. Leacock
effectively weaves together personal/political statements and
scientific   ones   and   demonstrates   their   crucial
interrelationships. The volume is a major synthesis of the
rapidly developing field of the anthropology of women. The work
is highly recommended, both as a critically presented state of
the art and as an account of how one's personal/political history
informs the process of scientific inquiry.

78. Lerner, G. (ed.)

    1977.   THE FEMALE EXPERIENCE: AN AMERICAN
             DOCUMENTARY. Indianapolis: Bobbs-Merrill
             Company, Inc.

    The focus of the book--what it has meant to be a woman in
America--examines women's life cycle from youth to death and how
they have defined themselves while developing various forms of
feminine consciousness. Lerner provides a new framework for the
study of women's history in the United States in her shift of
emphasis to the experiences of ordinary women and to ideas
expressed outside of formal organizations. Whereas, the
activities of women were considered to have been marginal and
insignificant to historical scholarship, the documents in this
collection show American women's ideas, values and participation
in social institutions from the woman's point of view. This
reveals the slow process by which women emancipated themselves
from the male-dominated and male-defined world in which they
live. The book has three parts: Part one traces the life stages
of women and turning points in individuals' lives. It centers on
the family. Part two deals with women's experiences in male-
defined institutions, such as the workplace, school, trade union,
and government. Part three examines the development of feminist
consciousness in its various stages: defiance of traditional
roles, definition of sisterhood, the search for new structures,
and finally, the experiences of feminist ideology. This is an
excellent sourcebook of original documents, many of which are
published here for the first time.

79. Lerner, G. (ed.)

    1973.   BLACK WOMEN IN WHITE AMERICA: A DOCUMENTARY
             HISTORY. New York: Vintage Books.

    The oppression of black women has been pervasive in America,
beginning with slavery, illiteracy and lynching in the nineteenth
century to current social oppressions: menial labor, rape, the
"bad" black woman myth, and the daily struggle for survival. The
author concludes the book with two sections on "race pride" and
"womanhood" among black women, and emphasizes the necessity for
liberation to begin among the oppressed themselves.

80. Marks, E. and I. de Courtivron (eds.)

    1981.   NEW FRENCH FEMINISMS. New York: Schocken
             Books.

    Modern feminism is said to have begun with Simone de
Beauvoir's THE SECOND SEX. Now readers can learn of the rich and
diverse history of French feminist theory since the publication
of that work. In this collection, the editors have included more
than fifty selections of recent French feminist writings, most

never before translated, and some never before published, along with a series of introductions that evaluate these writings in the context of American feminist thought.

81. Matthaei, J.A.

1982.   AN ECONOMIC HISTORY OF WOMEN IN AMERICA: WOMEN'S WORK, SEXUAL DIVISION OF LABOR, AND THE DEVELOPMENT OF CAPITALISM. New York: Schocken Books.

This ambitious examination of working lives explains women's role in labor within the broad sweep of American economic history. Matthaei's original analysis not only explains the evolution and economic implications of sexual division in labor; it provides a powerful tool for understanding the changing lives of women.

82. Njoku, J.E.

1980.   THE WORLD OF THE AFRICAN WOMAN. Metuchen, N.J.: Scarecrow Press, Inc.

The chronicle of the changing roles and growing political and economic influence of African women is rendered here with appreciation and brevity. Chapters focus on kinship and social organization, the market women, contemporary African women, women's migration and production, women's self-help and cooperatives, and rural development and women. The appendix is especially useful, including data on dozens of women's groups throughout the continent -- their leaders, aims and organizations.

83. Norton, M.B.

1980.   LIBERTY'S DAUGHTERS: THE REVOLUTIONARY EXPERIENCE OF AMERICAN WOMEN, 1750-1800. Boston/Toronto: Little, Brown, and Company.

It is not surprising to discover that in eighteenth-century America, women's lives centered upon their homes and their families. What Norton's research into the published and unpublished papers of approximately 450 eighteenth-century families questions are the historian's common assumptions about the lives of colonial women. The most widely accepted notion is that the preindustrial American woman's essential economic contribution to the household gave her a social status higher than that of both her European contemporaries and her nineteenth-century descendents. The reality is far different. White female colonialists were subordinate within the home, did not engage in business activities outside the household, experienced sharply defined gender roles, and as a consequence developed low self-esteem. Women's discontent, especially among frontier wives and daughters, was expressed, not to husbands or fathers, but to female relatives. And while Mary Wolstonecraft's A VINDICATION OF THE RIGHTS OF WOMEN was widely read in America, it was almost as widely criticized. Options for women during this period were highly restrictive: an educated woman in 1800 had only a fraction more control over her destiny than her uneducated grandmother 50 years earlier. Despite the legacy of the American Revolution which proposed an egalitarian rhetoric, women were confined to the feminine sphere. This offered her a private household and marital relationship, but little responsibility outside the domain of domesticity.

84. Ochs, C.

1977.   BEHIND THE SEX OF GOD: TOWARD A NEW CONSCIOUSNESS -- TRANSCENDING MATRIARCHY AND PATRIARCHY. Boston: Beacon Press.

To focus on the universal patterning of the opposition of matriarchy and patriarchy, the author borrows from a number of intellectual approaches: a Jungian approach, an anthropological approach (e.g. Levi-Strauss, Mary Douglas), a comparative religion approach, an archeological approach, a psychological approach (e.g. Freud, Jung), and a philosophical approach (e.g. Kant, Daly). In this original effort to make the patriarchal view explicit, thereby making conscious a value system unconsciously absorbed in Western society, the author explores five distinct themes: (1)the Frankenstein motif and its implications for ethics, (2)the Eleusinian mystery religion, a predominantly matriarchal system, (3)the biblical story of the sacrifice of Isaac, a story central to the entire Judeo-Christian tradition, (4)the stories of Cain, and (5)two chapters on the feminization of religion, Jewish and Catholic. The alternative views of religion proposed here are offered as part of the reconstruction of social reality, wherein oppositions can be transcended. The author suggests a monistic view of life can accomplish this transcendence and bring about the collapse of the archaic opposition between male and female, which has worked to the disadvantage of women.

85. Okin, S.M.

1979.   WOMEN IN WESTERN POLITICAL THOUGHT. Princeton, N.J.: Princeton University Press.

Although women have obtained formal citizenship rights, they remain far behind men in achieving substantive equality. The tradition of political philosophy helps to explain why the gaps persist between formal and real equality. In this discerning study of the works of Plato, Aristotle, Rousseau, and Mill, the author proposes that early thinkers took their view of women from interpretations of the family. Thus a patriarchal view of the family restricts women to sexual, procreative, and child-rearing functions. The wife/mother role thus becomes women's very "nature," rather than products of society. The philosophical tradition, then, rests largely on the assumption of the natural inequality of the sexes. Until women alter the traditional conception of the family there is little hope of altering women's subordination.

86. Quaife, G.R.

1979.   WANTON WENCHES AND WAYWARD WIVES: PEASANTS AND ILLICIT SEX IN EARLY SEVENTEENTH CENTURY ENGLAND. New Brunswick, N.J.: Rutgers University Press.

In the peasant world of seventeenth-century England, women formed an "inferior subworld" to the "patriarchal, parochial, public, and precarious" world of the male peasant. The center of peasant life for men and women alike was the household, yet the household was developed quite consciously as a major social vehicle of discipline. As head of the household, the adult male had nearly absolute power over his wife, children and servants. Although total power was curbed by the church, violence -- in the form of woman battering -- was very common. Because there was an excess of women over men, women were undervalued, exploited by men and consequently sought various expedient ways to escape or modify their oppression; for example, through drink, witchcraft or religious fanaticism. Women were denounced by church and state alike as inferior beings who were barely rational and governed by a voracious sexual appetite. In this exploitative milieu, chastity was not an economic asset for perhaps a majority of the rural population, who were either destitute or laborers. Children left home early in search of work, eliminating parental control. Thus, bastardy, drinking, non-marital sex, rape, and other violent acts were commonplace during this period.

87. Reed, E.

1978.   SEXISM AND SCIENCE. New York: Pathfinder Press.

A collection of essays meant as a sequel and supplement to WOMAN'S EVOLUTION, this book examines biology, sociology, anthropology, as well as their sub-areas, sociobiology and primatology. The author's purpose is to show how the scholarly fields have been influenced by the biases current in the established social system, and to demonstrate how "the infiltration of pseudo-scientific notions distorts the facts." She specifically examines the sexist stereotypes in the biological and social sciences. The first three essays are primarily concerned with the newer sciences of sociobiology and primatology, the last five with the status of anthropology.

88. Reiter, R.R. (ed.)

1975.   "Toward an Anthropology of Women." MONTHLY
REVIEW PRESS.

The eighteen essays in the volume are written by feminist
anthropologists who are making an attempt to move beyond the
pervasive male bias in anthropology. There are three papers that
relate directly to the issues of male bias in the interpretation
of the biological and cultural evolutionary record, three that
discuss aspects of sexual equality in groups organized primarily
along the lines of kinship, and two that offer theories
concerning the origin of gender relations. Of particular interest
to readers of the present volume is Judith Brown's
ethnohistorical analysis of Iroquois women.

89. Riencourt, A.

1974.   SEX AND POWER IN HISTORY. New York: David
McKay Company.

This historical treatment of women's role in pre-history
and culture adapts Jungian and structural perspectives to examine
the past that survives and the present civilization. Like Jung,
the author maintains that male and female differentiation is a
biological and cultural reality. Any attempts to reduce female
experience to androgyny could result in erasing women's
experiences altogether. The crisis of contemporary civilization
revolves around the predicament in the relations between the
sexes. The refusal of men to confront the "female principle"
within, and society's denial of independence for women, leads to
active revolt by women and angry male backlash. For example,
genetic engineering, hailed as the new emancipation by some
feminists, would most likely be used by those who control
biological research -- men. Eliminating women's procreative role
could leave women without biological or cultural roles; a
disposable being. A controversial work, the book offers a
provocative argument for the increasing differentiation of the
sexes and proposes a policy that would "refeminize" rather than
masculinize females.

90. Rohrlich-Leavitt, R. (ed.)

1975.   WOMEN CROSS-CULTURALLY: CHANGE AND CHALLENGE.
Ninth International Congress of
Anthropological and Ethnological Sciences,
Chicago, 1973. The Hague: Mouton Publishers.

In this collection of conference papers, anthropology
recognizes that the women's movement is international. The papers
in this volume were written for the session on women's status and
women's movements, and represent critical evaluations of women's
status in gathering and hunting bands, fishing clans, peasant

communities, agricultural chiefdoms, both in developing and developed societies, and in capitalist and socialist ones. Women are shown in their multiple roles as food gatherers, farmers, potters, weavers, traders, chiefs, miners, industrial workers, union organizers, servants, wives, mothers, and professionals: as victims of exploitation and as fighters against oppression. For example, an analysis of women in Bangladesh by R. Jahan clarifies the structural features of women's subordinate status as an issue not of law (inasmuch as Moslem law provides inheritance and other rights), but as an issue of the custom of male domination. Separatism between the sexes encourages wide disparities in status and lifestyles. This volume reports not only about the condition of women around the world, but also examines the relationship of anthropology to knowledge about and participation of women professionals in the field.

91. Rosaldo, M.Z. and L. Lamphere. (eds.)

    1974.   WOMEN, CULTURE AND SOCIETY. Stanford:
            Stanford University Press.

    This book explores what anthropologists have to say about women and how a professional interest in women might provide a new perspective in the field. With a few exceptions, cultural anthropologists have followed their own cultural biases in treating women as relatively invisible and describing only the activities of men. Recent anthropological concerns entail these questions: Are there societies that make women equal or superior to men? If not, are women "naturally" men's inferiors? Why do women accept a subordinate standing? How and when do women èxercise power?
    Essays in this volume include: (1)family structure and feminine personality; (2)women in politics; (3)strategies, cooperation, and conflict among women in domestic groups; (4)sex roles in an urban black community; (5)Engels revisited: women, the organization of product, and private property; (6)female status in the public domain; (7)sex and power in the Balkans; (8)why men rule in primitive societies; and (9)the mastery of work and the mystery of sex in a Guatemalan village. This book is rewarding to all who are willing to assess cultural variations and women's role changes.

92. Rossi, A.S. (ed.)

    1973.   THE FEMINIST PAPERS: FROM ADAMS TO DE
            BEAUVOIR. New York: Bantam Books, Inc.

    Alice Rossi, a noted sociologist and feminist, has assembled a comprehensive anthology of major feminist writings from the late 18th century to the mid-20th century. Here we meet religious women as well as atheists; conservative moralists as well as radicals; women in deep rebellion from their families and society; as well as women in comfortable, happy circumstances.

39

There are calls for political rights, but in addition, for economic, sexual and educational liberation. Dr. Rossi has made a careful choice of materials and has included extended introductory essays.

Rossi begins with the Enlightenment perspective and includes the writings of Abigail Adams, Juliet Sargent Murray, Mary Wolstonecraft, Frances Wright, Harriet Martineau, Margaret Fuller, and John Stuart Mill. Next she presents the Grimkes', the Blackwells, Elizabeth Cady Stanton, and Susan B. Anthony. She also treats feminism and class politics with the writings of Fredrich Engels, August Bebel, Emma Goldman, Margaret Sanger, Suzanne LaFollette, Charlotte Perkins Gilman, and Jane Addams. The writings of Virginia Woolf, Margaret Mead and Simone deBeauvoir bring us up to the modern epoch. It is overall a rich collection.

93. Sacks, K.

1979.   SISTERS AND WIVES: THE PAST AND FUTURE OF SEXUAL EQUALITY. Westport, Conn.: Greenwood Press.

Offering a combined Marxist and feminist perspectives, this study challenges the anti-feminist perspectives in anthropology. Biology has been an unconscious metaphor for social relations, with wifehood and motherhood, as dependent roles, considered to be women's essential and defining social relations. Drawing on African data, Sacks demonstrates that women are neither universally dependent nor subordinate. "Women have been making culture, political decisions and babies simultaneously and without structural conflicts in all parts of the world." The author discusses women's relationships as sisters, mothers and wives and shows that autonomy and political and economic decisionmaking have been common. Sisterhood and wifehood are critical roles for women in the precapitalist world. "Sister" is a kind of kinship shorthand for a women member of a community of owners; an adult, a decisionmaker. Wife is shorthand for a woman's relation to her spouse, which may entail her dominance or submission. Under the political organization of class rule, corporate kin control eroded and sometimes destroyed sisterhood with the commensurate elevation of wifehood. The book details various groups: Mbuti, Lovedu, Mponda, Ontisha, Buganda, and West Africa to show the impact of a ruling class on women's diminished relation to production.

94. Schramm, S.S.

1979.   PLOW WOMEN RATHER THAN REAPERS: AN INTELLECTUAL HISTORY OF FEMINISM IN THE UNITED STATES. Metuchen, N.J.: Scarecrow Press, Inc.

This comprehensive scholarly treatment of the history of

feminist thought offers a sophisticated analysis of feminist thought from the colonial period to about 1950. Schramm combines her findings about feminist thinkers, both well known and obscure, with American intellectual history and women's social history for a well-rounded approach.

95. Tax, M.

1980.   THE RISING OF THE WOMEN: FEMINIST SOLIDARITY AND CLASS CONFLICT, 1880-1917. New York: Monthly Review Press.

Women's participation in the labor movement should not be lumped with men's movement activities. Among women, intricate relations between workplace and home, union and community organizations, socialism and feminism, street and kitchen, and school and bedroom offer a web of connections that prevent women from moving with the degrees of freedom found among male organizers. There is strength in this web as well. Labor history for women comes "attached to community history and family history and the history of reproduction." This involves not only class consciousness and the awareness of systematic oppression, but also consciousness of sex oppression. Chapter six on "Rebel Girls and the First World War" shows how sexual radicalism among men was often a mask for sexual opportunism. Hence, the united front of women in the labor movement was necessary to confront exploitation in two spheres: change in the conditions of labor and change in sex roles, wherein women were sexually subordinated.

96. Tiffany, S.W. (ed.)

1979.   WOMEN AND SOCIETY: AN ANTHROPOLOGICAL READER. Montreal: Eden Press Women's Publications.

These crosscultural essays on women's social condition and statuses help to counterbalance the male bias in anthropology which has rendered women "invisible." There is a diversity of female-male relationships involving production, reproduction, power, marriage ritual, and ideology which has been almost totally ignored in the field. Part of the problem resides in the terminology, such as dominant and subordinate, used to describe woman-man relations. This language obscures rather than clarifies women's statuses. First, there are great cultural variations when considering women's position in different cultures. Second, status is a multidimensional attribute, which is continuously changing as women move through the life cycle. These writers stress that anthropology needs to assess what these variations are over space and time. The essays consider a variety of cultures and situations, revealing the complex roles assigned to women in preliterate societies. For instance, the woman-marriage in Africa entails a woman who takes on one or more wives, which is an indication of her resource accumulation and high status.

Westernization can sometimes weaken or destroy women's traditional autonomy or power, according to Allen, one of the contributors. Thus, social change may be a more accurate predictor of attitudes and behavior of people in modernizing society than traditional roles and rules.

97. Tilly, L.A. and J.W. Scott.

    1978.   WOMEN, WORK AND FAMILY. New York: Holt, Rinehart and Winston.

    This book describes and analyzes changes in patterns of women's productive activity. Focusing on the history of women in Britain and France since 1700, they show that patterns of women's work have been shaped by the intersection of economy, demography and family. Specific historical contexts differ; thus, the experiences, attitudes and choices women make in different situations have varied widely. But the family as a support unit for its members has maintained its essential function as providing a certain continuity in the midst of economic change. This study challenges the older view, which held that industrialization separated the family and work, isolating one sphere from another. They found that while industrialization eventually deprived the family unit of its productive activity, the family continued to influence various activities of its members. Domestic organization does not change quickly or easily. Families adopt complex strategies that enable them to preserve elements of customary practices in altered circumstances. The current family patterns that have emerged represent adaptations and compromises between tradition and new organizational and social structures.

98. Trescott, M.M. (ed.)

    1979.   DYNAMOS AND VIRGINS REVISITED: WOMEN AND TECHNOLOGICAL CHANGE IN HISTORY. Metuchen, N.J.: Scarecrow Press, Inc.

    These essays bring together some of the more significant pioneering works on the interaction between women and technology. Areas cover women's history, women's studies, history of science and technology, and economic and business history. Although the book emphasizes the United States over the last one hundred years, it also considers European and American topics from the 18th and 19th centuries. Women were active participants, these studies argue, in their roles as operatives in industry, and as inventors, engineers, scientists, and entrepreneurs. Technological change has also impacted on women in the domestic sphere: in home and reproduction, and in child-raising and socialization.

ABORTION

99. Arms, S.

1975.   IMMACULATE DECEPTION: A NEW LOOK AT WOMEN AND
CHILDBIRTH IN AMERICA. Boston: Houghton
Mifflin Company.

In this strong defense of home birth and midwife attendant,
Arms launches one of the most devestating and complete attacks on
mandatory hospital births (except in exceptional cases). The
testimony is damaging: hospital births occur in a context of
impersonality and coerciveness; over-dependence on drugs and
surgery; separation of mother and child; the required supine
positon; and episiotomy -- all increase the health risks for the
mother and child. The medical and psychological benefits of home
births are well documented. This book relates to the abortion
issue, inasmuch as abortion and home birth represent areas of new
choices for women.

100. Bates, J.E. and E.S. Zawadzki.

1964.   CRIMINAL ABORTION: A STUDY IN MEDICAL
SOCIOLOGY. Springfield, Ill.: Charles C.
Thomas, Publisher.

This collaborative effort by a sociologist and a physician
brings a new policy-oriented approach toward investigating
criminal abortion. The authors had three purposes: (1)describing
and analyzing the subculture of criminal abortion by means of
field research, drawing on case studies, statistics, and
interviews with detectives, medical personnel and women who have
had abortions; (2)isolating factors in American culture that
perpetuate the deviant institution of criminal abortion; and
(3)demonstrating how various cultural strengths could be utilized
to "slow down the spiraling circle of misery, invalidism and
death caused by the surprising prevalence of illegal abortion."
Abortion in the prelegal epoch is documented in this book as a
personal and social problem of monumental proportions.

101. Beauchamp, T.L. and L. Walters.

1978.   CONTEMPORARY ISSUES IN BIOETHICS. Belmont,
California: Dickenson Publishing Company.

This is a collection of contemporary articles on a broad

range of topics in medicine and bioethics. The section on abortion examines both pro- and anti-abortion viewpoints. The strongest attack on the feminist position -- the fetus as a person has a right to life -- is debated on philosophical and moral grounds with a strong case made for abortion. Other sections treat topics relevant to feminist concerns about the American health care system.

102. Calderone, M.S. (ed.)

1958. ABORTION IN THE UNITED STATES. New York: Hoeber-Harper.

Based on a Planned Parenthood Conference, this early pro-abortion book, now a pioneer study, summarizes the medical, scientific, sociological, and legal issues. Using the dialogue approach, participating speakers are directly quoted. This provides a view of the emergent role played by leaders in psychiatry and maternal health in pushing for abortion reform. The book offers an important contribution in the historical development for legal abortion.

103. Callahan, D.

1970. ABORTION: LAW, CHOICE, AND MORALITY. New York: The Macmillan Company.

In this balanced and comprehensive coverage, the author examines medical, legal, social, moral, religious, and philosophical issues of abortion. Steering a middle position, Callahan argues against both extremist views: restrictive abortion, the Roman Catholic position, on the one hand, versus abortion on demand, the radical-feminist view on the other. His recommended limits on abortion (up to the twelfth week of pregnancy), however, antagonizes both pro-life and pro-choice advocates. Overall, this is a useful book for summarizing a still unresolved issue.

104. Chandrasekhar, S.

1974. ABORTION IN A CROWDED WORLD: THE PROBLEM OF ABORTION WITH SPECIAL REFERENCE TO INDIA. London: George Allen and Unwin Ltd.

The special population problems in India are given attention in this study, which begins with a comparison of the Indian and the non-Indian view of abortion. The author's primary concern -- what lessons can India learn from the abortion experience of Asia, Europe and, particularly, that of Japan and Hungary -- leads to some questions that upset the taken-for-granted view of legal abortion in the West. According to Chandrasekhar, in India, the liberation of abortion laws does not necessarily or always lead to a decline in the number of illegal abortions, much less their complete disappearance. This is because legal and illegal abortions attract different kinds of patients. As legal abortion remains a stigmatized medical service, unmarried, widowed, divorced, or separated women may seek illegal abortion because of a desire for secrecy. Solving world population problems with a single set of assumptions derived from Western experience could be pernicious. Nevertheless, the author calls for a credo which emphasizes the right of privacy, a Western doctrine, for every woman. The fundamental right to choose whether to bear children or not should be a basic right in every human society.

105. Cisler, L.

1972.   "Abortion: A Major Battle is Over---But the War is Not." FEMINIST STUDIES. 1(2):121-133.

Written in the wake of the late 1972 pro-abortion court rulings, this article attacks the legal underpinnings of the Justice Berger-inspired decision. Because privacy rights of the woman were not absolute in the abortion case, there is a clear lack of a positive mandate. State interests increasingly intrude as the pregnancy progresses. In addition, physicians have a monopoly on the abortion procedure. The court straddled the abortion issue attempting to give "something to everybody," but failed to achieve a clear victory for either side. Protective proposals, the author emphasizes, underscore how "we are still owned by the state." This early critical article predicts correctly the issues over which the post-legal abortion struggle has concentrated.

106. David, H.P. (ed.)

1974.   ABORTION RESEARCH: INTERNATIONAL EXPERIENCE. Lexington, Massachusetts: Lexington Books.

This edited study, dedicated to World Population Year, 1974, is a useful survey of abortion legislation and practices. A number of countries and geographic areas are surveyed -- Japan, Great Britain, Rumania, Yugoslavia, People's Republic of China, the Middle East, North Africa, Sub-Saharan Black Africa, Turkey, Tunisia, and the Soviet Union -- with the central issue being that of fertility control. In an article by Malcolm Potts (Chapter 19), he questions whether future advances in fertility control can occur, unless researchers and practitioners take into account the available options, constraints of methods, costs, trained personnel requirements, and administrative roadblocks in distributive systems. The conclusion of the collected articles appears to be that abortion is necessary as part of a national family-planning policy. But risks to the health of the woman and the cost of medical services to the community suggest that this is "not the optimal way of controlling human fertility" on an international basis.

107. Davis, N.J.

1973.   THE ABORTION MARKET: TRANSACTIONS IN A RISK
         COMMODITY. Ph.D. Dissertation, Michigan State
         University.

An overview of the changing institutionalization of
abortion, this study is based on Michigan data and focuses on the
immediate period (1969-1973) preceding legal abortion. While
considering legal, medical and agency responses to change, reform
efforts by a group of crisis-counseling Protestant clergymen most
clearly emphasize how new service ideologies and networks emerge
and shape the human services environment without basically
altering the sex or class stratification order.

108. Frances, M.

1972.   "Abortion: A Philosophical Analysis."
         FEMINIST STUDIES. 1(2):49-63.

Drawing on the philosophical concept of "person" developed
by John Rawls (A THEORY OF JUSTICE. Cambridge: Harvard University
Press, 1971), the author asks: "What if we were to calculate the
rights and obligations of a woman and a fetus using a model
similar to one developed by Rawls?" This is based on "fair
arrangement." The unequal sacrifice of the woman for the fetus
(and never the reverse), if the pregnancy is unwanted, implies
that no woman need make such an unequal contribution. Hence,
abortion is morally permissible at roughly any time during
pregnancy. In this well argued, extreme pro-feminist position,
the writer concludes that the Supreme Court granted "too little
freedom to have abortions."

109. Frisez, G.G.

1970.   ABORTION: THE MYTHS, THE REALITIES, AND THE
         ARGUMENTS. New York: Corpus Books.

This scholarly work, written before legal change, summarizes
the major ethical, religious, medical, legal, sociological, and
public policy issues in the abortion debate up to that time. Each
chapter -- How Life Begins, A Sociological Review, A Medical
Review, Religious View of Abortion, The State of the Legal
Question, Ethical Arguments, Toward a Sound Public Policy, and
Abortion and Prejudice Against the Unborn -- presents a well-
documented, dispassionate analysis of facts, events, cases,
statistics, and interpretations, including primitive and
scriptural references. With the current abortion controversy
often a repetition of debates heard over a decade ago, the book
is recommended as an historically insightful, well-written
overview of major problematic topics in the still unresolved
abortion field.

110. Gordon, L.

1976-77.   WOMEN'S BODY, WOMEN'S RIGHT. New York: Viking
            and Penguin.

This history of the birth control movement, written from a
feminist perspective, offers a lively and insightful analysis of
the struggle to emancipate contraception from its negative label
as immoral and as associated with promiscuous women. The
discussion of how the sexist biases restricted birth control
information and distribution clarifies how labels serve as
significant barriers to a rational health program in human
reproduction.

111. Hall, R.E. (ed.)

1970.   ABORTION IN A CHANGING WORLD. VOL. 1 & 2. New
            York: Columbia University Press.

Following the early format established in Planned Parenthood
Conferences, this edited set of papers offers a cafeteria choice
of topics and viewpoints. The by-now-familiar categories --
ethical, medical, legal, social, and global aspects of abortion
(see Volume 1)--are presented by learned professionals and
buttressed by political supporters (e.g. John Rockefeller, III).
By the second volume, the issues are more selective, detailed and
specialized (e.g. abortion and animation, abortion and poverty,
abortion and constitutionality). Facts and figures abound, but
the collection remains highly readable. For instance, photographs
of a rabbit fetus in utero and a human fetus at the end of the
seventh week reveal the embryologist's rather restrictive view --
both rabbit and human are mere animals after all! The aim of the
study remains clear: overcome the obstacles to legalizing
abortion.

112. Hardin, G.

1978.   STALKING THE WILD TABOO. (2nd ed.) Los Altos,
            California: William Kaufmann, Inc.

In this five section book dealing with our most imposing
cultural taboos -- abortion, religion, technology, economic
competition, and "other superstitions" -- abortion is treated in
positive rather than in exclusively negative terms. Drawing on
lectures presented in the late 1960s, the author attacks the
language used to denigrate the abortion choice: "therapeutic
abortion" (a psychiatric term), "lynching in the womb", and "the
slaughter of the innocents." Reconceptualizing abortion, Garrett
proposes terms such as "humane, self-fulfillment and valuable."
Although the arguments for legal abortion are no longer original,
(such as the rape justification or fetal deformity), the writer
served as a pioneer in opening up the abortion issue to public
discourse.

113. Hilgers, T.W., D.J. Horan, and D. Mall. (eds).

    1981.   NEW PERSPECTIVES ON HUMAN ABORTION.
                Frederick, Md.: University Publications of
                America, Inc.

This sophisticated version of the pro-life message offers
"new perspectives" on this well debated topic. Emphasizing the
"human characteristics of the early fetus" and "a day in the life
of a fetus," the ethics of abortion are examined in detail. These
articles take a highly critical view of the Supreme Court's
interpretation of abortion as a privacy issue. Instead, there are
human (fetal), ethical and religious issues that transcend the
woman's freedom. The abortion movement is also interpreted in
reversal terms, as "inaugurated by the desire to eliminate the
abnormal and the unwanted by unimaginable acts of violence." The
arguments are well developed, but totally lacking in a
relativistic or situational perspective. There is little
appreciation in these papers for such varied issues as single
parenting or moral responsibility in situations such as rape,
incest, teenage pregnancy, and the overburdened mother (or
father), economic issues, and the changing roles of women.
"Human" becomes translated narrowly as "fetus," or "baby,"
without attention to the wider scope of the quality of life.

114. Jaffe, F.S., B. Lindheim, and P. Lee.

    1980.   ABORTION POLITICS: PRIVATE MORALITY AND
                PUBLIC POLICY. New York: McGraw-Hill Book Co.

This book, published after the death of Fred Jaffe, former
president of the Alan Guttmacher Institute, reflects its senior
author's long involvement with family planning and population
policy. Avoiding the moral issue of whether abortion is right or
wrong, the writers focus on a key policy question: What kind and
what amount of information should be available to women about
their options in coping with pregnancy? Sample chapters include,
"The Impact of Legal Abortion," "The Leadership Equivocates,"
"Vox Populi," "The Holy Wars," and "Her Right to Be." In
detailing the scientific evidence in favor of safe, early
abortion, the study takes a strong stand in the struggle for a
permissive abortion policy.

115. Lader, L.

    1966.   ABORTION. Indianapolis: The Bobbs-Merrill
                Company.

This pro-abortion defense of legal abortion was a
significant document in the creation and development of the
abortion movement. Lader examines the social status of abortion
and concludes that illegal abortion results in a "system of fear
and privilege" among physicians and an "underworld" for most

consumers. Calling legalized abortion the "final freedom," in that all children will be wanted, Lader outlines a blueprint for changing U.S. abortion laws.

116. Lader, L.

     1973.   ABORTION II: MAKING THE REVOLUTION. Boston: Beacon Press.

     As chairman of the National Association for Repeal of Abortion Laws and other executive positions in the Association for Voluntary Sterilization and Zero Population Growth, Lader writes from the organizational insider's perspective. This book documents the abortion movement as a dual effort: the revolt by women against traditional reproductive roles, and the organizational efforts by various crusading groups, especially the National Association for Repeal of Abortion Laws (NARAL). As a descriptive book, it fills an important gap in the abortion reform literature. It lacks, however, the in-depth structural analysis that would help to explain why abortion remains a controversial health policy.

117. Manier, E., W. Liu and D. Solomon.

     1977.   ABORTION: NEW DIRECTIONS FOR POLICY STUDIES. South Bend: University of Notre Dame Press.

     This book includes position papers presented at an abortion conference held at the University of Notre Dame in March 1975, as well as papers written by four additional authors one year later. The published papers represent the separate disciplines of comparative constitutional law, sociology and philosophy, and attempts to clarify the differences in opinion, not silence them. The senior author recognizes that the Catholic position, which stands firmly on a pro-fetal life stance, must take into account the secularization trends, including women's autonomy and increasing participation in the job market, conditions that leave them vulnerable. Women thus confront the terrible prospects of unwanted pregnancy much more directly than men, and are often left alone to deal with those prospects. Some chapters and authors include, "The Abortion Decisions: Judicial Review and Public Opinion" by Judith Blake, "Membership Decisions and the Limits of Moral Obligation" by Edmund L. Pincoffs, "Abortion and Public Policy in the U.S.: A Dialectical Examination of Expert Opinion" by Edward Manier, and "Abortion and the Social System" by William Liu.
     This is a thoughtful, well reasoned book, whether the reader accepts the moral premises of some of the arguments or not.

118. Mohr, J.C.

> 1978.   ABORTION IN AMERICA: THE ORIGINS AND
> EVOLUTIONS OF NATIONAL POLICY: 1800 -1900.
> New York: Oxford University Press.

This is the most authoritative book written on the nineteenth-century history behind the issue of abortion. Well written and dispassionate, Mohr's meticulous legal and historical analysis shatters the assumption that religious objections were at the bottom of anti-abortion legislation in the 19th century. Instead, it was organized medicine which waged a moral crusade against abortion and the irregular practitioners who profited from this practice. This is required reading for close observers of the conflict over women's reproductive rights.

119. Noonan, J.T., Jr. (ed.)

> 1970.   THE MORALITY OF ABORTION: LEGAL AND
> HISTORICAL PERSPECTIVES. Cambridge, Mass:
> Harvard University Press.

This collection includes some of the most important papers by leading theorists of the anti-abortion position. Noonan takes an historical approach to trace the opposition of abortion within the Catholic Church from St.Augustine and Tertullian to the Second Vatican Council in 1965. An argument by Paul Ramsey proposes no intervention at either the beginning or the end of human life. This excludes not only abortion and euthanasia, but in addition, rules out any extraordinary measures to prolong the lives of severely defective fetuses or neonates or even of the terminally ill. A strong case for fetal protection by David Louisell and John Noonan is based on English common law and the U.S. Constitution, which the authors contend has always supported the legal concept of fetuses as persons, hence deserving of protection. This is a recommended overview of the conservative Judeo-Christian position.

120. Sanger, M.

> 1959.   MY FIGHT FOR BIRTH CONTROL. Elmsford, New
> York: Maxwell Reprint Co. Original Edition,
> 1931.

An adequate history of the abortion movement requires a first-hand account of the original struggle to emancipate birth control from traditional anti-contraceptive laws and practices. Margaret Sanger's personalized account furnishes conclusive information about the forces of women's reproductive repression -- the church, law, medicine, and the criminal justice system combined to eliminate and deny reformers' efforts to provide women with reproductive options. Sanger was probably one of the last of the single-minded crusaders. Social movements today require far more elaborate resources and distribution systems to win over public opinion. This is an interesting, biographical account of an earlier epoch, in which one woman could mount a moral crusade to change women's health care.

121. Sumner, L.W.

      1981.   ABORTION AND MORAL THEORY. Princeton, N.J.: Princeton University Press.

A philosophical treatment of the abortion debate, this recent study examines both the liberal and conservative views, and proposes a "third way." The morality of abortion is not an absolute, Sumner argues. The criterion of "moral standing" implies continuity. Thus, there is a point at which fetal rights asserts itself. This occurs when the fetus is at the "threshold of sentience." Before that point, abortion, like contraception, must be treated as a "private act," or "one requiring no special justifying conditions."

122. Warren, M.A.

      1980.   THE NATURE OF WOMEN: AN ENCYCLOPEDIA AND GUIDE TO THE LITERATURE. Inverness, California: Edgepress.

In a brief, but succinct, section on abortion, Warren writes from a philosophical viewpoint, examining feminist and anti-feminist interpretations of abortion. On one side, feminists argue that personhood entails the capacity (not merely potential) for consciousness: rationality, self motivation, self awareness, and usually, but not always, linguistic communication. On the other, anti-feminists argue that there is a prima facie obligation to permit potential people (not just fetuses but every ova and spermatazoa) to become actual people. Warren's position stresses the necessity for educated public opinion and for sexual equality to overcome the forces of reaction to abortion as a personal choice. The Encyclopedia also reviews works on abortion under the heading "Biology and Medical/Sexual Ethics."

Alcohol and Drugs

123. Anderson, S.C.

 1980.   "Patterns of Sex-Role Identification in
          Alcoholic Women." SEX ROLES. 6(2):231-243.

     Anderson studied alcoholic women and their biological
sisters to determine the differential presence of sex-role
identification conflict. Findings reveal that in accordance with
Sharon Wilsnack's earlier study ("Sex-Role Identity in Female
Alcoholism." JOURNAL OF ABNORMAL PSYCHOLOGY. 82, 1973; 253-261),
female alcoholics do not exhibit conscious sex-role
identification conflict. Anderson's study failed, however, to
confirm Wilsnack's contention that on an unconscious level female
alcoholics experienced more sex-role conflict than non-alcoholic
women. Anderson did, however, discover that there was less
consistency evidenced "between the expressed attitudes and actual
behavior" in women alcoholics than in their sister controls. This
phenomenon, together with a strict adherence to playing out a
stereotypical role, be it masculine or feminine, may result in
conflict. Whether this is directly related in a cause-effect
relationship to alcohol abuse needs further research.

124. Beckman, L.

 1975.   "Women Alcoholics: A Review of Social and
          Psychological Studies." JOURNAL OF STUDIES ON
          ALCOHOL. 36(7):797-824.

     In an extensive review of the literature on alcoholism,
Beckman focuses on the etiology of female alcoholism. Her study
compares and contrasts the characteristics of male and female
abusers, the effects of alcohol on males and females, as well as
treatment opportunities available to each.
     Research on divergent theories are critically analyzed,
including the concepts of dependency needs, the search for power,
conflict in sex-role identification, the lack of self-concept and
self esteem, and psychological determinants, especially
menstruation and menopause.
     Beckman's review article suggests that generalizations about
why women abuse alcohol is, at best, a precarious task, as
indicated by the contradictions that abound in the literature on
women and alcohol.

125. Belfer, M., R. Shader, M. Carroll, and J. Harmatz.

1971.   "Alcoholism in Women." ARCHIVES OF GENERAL
         PSYCHIATRY. 25(6):540-544.

This study, based on the evaluation of thirty-four alcoholic
and ten nonalcoholic women, focuses on "premenstrual function,
depression, anxiety, femininity, and other parameters." The
authors conclude that there is sufficient evidence to produce a
positive correlation between alcohol intake and menstrual cycle.
Results showed that over 50 percent of the women in this study--
67 percent of the menstruating women and 46 percent of the non-
menstruating women--related their drinking to their menstrual
cycles, and overwhelmingly to the premenstruum as a key time.
Findings also revealed that the alcoholic women in this sample
expressed more anxiety and depression than nonalcoholic women.

126. Beyer, J.M. and H.M. Trice.

1981.   "A Retrospective Study of Similarities and
         Differences Between Men and Women Employees
         in a Job-Based Alcoholism Program from 1965-
         1977." JOURNAL OF DRUG ISSUES. 11(2):233-262.

An increase in female participation in the working world,
coupled with a rise in female alcoholism, has motivated a re-
examination of male-oriented alcohol abuse programs. Male/female
differences, thought to be most significant in treatment,
include; (1)women are more influenced by their environment than
men; (2)women are more apt to obtain treatment for their health
problems; (3)female drinking problems often follow "stressful
life events;" and (4)females reveal a higher rate of suicide
attempts than males.
    With these differences in mind, it is advised that instead
of abandoning constructive confrontation strategies employed so
successfully with males, therapists adapt these techniques to the
special needs of female clients. By placing greater emphasis on
constructive components and deemphasizing direct confrontation,
women alcoholics can be helped. In addition, women's greater
response to social and environmental elements can be utilized as
a therapeutic tool to aid prevention and to facilitate treatment
for women alcoholics.

127. Brahen, L.S.

1973.   "Housewife Drug Abuse." JOURNAL OF DRUG
         EDUCATION. 3(1):13-24.

Drug abuse, not limited to the counterculture and street
people, is becoming problematic in the lives of middle class
housewives. While American women tend to use less illegal drugs
than men, they are prone to be heavy users of "tranquilizers,
antidepressants, strong sedatives, dangerous diet pills, and

powerful analgesics." In order to obtain their prescriptions from physicians, they often find it necessary to "shop around" from doctor to doctor to assure a constant supply.

This article discusses the nature of amphetamines and barbiturates, their medical use, effectiveness, the hazards of prolonged use, and the prevention and treatment of addiction. Newer drugs with diminished addictive-related problems are suggested as a preferred alternative to the use of amphetamines and barbiturates for most women.

128. Burtle, V. (ed.)

1979.   WOMEN WHO DRINK: ALCOHOLIC EXPERIENCE AND PSYCHOTHERAPY. Springfield, Illinois: Charles C. Thomas.

Theoretical constructs concerning alcoholism are illustrated by a self-revealing case study of one woman's experience of drug and alcohol abuse. An excellent article by Edith S. Gomberg on the drinking patterns of female alcoholics provides a review of pertinent literature accompanied by an extensive bibliography. Vernelle Fox also contributes an interesting chapter in which she relates her clinical experiences in an Atlanta treatment clinic for alcoholics. Burtle makes a special contribution to the literature concerning treatment for female alcoholics by offering chapters that focus on the cognitive/behavioral therapy, psychoanalytic therapy, Jungian therapy, Alcoholics Anonymous, gestalt therapy, family therapy, and developmental and learning theories, including their specific approaches to the problems of the woman alcoholic.

129. Coney, J.

1978.   EXPLORING THE UNKNOWN FACTORS IN THE RATES OF ALCOHOLISM AMONG BLACK AND WHITE FEMALES. San Francisco: R&E Research Associates.

This research project attempted to determine whether black females have a higher rate of alcoholism than their white counterparts; what accounts for this difference; whether the rate of alcoholism has risen among black and white females since World War II; and, if so, what factors are responsible for this increase. An extensive array of journals and books were consulted and key citations annotated with additional information gathered from interviews with individuals from 3959 households.

The chapter, "Critical View of Empirical Findings," includes research projects focusing on alcohol problems and concludes with a summary of pertinent information. Findings clearly indicate that alcoholism among women is increasing. It is unknown, however, whether this phenomenon is due to an actual increase or to a greater visibility due to more public drinking. Other factors accounting for increased rates of alcoholism among women are women's changing roles and their greater utilization of treatment facilities.

Coney's research also presented a study of subgroups that indicated a higher percentage of alcoholism among black and Protestant women (the lowest rate was among Jews) and a high rate of abusive drinking among women who are separated, divorced, widowed, or experiencing marital problems. Research also revealed a higher rate of alcoholism among lower-class women, who tend to indulge in heavy drinking at an earlier age. The highest rate of abusive drinking was found among women between the ages of 40 and 59. Unfortunately, much of the research is inconclusive, often clouded by the uncertainty of the rate of secretive drinking, especially among the white female population.

130. Corrigan, E.

    1980.   ALCOHOLIC WOMEN IN TREATMENT. New York: Oxford University Press.

Corrigan presents longitudinal research based on interviews with 150 women who had sought treatment for their alcohol problem, as well as additional interviews with 33 nonalcoholic sisters and 20 husbands.

A review of earlier research findings in the field of women and alcohol reveals that there is insufficient "descriptive data" concerning women who are problem drinkers. Some of the issues that Corrigan feels are important to address include: patterns of drinking; consequences of drinking; the effect of a wife and mother's drinking on a marriage; family life and children; the history of family drinking patterns; and the family's effect on the alcoholic in treatment.

131. Diamond, D. and S. Wilsnack.

    1978.   "Alcohol Abuse Among Lesbians: A Descriptive Study." JOURNAL OF HOMOSEXUALITY. 4(2):123-142.

Ten lesbian alcoholics were interviewed at length to determine the etiology and effect of alcohol on this female subgroup. Hypotheses concerning dependency, power, sex-role expectations, and conflicts and self-esteem were tested. The conclusions were that these ten women evidenced "strong dependency needs and low self-esteem, and a high incidence of depression." While drinking seemed to help respondents cope with dependency needs and self-esteem, it also tended to increase depression with suicidal behavior a common phenomenon.

Diamond recommends that therapists accept the client's homosexual orientation, stressing "acceptance of lesbian and gay males as legitimate sexual minorities rather than deviant and pathological subgroups." Research comparing nonproblem drinking lesbians with alcohol-abusing heterosexual and homosexual female drinkers could enhance our knowledge concerning lesbians and alcohol abuse.

55

132. Dowsling, J. and A. MacLennan. (eds.)

   1978.   THE CHEMICALLY DEPENDENT WOMAN: R$_x$.
            RECOGNITION, REFERRAL, REHABILITATION.
            Toronto, Canada: Addiction Research
            Foundation.

   Based on the proceedings of a conference sponsored by the
Dunwood Institute, this study examines a public hospital that
specializes in the treatment of chemically-dependent patients.
Each chapter represents a presentation covering some aspect of
drug abuse among women, for example, special issues of women in
therapy and psychotropic drug use. Various perspectives are
explored with both patient and physician views well represented.

133. Freedman, T. and L. Finnegan.

   1976.   "Triads and the Drug-Dependent Mother."
            SOCIAL WORK. 21(5):402-404.

   The authors recommend family therapy as an alternative
treatment modality for drug-dependent mothers. Choosing to focus
on the client's environment rather than individual pathology, the
book explores intergenerational conflicts between the addicted
mother's family of origin and her children, and intragenerational
conflicts with the child's father, as well as the client's
friends. Additional contributing factors deemed influential in
her illness are the pressures imposed upon her by her culture
(especially economic) and the intrapersonal stresses of the
client.
   Utilizing the concepts of the "triangularity of family
relationships" and the "individual development process" as aids
in this family systems model, social service practitioners are
advised to focus on the entire family system. Enlisting all
members in tasks and goals implies that the responsibility for
success will be shouldered by the family rather than by the
therapist.

134. Garrett, G. and H. Bahr.

   1973.   "Women on Skid Row." QUARTERLY JOURNAL OF
            STUDIES ON ALCOHOL. 34(4):1228-1243.

   Based on data concerning the drinking patterns of homeless
women in New York's Bowery district and homeless men at a
rehabilitation camp, the authors attempt to compare the
proportion of heavy drinkers among homeless men and women: their
consumption patterns; the degree of heavy drinking for each
group; their preference of beverages consumed; the propensity
towards solitary drinking; the age that drinking commenced; and
the onset of heavy drinking for each sex.
   Research indicates that the number of abstainers among the
men and women are almost equal. Women mistakenly perceive

56

themselves to have similar drinking problems as their male counterparts. Men have a tendency to underreport their "perceived drinking status," but when classified on a quantity-frequency index, they were actually heavier drinkers than women. Other findings revealed that the taking of the first drink, as well as the onset of heavy drinking, occurs later in life for women.

The conclusion that "homeless women alcoholics may very well be the most isolated and disaffiliated residents of skid row" was based on the fact that skid row women are significantly less involved in group activities and receive less aid from the various helping institutions located in their downtown living area than any other poverty group.

135. Hornik, E.L.

1977. THE DRINKING WOMAN. New York: Association Press.

THE DRINKING WOMAN touches lightly on the historical background and common myths concerning women's alcoholism, its etiology, as well as the effects of the drug on the human body. Cultural stresses, especially affecting women, are explored with special attention given to black, Jewish, Indian, and elderly women.

Feminine issues, such as abortion, divorce, the working woman, and overcoming dependency needs are explored, as well as the relationship between marriage, family life and female alcoholism. Poignant case histories are included throughout the book.

Hornik advises that help for the alcoholic woman may be sought through a number of agencies, including treatment centers, detoxification facilities, doctors and counselors specializing in the field, and Alcoholics Anonymous.

136. Kinsey, B.

1966. THE FEMALE ALCOHOLIC: A SOCIAL-PSYCHOLOGICAL STUDY. Springfield, Illinois: Charles C. Thomas Publisher.

As the subtitle suggests, three theoretical categories (physiological, psychological and sociological) concerning the etiology of alcoholism are examined and evaluated. The authors employed a symbolic-interactionist construct to interpret the outcome of research conducted on 46 female respondents ranging in age from 28 to 66.

The importance of this study derives from the paucity of earlier research on female alcoholism and the author's attempt to explain the phenomenon within a more sophisticated psycho-social framework.

137. Langone, J. and D. de Nobrega Langone.

    1980.   WOMEN WHO DRINK. Reading, Massachusetts: Addison-Wesley Publishing Company.

The Langones examine situations that contribute to the rise in female drinking as well as the effects of alcohol on women, their families and friends. A brief historical perspective together with present societal attitudes concerning women's drinking provides a backdrop for an examination of why women drink to excess. Psychological, genetic, environmental, and cultural theories are offered as explanations for the etiology of alcoholism in women. The heterogeneity of female alcoholics along with commonalities and differences between alcohol-abusing males and females provide major findings.

Research garnered from journals, papers presented at scientific meetings, and interviews (including first hand testimony from alcoholics, their families and friends) focus on some of the following issues: the nature of alcoholism and menopause, alcohol and drugs, alcohol and pregnancy (including data on its effects when mixed with contraceptive pills) and the phenomenon of fetal alcohol syndrome(FAS).

Implications for treatment are explored with feminist and family therapy viewed as positive treatment modalities. Several concrete programs that are highlighted include: Alcoholics Anonymous; the women's alcohol program of CASPAR; the Alcohol Center for Women which specializes in lesbian clients; Dr. Jean Kirkpatrick's Women for Sobriety; the Menninger Foundation recovery program; as well as the Alcohol and Drug Rehabilitation Service at the California Naval Hospital in Long Beach, the latter having treated many celebrities, such as Betty Ford and Billy Carter. Numerous facilities which specialize in aiding the alcoholic are conveniently listed with addresses and phone numbers for persons seeking help.

138. March, J., M. Colten, and M. Tucker.

    1982.   "Women's Use of Drugs and Alcohol: New Perspectives." JOURNAL OF SOCIAL ISSUES. 38(2):entire issue.

The focus of the 1982 summer JOURNAL OF SOCIAL ISSUES examines new perspectives on female substance abuse. Representing many of the alcohol and drug experts in the field, March, et.al. look at the legal, historical and political implications of alcohol and drug use.

139. Nellis, M.

    1981.   FEMALE FIX. New York: Penguin Books.

The author, herself the director of the first national conference on women and drugs, examines the problem of female drug dependency in America. Social catalysts, which may drive women to such dependency, are analyzed, as well as the role of the medical profession and pharmaceutical companies in perpetuating female addiction.

140. Norback, J.

1980.   THE ALCOHOL AND DRUG ABUSE YEARBOOK/DIRECTORY. New York: Van Nostrand Reinhold Co.

This publication provides a wealth of material that focuses on educating the reader about the etiology, treatment and prevention of drug abuse. Of special interest are the chapters devoted to alcohol abuse and women; the effects of alcohol on the human body; and the structure and goals of Alcoholics Anonymous and Al-Anon. An extensive listing of alcohol and drug treatment centers (by state) is included for those seeking help.

141. Rosenbaum, M.

1981.   WOMEN ON HEROIN. New Brunswick, N.J.: Rutgers University Press.

This "street study" of one hundred women of varying races and ages presents an insightful sociological view of what it is like to be a woman locked into the heroin culture. The author traces the entire "career" of the woman addict, asking such questions as: How and why does a woman become addicted to heroin? Is she a liberated woman, breaking through sexual barriers and functioning alongside men in the heroin world? Or is she doubly oppressed as an addict and a woman? The study shows that the experience of addiction is vastly different for men and women, and that treatment programs must therefore also differ.

142. Sandmaier, M.

1980.   THE INVISIBLE ALCOHOLICS: WOMEN AND ALCOHOL ABUSE IN AMERICA. New York: McGraw-Hill Book Company.

Sandmaier captures the experiences of alcoholic women living in a culture which simultaneously ignores and stigmatizes them. She offers a brief history of alcohol use among women and updates it with a chapter on the scope of the problem today. The etiology of female alcohol abuse is examined, followed by a focus on such female subgroups as housewives, employed women, minority women, adolescents, lesbians, and skid row women.
Hazards that women encounter when seeking treatment are addressed as well as the often symbiotic relationship between sexism and alcoholism. The final chapter offers a range of approaches for helping the alcoholic woman, including treatment

programs, support groups, related services, and recommended readings for further information.

143. Schuckit, M.

1972.   "The Alcoholic Woman: A Literature Review." PSYCHIATRY IN MEDICINE. 3(1):37-43.

This comparative study on the effects of alcohol on male and female abusers was conducted in an effort to establish a more accurate picture of the female alcoholic. Schuckit has compiled information from 28 studies that show characteristics of female alcoholics, including: age of onset of disease, time of first hospitalization, marriage status, satisfaction in marriage, intelligence testing, and family background. Findings also reveal that alcoholism in women frequently follows an affective illness and is often accompanied by suicidal behavior.

144. Tamerin, J.

1978.   "The Psychotherapy of Alcoholic Women." In S. Zimberg, J. Wallace and S. Blume (eds.) PRACTICAL APPROACHES TO ALCOHOLISM PSYCHOTHERAPY. New York: Plenum Press. p.183-203.

Several chapters in the book are devoted to the treatment of different populations of abusive drinkers with one concentrating specifically on the psychotherapy of alcoholic women. A literature review includes Tamerin's own data on male and female alcoholic's spouses and self perceptions. Females were more frequently depicted as guilty or depressed, these findings show.
Drinking patterns of male and female alcoholics are contrasted as are etiological features. These include psychological problems, sex role conflicts, the influence of family history, and the influence of stressful life events. The evaluation and treatment of alcoholic women are discussed with illustrations from several case histories. Tamerin's bibliography includes many of the leading studies concerning women's alcohol use available in the field.

145. Tyler, J. and M. Thompson.

1980.   "Patterns of Drug Abuse Among Women." THE INTERNATIONAL JOURNAL OF THE ADDICTIONS. 15(3):309-321.

Authors Tyler and Thompson identify patterns in the abuse of heroin, marijuana, barbiturates, and amphetamines as linked to such variables as age, education and race. The study sample included 14,428 women attending a federally funded drug treatment center. Findings indicate that in the 19 to 20 year age group, heroin was the most abused and marijuana the second most abused drug. Women with a high school education were more likely to abuse heroin than those with less than a 9th grade education.

Implications for treatment include the area of primary prevention, which entails "community-based, socially acceptable alternatives to drug-taking behavior."

V

Bisexuality

146. Bode, J.

1976.   VIEW FROM ANOTHER CLOSET: EXPLORING
BISEXUALITY IN WOMEN. New York: Hawthorne
Books, Inc.

Utilizing both an in-depth interview and a questionnaire,
Bode records the "experiences and philosophies of bisexual
women." The average age of these women was 27.8 years with 17
percent married at the time of the research (23 percent had been
married at least once). VIEW FROM ANOTHER CLOSET reveals the
dilemmas that bisexuals face ("that unique double-pressure
situation") together with the advantages and disadvantages of
their alternative sexual lifestyle. The variables of family
background, parental dominance, sibling relationships, self-
image, religious influence, sexual identity, and environmental
influences are related to the phenomena of bisexuality.
In conclusion, the women interviewed believed that sexual
mores and attitudes are changing "toward a more rounded,
androgynous society free of all sex-role stereotyping."

147. Blumstein, P.W. and P. Schwartz.

1976.   "Bisexuality in Women." ARCHIVES OF SEXUAL
BEHAVIOR. 5(2):171-181.

Interviewing women with a history of bisexual behavior
and/or a bisexual self-identification, the authors show that
there is only a moderate correspondence between identity and
behavior. Blumstein and Schwartz provide a general description of
the sexual relationships of the study participants. The major
focus is on the wide diversity of self-identified bisexual women,
especially in terms of self-perceived sexual and emotional needs.
These circumstances precipitate both heterosexual and homosexual
behavior, and support a bisexual lifestyle. Heterosexuals in the
study group reported that, while they responded to different
kinds of situational exigencies which made homosexual relations a
possibility, they evidently neutralized the homosexual stigma in
maintaining their heterosexual self-identification.

148. MacInnes, C.

      1973.   LOVING THEM BOTH: A STUDY OF BISEXUALITY AND BISEXUALS. London: Martin, Brian, and O'Keeffe.

    MacInnes' personal essay incorporates his views on the phenomenon of bisexuality by describing the "types and practices among men and women I have encountered." Although not a scholarly sociological study, LOVING THEM BOTH is interesting reading in an area of alternative sexual lifestyles in which little has been written.

149. Wolff, C.

      1977.   BISEXUALITY: A STUDY. London: Quartet Books.

    BISEXUALITY: A STUDY, a sequel to LOVE BETWEEN WOMEN, is directed towards both the lay and professional reader, and covers numerous interpretations of bisexuality, including the views of Jung, Freud, Mead, Kinsey, and Harvey. The author discusses the biological origins of bisexuality and distinguishes between gender identity and sexual orientation. Several chapters are devoted to the investigations of the origins and influences prevalent in the life of a bisexual with the latter portion of the book devoted to three extensive in-depth interviews with three bisexuals.

    The appendix, consisting of 31 tables of questionnaire data returned by the respondents, is accompanied by helpful instructions for reading the tables. A glossary is also included.

VI

Corrections and Punishment

150. Alpert, G.P. and J.J. Wiorkowski.

> 1977.   "Female Prisoners and Legal Services."
> QUARTERLY JOURNAL OF CORRECTIONS. 1(4):28-33.
> Special Issue.

The effects of sociolegal background and attitudes on the use of legal services by female inmates are explored in a study of 71 females sentenced to the Texas Department of Corrections. The subjects were interviewed as they were admitted to the prison system and again six or seven months later to determine whether they had used the system's legal services program. Data were gathered on sociodemographic characteristics, attitudes and experiences with the law and the legal system. The data show that the number of times a woman has been adjudicated delinquent appears to be the best predictor of her use of legal aid. Other important factors are number of criminal convictions, age (younger women seem reluctant to seek legal aid), degree of imprisonization (those less caught up in prison culture are more likely to seek legal aid), and attitudes toward lawyers, the law, the judicial system, and work. The findings support those of a similar study in Washington State. Although the variables in the two studies are not identical, both investigations suggest that attitudes, values and experiences brought into prison from the outside world are predictors of legal aid usage. Supporting data and a list of references are included.

151. Anderson, E.A.

> 1976.   "The Chivalrous Treatment of the Female
> Offender in the Arms of the Criminal Justice
> System: A Review of the Literature." SOCIAL
> PROBLEMS. 23(3):350-357.

This article reviews the available literature on the management of the female offender by the criminal justice system to ascertain the extent and nature of differential treatment. In addition, an attempt is made to identify the major assumptions about the nature of female criminality which underlie the notion that women are, in general, more likely to be exposed to a "chivalrous" justice system. Three characterizations of the female offender, which have influenced the perpetuation and survival of the "chivalry" proposition are discussed: the instigative female offender (a manipulative female who cons male criminals into displaying a chivalrous attitude toward her); the sexualized female offender (women who turn to crime for purely sexual reasons); and the protected female offender (the idea that female criminals need to be protected by the criminal justice system). The author concludes that the notion of a chivalrous justice system is largely a myth. Directions for future research and a two page list of references are included.

152. Arditi, R.R., F. Goldberg, M.M. Hartle, J.H. Peters, and W.R. Phelps.

1973.   "Sexual Segregation of American Prisons." MENTAL HEALTH DIGEST. 5(9):18-26.

This study examines differential treatment of male and female inmates with an assessment of the constitutionality of such practices in light of the 14th and equal rights amendments. Data were obtained from state corrections departments, U.S. Bureau of Prisons, women's prisons of nine states, four federal correctional institutions, and 15 sample states chosen on the basis of size and geographic location. Differences between prison systems include: women's prisons were found to be considerably smaller and more remote than men's prisons. For male prisoners there are different institutions for the various categories of offenders, while women's institutions include inmates with more diverse offenses, sentences and ages. Men's institutions were found to have more complete medical and religious services than female institutions. Women's prisons provide architectural and security arrangements which emphasize rehabilitation, and show less concern with custody than is the case for men's prisons. The article discusses the constitutionality of differential treatment of male and female inmates, and summarizes the impact of the proposed equal rights amendment in this area.

153. Baunach, P.J.

1977.   "Women Offenders: A Commentary--Current Conceptions on Women in Crime." QUARTERLY JOURNAL OF CORRECTIONS. 1(4):14-18. Special Issue.

The author presents an overview of the status of the female offender, especially those who experience incarceration. Possible causes for the increase in the number of women offenders are analyzed along with the conditions of women's confinement, the problems confronting incarcerated women and the need for research about the female offender. As the population of women offenders increases, the problems inherent in the imprisonment process become more acute. The writer critically assesses the rationale for the apparent increase of incarceration. The major policy conclusion is the need to explore alternatives to current approaches for dealing with women offenders.

65

154. Baunach, P.J. and T.D. Murton.

   1973.   "Women in Prison--An Awakening Minority."
            CRIME AND CORRECTIONS. 1(2):4-12.

   This article examines a wide array of previously neglected
research issues, including the conditions of imprisonment for
women, reactions of female inmates to such conditions, prison
strikes and riots in women's institutions, and innovations in the
women's correctional system. According to the authors, the
criminal justice system is overwhelmed with problems caused by
the increase in female criminality, leading to higher arrests,
prosecution rates and a growing female inmate population.
   Prison conditions in women's institutions located in
Georgia, South Carolina, Illinois, and Iowa, the sites for the
study, demonstrate a wide range of prison types. Little
publicized strikes and riots by female inmates protesting prison
conditions have led to innovations. The authors recommend that
coed prisons, inmate councils and allowing female prisoners to
keep their babies provide needed changes in women's institutions.

155. Berecochea, J.E. and C. Spencer.

   1972.   RECIDIVISM AMONG WOMEN PAROLEES: A LONG-TERM
            SURVEY. Sacramento, California: California
            Department of Corrections.

   This study describes the effects of agency decision-making
on long-term parole outcomes among California's women parolees.
Of the test group of 626 women released in 1960 and 1961, 40
percent were returned to prison over an eight year period--a rate
almost twice the national average. Of this group, 80 percent were
returned to prison for parole violations rather than commission
of new felonies, and half were multiple returnees. Such returnees
increased the original incarceration time and costs by 44
percent, of which two-thirds can be attributed to parole
violators. Parole violators were characterized by narcotics use,
a prior commitment record, minority group membership, and
comparatively low educational and intelligence test scores.
Additionally, it was found that these characteristics were
associated with differential treatment, indicating that they were
viewed by the agency as highly likely to become involved in new
criminality. Thus, the study's tentative conclusion was that high
recidivism rates among women were a function of agency decisions
based on factors unrelated to the criminal behavior of the
parolee.

156. Bertcher, H.J.

> 1974.   ATTITUDES OF GIRLS TOWARD STAFF IN A
>   CORRECTIONAL INSTITUTION. Michigan:
>   University Microfilms, Inc.

The purpose of this study was to examine selected factors presumed to be associated with the development of inmates' attitudes toward staff in a female correctional institution. Many factors in addition to peer group pressure affect the attitudes of inmates toward staff, and such attitudes can be positive as well as negative. Factors that were thought to affect inmate attitudes toward staff and that were selected for study were inmate interaction with staff, inmate interaction with other inmates, inmate attitudes towards discharge, the attitudes of inmates toward themselves, and the length of time inmates' stay in the institution.

157. Burkhart, K.W.

> 1973.   WOMEN IN PRISON. New York: Doubleday and Co.,
>   Inc.

This well received book deals with prison life from the women's perspective, revealing their experiences and feelings. The author conveys the meanness of prison existence without distortion or bias. Realities are opposed to myths concerning women's prisons. Looking at the impact of the system for alleviating crime, the author concludes that prison creates the criminal. The research is based on visits to twenty one jails and prisons for women; sixteen county and city jails (thirteen housing both men and women and three exclusively for women), five state, and one federal prison for women. Her data consisted of 400 in-depth interviews with women in prison and 500 more women located in various jails or who were formerly jailed.

158. Chandler, E.W.

> 1973.   WOMEN IN PRISON. New York: Bobbs-Merrill.

This work deals with prison programs, inmate characteristics, parole procedures, and institutional life at the California Institution for Women (CIW). The author presents a brief discussion of the admittance procedure at CIW and the rehabilitative goals of the prison. Several chapters are devoted to the development and maintenance of interpersonal relationships between inmates and staff, inmates and their families and between recently admitted inmates and older residents. Discussion centers on the psychological impact of the prison experience on a woman, especially the problems she has adjusting to institutional life and its controls, and later, the reverse problems of readjustment to life in the free world. The parole program in California and the halfway house are cited as means of helping women released from prison to readjust to society. This work discusses data obtained from a questionnaire (which is included) sent to other institutions for women in the United States. The appendices also contain summaries of institutional trends and practices from eighteen other women's prisons.

159. Cook, M.E. and S. Jasper.

    1976.   AN EXPLORATORY STUDY OF RUNAWAY FEMALE ADOLESCENTS IN A RESIDENTIAL TREATMENT CENTER. Portland State University. (Unpublished Manuscript, Masters in Social Work).

This study specifically focuses on the factors that influence a teenage girl to run away and what factors encourage her to stay at Villa St. Rose, a residential treatment center in Portland, Oregon. The authors researched the influencing factors regarding runaways by investigating the differences of functioning between girls placed in different treatment teams and the differences in attitudes and behavior between the residential groups. This is an exploratory study of the various influences that motivate girls to run away. The study also aims to reduce the likelihood of this occurring by recommending improvements of overall treatment of female adolescents in such institutions.

160. Eyman, J.S.

    1975.   PRISONS FOR WOMEN: A PRACTICAL GUIDE TO ADMINISTRATION PROBLEMS. Springfield, Illinois: C.C. Thomas.

Distinct areas in which women's prisons differ from men's are often ignored. This study shows that because women represent only a small proportion of the total inmate population, prison facilities are grossly under-budgeted, and, hence, wholly inadequate. Only one state provides more than one state facility for female offenders.

This guide addresses the issue of the special needs of the female offender. It recognizes the neglect involved in housing women in institutions designed for men, and observes how small numbers of female inmates supposedly make it economically unsound to establish separate institutions. For example, states could join together to establish regional correctional institutions. The author emphasizes that "some women's institutions have made notable contributions to penology, but far more are still disgraceful and guilty of criminal neglect."

161. Feinman, C.

    1980.   WOMEN IN THE CRIMINAL JUSTICE SYSTEM. New
                  York: Praeger Publishers.

    This is a study of women in the criminal justice system,
based on the author's interviews with the prisoners, corrections
personnel in prisons and jails, and observations in the New York
Corrections Institute for Women on Rikers Island. In addition,
police personnel, lawyers and judges in a number of cities were
interviewed.

162. Giallombardo, R.

    1966.   THE SOCIAL WORLD OF IMPRISONED GIRLS. New
                  York: Wiley.

    This study offers an insightful analysis of women's prison
life based on research in three institutions for adjudicated
delinquent girls. Examining the impact of organizational goals
and age statuses on inmate organizations, the author shows the
impact of cultural definitions of sex roles on the informal
social organization. Differences were then identified between
female and male methods of coping with prison life. Findings
suggest that the informal culture evolved by the girls at the
three institutions is similar in structure, and that girls in
each institution faced similar problems of incarceration. These
are attributed to a nonresponsive formal organization which
ignored the girls' needs and their informal organizations.

163. MacArthur, V. (ed.)

    1974.   FROM CONVICT TO CITIZEN: PROGRAMS FOR THE
                  WOMAN OFFENDER. Washington, D.C.: District of
                  Columbia Commission on the Status of Women.

    This is a presentation of women's correctional programs and
recommendations. It is a very broad overview of what programs are
available nationally to the female offender. The report is
available from the Commission: Rm.204 District Building, 14th and
E street N.W., Washington D.C.

164. Mitchell, A.

    1969.   SOCIAL STRUCTURE IN PRISONS FOR WOMEN.
                  University of Washington Ph.D. Dissertation.

    Mitchell is concerned with one aspect of the process of
adult socialization, namely, the impact of institutional goals on
the structure of informal inmate social structure. Two prisons
were selected on the basis of their contrasting organizational
goals. The study was guided by the general hypothesis that

variations in formal prison organization are closely associated with variations in informal inmate social structures. The study concluded that (1)inmates in custody-oriented institutions have more negative attitudes toward the prison staff than those in the treatment-oriented institutions; (2)inmates in the custody-oriented institution have more positive attitudes toward other inmates than those in the treatment-oriented institution; and (3)the frequency of homosexual activity will be greater in the treatment-oriented institution than in the custody-oriented institution.

165. Mosely, W.H. and M.H. Gerould.

   1975. "Sex and Parole: A Comparison of Male and Female Prisoners." JOURNAL OF CRIMINAL JUSTICE. (3):45-58.

  Surveying personal attitudes, time served and parole outcome among women offenders, this article emphasizes that men's and women's attitudes are varied, but that no conclusive findings can be made. This comparison of men's and women's prisons is empirically documented. The study also includes tables and a bibliography.

166. Rafter, N.H.

   1983. "Female State Prisoners, 1790-1980." In N. Morris and M. Tonry. (eds.) CRIME AND JUSTICE: AN ANNUAL REVIEW OF RESEARCH, VOL. 5. Chicago: University of Chicago Press.

  Nicole Hahn Rafter poignantly illustrates the unequal justice of incarcerated women over the last 200 years. She provides a chronological and regional perspective of an unequal prison system based on sex role stereotyping.
  Rafter argues that women's institutions and their inmates have received little attention in the literature on prisons. She argues that this neglect is based, in part, on two mistaken assumptions: (1) that the experience of female inmates in the prison system and the development of the women's prison system, have closely resembled those of men; or alternatively, (2) that if the two systems are different, then the experiences of female inmates and the history of the development of the women's prison system are irrelevant to mainstream penology. This is because such variations are believed to shed little light on the nature of the prison system as a whole. Both assumptions are false, Rafter argues persuasively.

167. Smykla, J.O. (ed.)

   1980. COED PRISON. New York: Human Sciences Press.

In this collection, the editor presents the administrative, interpersonal and research issues related to sexually integrated prisons. The various articles explore such diverse aspects as sex differences in the ways inmates adapt to prison; recidivism rates in coed vs. segregated prisons; feminist perspectives on sexual equality in integrated prisons; interpersonal relationships among inmates; examination of specific facilities and programs; and a special section which focuses on the role of the female offender. The articles indicate some new directions in the organization of prison life.

168. U.S. Department of Labor, Office of the Secretary, Women's Bureau.

    1980.   THE WOMEN OFFENDER APPRENTICE PROGRAM: FROM INMATE TO SKILLED WORKER. Pamphlet 21.

The result of a ten year study by the Women's Bureau of the U.S. Department of Labor, this pamphlet deals mainly with remedies for the problem of institutional limitations placed on women offenders and ex-offenders to achieve economic independence. The women offender's apprenticeship program is explained in some detail, as this program aims to improve the chances of women offenders becoming productive members of society.

169. Weintraub, J.F.

    1981.   "Delivery of Services to Families of Prisoners." In P.C. Kratcoski, CORRECTIONAL COUNSELING AND TREATMENT. Monterey, California: Duxbury Press.

This article deals with the special needs of the families of prisoners, i.e. "discrete client group." It is based on the premise "that the problems of the family are the problems of the defender." Weintraub identifies four specific crisis points for the family of an individual passing through the criminal justice system, and how each crisis point represents a special family problem. To meet these special problems, Weintraub outlines ways to establish an information office for families and further reinforces the importance of such a program. "The family (of the offender) exists and it behooves the public and the private correctional establishment to recognize the fact."

VII

Crimes Against Women

A. Domestic Violence

1. General

170. Dobash, R.E. and R.P. Dobash

1981.   "Community Response to Violence Against
            Wives: Charivari, Abstract Justice and
            Patriarchy." SOCIAL PROBLEMS. 28(5):563-81.

     The authors analyze community response to wife battering,
its history from the fifteenth century to the present, beginning
with direct and personal responses by members of the community
and developing into the more abstract and impersonal responses of
the state institutions that emerged during the eighteenth and
nineteenth centuries. Within both of these types of responses the
intent has not been to stop the violence but rather to set limits
on how much violence the husband may use in pursuing his rights.
The development of abstract institutional regulation in society
from the former informal means forces battered women to seek help
from such impersonal institutions as the police, which were not
established or trained to deal with domestic order, and so remain
relatively unconcerned with the problem of wife abuse.

171. Gibbens, T.C.N.

1975.   "Violence in the Family." MICRO-LEGAL
            JOURNAL. 43(3):76-88.

     The author presents an overview of statistics from the
literature on violence in the family, spouse abuse, child abuse,
and intra-sibling violence. In discussing wife beating, the
author states that, once a husband is really worked up, police
intervention will probably result in harm to the officer. The
police are said to be popular with "this sort of woman," because
they step in, stop the violence, and leave without the prying
questions of social workers regarding their marriage, background,
etc.

172. Green, M.R. (ed.)

      1980.   VIOLENCE AND THE FAMILY. Boulder, Colorado: Westview Press, Inc.

This set of papers reports and interprets data on several types of family violence and suggests that the factors responsible for most of the violence in families stem from the prevailing idea that physical punishment is "morally right," as confirmed repeatedly by societal norms. There is a delicate balance in human relationships, in which violence acts as another "unfortunate" event in a system of negative family experiences. The articles explore ethnic and subcultural factors, as well as the presentation of new material about cultures that do not permit violence. A final paper explores the potential role of the police in preventing the escalation of violence and in teaching alternatives to violence-prone families.

173. Nichols, B.B.

      1976.   "The Abused Wife Problem." SOCIAL CASEWORK. 57(1):27-32.

This article examines aspects of wife abuse the author deems pertinent to caseworkers. Examined are: concepts which tend to maintain the pattern of abuse rather than treat it; the issue of differential police intervention; a comparison of police response to wife assault and stranger assault. The protection of the abused is crucial, while legal aid in this direction is slow and costly. The author calls on caseworkers, the majority of whom are women, to be more assertive in designing interventions.

174. Parnas, R.I.

      1973.   "Prosecutorial and Judicial Handling of Family Violence." CRIMINAL LAW BULLETIN. 9(9):733-69.

The purpose of the article is to define the problem of family violence, emphasize its importance, and describe the various beginning efforts being made to handle intra-family violence. Data was gathered on various aspects of the criminal justice response to domestic violence, including the prosecutor, joint police/prosecutor methods, the courts, and community-based programs and agencies. The author feels an effort must be made to divert cases away from the criminal process.

175. Schechter, L.F.

> 1982. "The Violent Family and the Ambivalent State:
> Developing a Coherent Policy for State Aid to
> Victims of Family Violence." JOURNAL OF
> FAMILY LAW. 20(1):1-42.

This article examines the state's role in aiding victims of
family violence, reviewing programs adopted in the past and
recommending policies for the state to follow in the future. The
author points out that legislative efforts on both the federal
and state level have focused on separate groups of individuals--
abused children, battered wives, and abused elders--rather than
on the problem of family violence as a whole. Policies for the
future must be based on the knowledge that the various
manifestations of family violence are interrelated, and any
attempt to cope with one of them in isolation is a fundamental
error.

176. Steinmetz, S.K. and M.A. Straus. (eds.)

> 1974. VIOLENCE IN THE FAMILY. New York: Dodd, Mead,
> and Company.

The National Council on Family Relations offered the
principle impetus for a summary of publications focusing on
violence in the family. The articles in this book were selected
from an extensive bibliography (400 items) acquired by the
editors during their own research. In this work, the authors
emphasize that their primary goal involved raising society's
consciousness concerning domestic violence and its serious
implications for all citizens.
    Each of the volume's four sections-- overview: intra-family
violence; violence between spouses and kin; violent parents; and
the family as training ground for societal violence--is prefaced
by an informative introduction.

2. Battering

177. Ahrens, L.

    1980.   "Battered Women's Refuges: Feminist Cooperatives Vs. Social Service Institutions." AEGIS. Summer:9-15.

Refuges for battered women, like rape crisis centers, seem to be undergoing a transformation throughout the United States from feminist, non-hierarchical, community-based organizations to institutionalized social service agencies. The author discusses her experience in an Austin, Texas shelter as a typical example of this trend.

178. Bass, D. and J. Rice.

    1979.   "Agency Responses to the Abused Wife." SOCIAL CASEWORK: THE JOURNAL OF CONTEMPORARY SOCIAL WORK. 60(6):338-342.

Largely ignored in the context of family violence, wife abuse is defined in this study as "a situation in which an adult woman is intentionally physically harmed by a man with whom she has an established relationship, regardless of marital status."
Conditions influencing wives to stay in an abusive relationship depend on such variables as the frequency and severity of the violence and whether alcohol was a factor in the violent behavior. Other conditions include the acceptance of cultural norms that promote sexual inequality and the lack of support resources available to the victim.
When studying the type of treatment provided to abused wives by social service agencies, researchers discovered that agencies fail to treat wife abuse as a problem in and of itself. Instead, they tend to view it simply as a symptom of other family problems. Findings indicate that abused wives need multiple services which are often limited due to the lack of networking within the social service community.

179. Chapman J.R. and M. Gates. (eds.)

    1978.   VICTIMIZATION OF WOMEN. Beverly Hills, Ca.: Sage Publications.

The editors have collected eleven articles by practitioners, planners and policy-oriented professionals to present current research and data on violence against women, including rape, the

sexual abuse of children, battered women, the prostitute, and
sexual harassment. This is recommended reading for courses on
victimology, women's studies, and especially those dealing with
female deviance.

180. Davidson, T.

　　　1978.　　　CONJUGAL CRIME: UNDERSTANDING AND CHANGING
　　　　　　　　　THE WIFEBEATING PATTERN. New York: Hawthorn
　　　　　　　　　Books, Inc.

　　　In this thoughtful book, the author presents alternatives
for all members should a family be involved in violence: the wife
to seek counseling or a shelter; the husband to recognize that he
cannot control himself, but desires to change; the witnessing
children that are trapped at home without the ability to help,
and who need guidence to survive the family crisis. There is
practical advice and hope for many families, while providing a
new perspective toward understanding a complex social problem.
　　　The author includes a complete index of hotline numbers,
referral addresses of over fifty shelters in the United States
and a look at the daily life inside one shelter. In addition
there is a list of "grassroots publications" that are not
available elsewhere.
　　　Ms. Davidson's book is one of the more practical
contributions to the field.

181. Dobash, R.E. and R. Dobash.

　　　1978.　　　VIOLENCE AGAINST WIVES. New York: The Free
　　　　　　　　　Press.

　　　Based on interviews with battered wives and a review of
police and court records in Edinburgh and Glasgow, Scotland, the
authors have written an important contribution to the literature
on wife abuse and violence. Dobash and Dobash used case histories
of violent marriages that are based on an in-depth assessment of
the history of marriage, the violent events within it and the
response of friends, relatives and social agencies.
　　　The authors' approach places wife abuse in the context of
the husband's power and domination over all within the family
unit and society's support of this arrangement. The book also
documents agency failure to support egalitarian marriage.

182. Dobash, R.E. and R.P. Dobash.

　　　1977.　　　"Love, Honor, and Obey: Institutional
　　　　　　　　　Ideologies and the Struggle for Battered
　　　　　　　　　Women." CONTEMPORARY CRISES. 1(4):403-15.

　　　The authors view the struggle for battered women as not just
the struggle for women beaten by their husbands or a struggle

against men who batter their wives. It is a struggle against the structure and ideologies which support wife beating and the oppression of women in marriage. They demonstrate how it is possible to want to help battered women while still adhering to the general principles which contribute to their battering. This is possible because the problem is defined as an individual one and not as one inherent in our social institutions. This is followed with a critique of the patriarchal family as a social institution in which wives are seen as property subject to control, including physical coercion. Sympathetic individuals do not want women to be battered, and yet they do not want to question the structure of the family which allows it. The two desires are mutually exclusive.

183. Langley, R. and R.C. Levy.

       1977.   WIFE BEATING: THE SILENT CRISIS. New York: E.P. Dutton.

     Offering evidence that will shatter popular myths about domestic violence, the authors present vivid case histories of victims, using original data to present what psychologists, criminologists and sociologists have discovered about wifebeating.
     Examining several interviews with doctors, lawyers and judges, Langley and Levy provide information for the victim that can help in dealing with social agencies and courts. This book presents an excellent introductory reference to the issues of wifebeating.

184. Miller, N.

       1975.   BATTERED SPOUSES. London: G. Bell and Sons.

     A revised and extended version of the author's dissertation, this book breaks the subject down into three areas: the "problem," consisting of introductory definitions and causal explanations; the needs of the battered woman, including issues of public policy, functions, orientations, and responses of specific agencies, the police, legal advice, and the criminal law and the courts; the third section looks toward the future, calling for an improvement of current official provisions and explores future trends in the role of the voluntary provider. A 120-citation bibliography is provided.

185. Pizzey, E.

       1977.   SCREAM QUIETLY OR THE NEIGHBORS WILL HEAR. New York: R. Enslow Publishers.

     With letters and case histories of several battered women and children together with original research by the author,

Pizzey discusses the first shelter for battered women and their
children. This initiated a much needed focus and awareness of
violence in the family in the United States and England. The
shelter opened in Cheswick, England in 1971 as a community center
where desperate women and children could come to meet others,
while escaping loneliness. Within a year it was home for thirty-
four women and children from violent homes.

Erin Pizzey discusses the legal problems facing battered
women in receiving assistance from law enforcement, medical and
social services when they attempted to report the violence and/or
tried to get away from the home. She also discusses the pattern
of violence in the families, continuing through the next
generation.

The letters and case histories document how children as well
as the wives are victims of violence, regardless of whether they
were battered or not. This book is a necessary contribution to
both the treatment and social science fields.

186. Renvoize, J.

    1978.   WEB OF VIOLENCE: A STUDY OF FAMILY VIOLENCE.
                 London: Routledge and Kegan Paul.

With documented case histories of both victims and
batterers, Jean Renvoize traces the web of violence along several
different strands. In this exploration of baby-battering, child
abuse, violent husbands and wives, "granny-bashing" and incest,
the author examines the psychological roots and social patterns
of family violence, including the agencies involved in treating
or preventing family violence, such as social workers, shelters,
police, and doctors. This book documents a major social problem
with insight and objectivity.

187. Roy, M. (ed.)

    1977.   BATTERED WOMEN: A PSYCHOSOCIOLOGICAL STUDY OF
                 DOMESTIC VIOLENCE. New York: Van Nostrand
                 Reinhold Co.

Beginning with a succinct history of wifebeating, Maria Roy
shows how the American culture has tolerated and condoned the use
of physical force to resolve marital conflicts. Included in her
book is a recent survey of 150 wifebeating cases and an extensive
examination of the social dynamics of the battering syndrome.

With a view towards understanding the phenomena while
finding practical solutions the author explores two questions:
(1)why do women stay with men who abuse them? (2)what is the role
of alcohol, drugs, sexual, and financial problems in
precipitating assault?

Also examined are the legal aspects, including ways in which
battered women can obtain equal protection under the law. Roy's
book is an invaluable source of information for anyone concerned
with wifebeating and its social repercussions.

188. Straus, M.A.

1976.   "Sexual Inequality, Cultural Norms, and Wife-Beating." VICTIMOLOGY. 1(1):54-70.

This article examines how the cultural norms built into the structure of contemporary Euro-American societies legitimize wife beating through the sexist organization of the family system. Sexism is seen as contributing to wife beating in significant ways: (1)the male oriented organization of the criminal justice system, (2)the social role of the woman, which gives her the full burden of childcare, denies equal opportunities, and makes her depdendent upon her husband.

189. Straus, M.A. and G.T. Hotaling.

1980.   THE SOCIAL CAUSES OF HUSBAND-WIFE VIOLENCE. Minneapolis, Minn.: University of Minnesota Press.

Straus and Hotaling present research findings that contribute not only to empirical knowledge but also to the development of theory in the study of family relationships as well as the larger field of social conflict and violence. Writing within the ironic perspective, the authors show that family living may lead to forms of conflict and violence rarely found outside the family context.
Since the social causes of husband-wife violence are diverse and complex, seven of the chapters show how different sets of these factors might operate to produce violence. Five of the chapters illustrate different methods of research such as case studies, content analysis of popular literature, brief questionnaire studies, and a survey of a nationally representative sample of couples. This book makes a significant contribution to the analysis of family violence.

190. Walker, L.E.

1979.   THE BATTERED WOMAN. New York: Harper and Row Publishers.

This book is based on an extensive three year research project by Dr.Walker on wifebattering. The author explains how women become trapped in a "learned helplessness" syndrome through a three stage battering cycle. The book also explores the different types of battering such as economic deprivation, family discord, social battering, and physical and sexual abuse, and offers several illustrative cases. The final section of the book, "The Way Out," deals with the new possibilities for help-safe houses, legal and medical alternatives and possible future programs. This book is "must" reading for both professional and lay people.

191. Walker, L.E.

1978.   "Treatment Alternatives for Battered Women."
          In J.R. Chapman and M. Gates (eds.) THE
          VICTIMIZATION OF WOMEN. Beverly Hills, Ca.:
          Sage Publications, Inc.

This article provides a well written, comprehensive approach
to the problems and needs associated with providing treatment for
battered women. The author first outlines the three cycle theory
of battering incidents, in which stage one, or the tension
building stage, is characterized by minor battering incidents
which get worse as tension builds; stage two is the explosion, or
acute battering stage where incidents generally last from two to
24 hours, and is characterized by the uncontrolled discharge of
the tensions built up in the previous stage; stage three
represents the end of this phase of the cycle, and is
characterized by loving, kind, and contrite behavior on the part
of the husband, who realizes he has gone too far and attempts to
make it up to her. This cycle can be repeated many times, ending
only with separation or death. The author then goes on to
describe specific treatment alternatives available to women in
England and America; refuges, safehouses, and shelters, comparing
the systems in the two countries and critiquing their
limitations. Naturally occurring support systems in the community
which the battered woman can utilize are discussed, as are
various psychotherapy modalities. A critique of the criminal
justice system is presented, in which she examines police
protection, restraining orders and legal rights in divorce
actions.

3. Child Abuse

192. Burgess, A.W., A.N. Groth, L.L. Holmstrom, and S.M. Syvoi.

      1978.   SEXUAL ASSAULT OF CHILDREN AND ADOLESCENTS.
                Lexington, Mass.: Lexington Books.

The authors focus on three general areas of child abuse: the
human dimension, community program planning and interagency
cooperation. They define sexual assault as "forced, pressured or
stressful sexual behavior committed on a person under the age of
17 years."
The book provides a complete needs assessment, including a
plan for education on prevention and treatment of sexual assault,
focusing on victims and services.

193. Chase, N.F.

      1976.   A CHILD IS BEING BEATEN: VIOLENCE AGAINST
                CHILDREN, AN AMERICAN TRAGEDY. New York:
                McGraw-Hill.

Naomi Chase has written a critical document on the "battered
child syndrome," which reveals widespread failures in our
families, schools, welfare, unemployment, legal, and child
custodial systems. Institutional neglect is rampant, she
concludes. Children have been beaten to death even though the
parent in question was working with professional social workers.
She argues that the effects of a capitalistic system on family
life and human development are crippled by an impersonal economic
order, which, in turn, fosters the type of violent psychology
inherent in the battered child syndrome.

194. Fontana, V.J.

      1976.   SOMEWHERE A CHILD IS CRYING: MALTREATMENT--
                CAUSES AND PREVENTION. New York: Macmillan
                Publishing Co.

Fontana examines the extent and nature of child
maltreatment, including society's failure to come to terms with
the problem and the urgent changes needed to help the child
victim. The book is filled with explicit case histories of child
murder, abuse, maltreatment, sexual exploitation, and extreme
neglect. The author also discusses several attempts to rescue

endangered children -- some successful, others not -- underscoring the inadequacy of our institutions in dealing with the problem. Included is a directory of child abuse programs.

195. Frude, N. (ed.)

1981.   PSYCHOLOGICAL APPROACHES TO CHILD ABUSE. Totawa, N.J.: Rowman and Littlefield.

Written from a psychological viewpoint, Frude's book provides an up-to-date guide on the problem of child abuse. Written in a non-technical language the book demonstrates how a fuller knowledge of stress, discipline styles and anger within the family can aid in understanding the situation in which child abuse takes place. There are several observational studies of parent-child interaction in both abusing and non-abusing families. After effects of parental attack and problems involved in setting up a treatment program are understudied topics relevant to child abuse. This book treats these issues in comprehensive fashion.

196. Geiser, R.L.

1979.   HIDDEN VICTIMS: THE SEXUAL ABUSE OF CHILDREN. Boston, Mass.: Beacon Press.

In this book, Robert Geiser pulls together what is currently known about the sexual abuse of children and discusses why it happens in order to facilitate intervention and change.
The seventeen chapters are divided into five parts: sexual misuse of female children; incest-our special secret; sexual misuse of male children; pornography, obscenity and prostitution; and deviant sexual environments. The author discusses ten steps for dealing effectively with the sexual abuse of children. This is one of the most complete works on sexual abuse of children, written with much understanding and compassion.

197. Gil, D.G.

1970.   VIOLENCE AGAINST CHILDREN: PHYSICAL CHILD ABUSE IN THE UNITED STATES. Cambridge, Mass.: Harvard University Press.

In an attempt to unravel the context of social and cultural forces that are associated with violent behavior against children, Gil explores and interprets several of the nationwide studies conducted from 1965 to the early 1970's. In this book he compiles findings from the press and public opinion surveys together with an analysis of almost 13,000 reported cases of child abuse across the country during 1967 and 1968 and a comprehensive study of 1300 nationally reported cases.
Included in this book are thirty tables of national

statistics on various aspects of child abuse, child abuse report forms, sample design and sampling units, research on the sexually-abused child, the sexual perpetrator, the circumstances of child abuse, and testimony at a United States Senate hearing in March 1973.

Gil concludes that the most serious type of child abuse is inflicted by society's norms, as American culture encourages the use of a certain measure of physical force in the rearing of children.

198. Helfer, R.E. and C.H. Kempe. (eds.)

1976.   CHILD ABUSE AND NEGLECT: THE FAMILY AND THE COMMUNITY. Cambridge, Mass.: Ballinger Publishing Company.

This is the third book in a series of anthologies that focus on child abuse and the families caught up in the cycle of violence.

The book is divided into six sections, including (1)dysfunction in family interaction, (2)evaluating the family, (3)family-oriented therapy, (4)the community, (5)the family and the law, and (6)early recognition and prevention of potential problems in the family interaction.

The authors also include over forty tables of statistics on subjects ranging from pregnancy and delivery abnormalities to family patterns. This in a valuable contribution in the child abuse field.

199. Herbruck, C.

1979.   BREAKING THE CYCLE OF CHILD ABUSE. Minneapolis, Minn.: Winston Press, Inc.

Interviewing abusive parents that were members of Parents Anonymous, Christine Herbruck analyzes five identified types of child abuse. First, she defines each type, showing the cycles and causes, then offers alternative solutions. It was discovered that abusive parents were themselves often victims of child abuse, following the learned pattern of abuse by bringing it into their own families until recognizing it as a serious problem. Many parents continued abusive patterns until a severely abusive episode made them aware they would lose their children either to the courts or to death. The author also examines therapies for these violent parents, such as how to rechannel their abusive behavior into constructive behavior that is nonabusive to their children as well as to themselves.

200. Leavitt, J.E. (ed.)

1974.   THE BATTERED CHILD. Fresno, Calif.: California State University.

Articles from medical, legal, education, and social science fields were selected for this now classic book on child abuse. The articles range from the historical materials to the detection and prevention of this problem.

The book is divided into seven sections that explore important facets in the field of child abuse: (1)who are the battered children, (2)the psychologist takes a look, (3)the criminologist takes a look, (4)the sociologist takes a look, (5)the medical worker takes a look, (6)the educator takes a look, and (7)what can be done for battered children.

Illustrations and case histories are important additions to the book, as are the list of readings for further reference.

201. Piers, M.W.

    1978.   INFANTICIDE: PAST AND PRESENT. New York: W.W. Norton and Company.

Infanticide, the deliberate killing of infants, most of whom have been female, was once an economic necessity, but now exists today as a social atavism. Dr. Piers explores the origins and motives of infanticide, beginning with the period in history when infanticide became an ambiguous custom, which eventually led to communal systems of defense. This protected the community from guilt, and allowed the continuation of infanticide.

The cases of infanticide cited in the book indicate that the killers, invariably mothers or mother-figures, were deficient in their level of parental caring because of emotional starvation and negative life experiences. Throughout history, oppression has kept women from realizing their full human potential. Infanticide is one expression of this experiential stunting. This book makes a useful contribution to the understanding of maternal-caused infanticide as an outcome of cultural pressures and normal sex-role socialization.

202. Rush, F.

    1980.   THE BEST KEPT SECRET: SEXUAL ABUSE OF CHILDREN. Englewood Cliffs, N.J.: Prentice-Hall, Inc.

This is a very powerful, clinically-based analysis of sexual abuse of children. Florence Rush, a psychiatric social worker, reveals the historic patterns that have been instrumental in sanctioning and perpetrating adult/child sex throughout the ages. She explores several modes of social control, such as religious interpretations and Freudian doctrines that have been encouraged by society's double standard. These cut across all economic, social and racial lines. Possible emotional consequences of child/adult sex include psychosis, depression and suicide, and argues that these repercussions should be a major focus for policymakers.

203. Spinetta, J.J. and D. Rigler.

   1977.   "The Child-Abusing Parent: A Psychological
              Review." PSYCHOLOGICAL BULLETIN. 77:296-304.

     This review of the psychological literature on the child-
abusing parent attempts to identify the "etiological factors"
involved in this violent offense. Divorce, separation and
unstable marriages tend to be typical of the child-abusing
parent, along with a marked absence of love and tolerance in
their early childhood. Family stress, too, appears frequently in
child abuse cases. One basic factor they emphasize is that
abusing parents were themselves abused or neglected, physically
or emotionally, as children. Some authors also point to character
defects (without indicating how such amorphous qualities can be
measured). Child abuse is ultimately the result of chance
environmental factors, especially poverty. They propose a
structural solution, which focuses on the elimination of poverty
and social and community services geared to the problem of child
abuse. On the whole, these authors prefer the psychological
causation, i.e. weakness in the personality structure.
Socioeconomic factors, they conclude, place added stress on the
already weakened psychological state. This explanation would also
account for child abuse in middle- and upper-middle class
families.

204. Walters, D.R.

   1975.   PHYSICAL AND SEXUAL ABUSE OF CHILDREN: CAUSES
              AND TREATMENT. Bloomington/London: Indiana
              University Press.

     Using a humanistic approach, David Walters has written a
book for professionals who treat abused children and their
parents. The author's primary thesis is that child abuse is
rooted in our cultural heritage of denigrating children and
institutionalizing violence. His data show that a significant
proportion of abusers are repeating their own childrearing
patterns. While focusing primarily on the practical aspects of
the diagnosis and treatment of child abuse, the author provides a
valuable typology of physical child abusers.
     After discussing how sexual abuse differs substantively from
physical abuse of children, Walters discusses causation and
therapy and offers suggestions for changing attitudes, treatment
procedures and legislation for the protection of children.

4. Police Relations

205. Auten, J.

1972.   "The Domestic Disturbance: A Policeman's Dilemma." POLICE CHIEF. 39(10):16-22.

It is the policeman's dilemma to try and deal with domestic disturbances in such a way that it is unlikely they will occur again. The author reviews and comments on the 19-step intervention guideline developed by the New York City Police Department Family Crisis Intervention Unit. Social service agencies must accept their share of the responsibility, however, as must the community. Police crisis intervention units are overburdened and understaffed, and so need social service agencies to provide the necessary support, while the community needs to provide more personnel and adequate funding.

206. Barocas, H.A.

1973.   "Urban Policeman: Crisis Mediators or Crisis Creators." AMERICAN JOURNAL OF ORTHOPSYCHIATRY. 43(4):632-9.

In rendering police sevices during family crisis situations, the very actions undertaken to reduce interpersonal conflict may precipitate or intensify violent reactions. When policemen feel they lack the expertise, usually associated with authority, feelings of ineptness, anxiety, or of being threatened may cause them to act hastily, irrationally, and in a stereotypical fashion. Unfortunately, authoritarian or belligerent intervention techniques may only heighten resistance and invite counter-attacks. If we acknowledge the existence of iatrogenic effects, then police officers can be trained to avoid them, and thus contribute to community mental health.

207. Hepburn, J.R.

1978.   "Race and the Decision to Arrest: An Analysis of Warrants Issued." JOURNAL OF RESEARCH ON CRIME AND DELINQUENCY. 15(1):54-73.

86

All 1974 adult arrests of a large midwestern city were analyzed examining race and the issuance of warrants for arrest to determine whether nonwhites were more likely than whites to be arrested on less than sufficient evidence. The author controls for age, type of offense, sex, and racial composition of neighborhoods, and shows that nonwhites continue to have a larger proportion of arrests not upheld by an issuance of a warrant.

208. Langley, R. and R.C. Levy.

    1978.   "Wife Abuse and the Police Response." F.B.I. LAW ENFORCEMENT BULLETIN. 47(5):4-9.

Wifebeating can be handled by the law as a civil or a criminal matter. Traditionally, it has been handled as a civil one, the result that police officers are trained to avoid making arrests in such cases. The authors of this article believe that, since police work is designed to deal with crime, it makes more sense for law enforcement officers to concentrate on the criminal aspects of wife abuse, and to leave the psychological and sociological elements to other agencies; especially those trained for it. Police enforcement only leads to "paper chase and clogged courts," and, therefore, is not the concern of the street officer, but of his superiors and other government agencies.

209. Muller, A.

    1979.   "Police Service in Psycho-Social Problem Situations." POLICE CHIEF. 46(9):32-4.

This article presents the results of a study on relations between the public and the precinct officer, the officers in the municipal police organization of The Hague who offer assistance to citizens facing problems of a psycho-social nature. The precinct officer is confronted with a large range of problems, largely concerning disturbance of relations with neighbors or within the family. Contact between citizen/client and precinct officers is initiated by other policemen or by the clients themselves. Their service is found to be appreciated by most of their clients. The fact that they are policemen is seen as an advantage, due to the authority vested in that role.

210.

    1980.   "On Powerlessness." OFF OUR BACKS. 10:14.

This article discusses the August 1980 workshop on "Poverty, Police Brutality and Woman Abuse: The Consequence of Powerlessness," in Washington, D.C., sponsored by the D.C. Afro-American Police Officers Association, the D.C. area Feminist Alliance, the Citizen's Party, and My Sister's Place, a feminist shelter for abused women.

B. Pornography

211. Baron, R. and P. Bell.

       1977.   "Sexual Arousal and Aggression by Males: Effects of Types of Erotic Stimuli and Prior Provocation." JOURNAL OF PERSONALITY AND SOCIAL PSYCHOLOGY. 35(2):45-58.

Eighty-five undergraduate males participated in an experiment designed to investigate the impact of various types of erotic stimuli upon aggression. It was determined that mild levels of sexual arousal inhibit aggression, moderate levels neither facilitate nor inhibit such actions, and high levels enhance such behavior. Baron and Bell therefore conclude that there is an important link between sexual arousal and aggressive behavior. Their comments regarding future research call for the development of a standardized set of test materials that control for the type of erotic materials employed; (i.e., nudes vs. acts) and the function of the specific content of these materials (i.e., affectionate lovemaking vs. bondage and beastiality).

212. Benjamin, J.

       1980.   "The Bonds of Love: Rational Violence and Erotic Domination." FEMINIST STUDIES. Spring:144-174.

In this paper, Jessica Benjamin voices her concern with the fantasy of rational violence, which she maintains, can be attributed to the interplay of great social forces and deep human needs. The root of this fantasy have their source in the contradictions in the early mother-child relationship where issues of differentiation, separation and recognition arise. She states that the way males experience differentiation is linked to a form of rationality that pervades our culture and is essential to sado-masochism: rational violence. Benjamin supports her thesis with the works of Hegel and Bataille, and then relates the bondage and domination themes in the "Story of O" to their works.

213. Berger, F.

       1977.   "Pornography, Sex and Censorship." SOCIAL THEORY AND PRACTICE. 4(2):183-209.

The author of this article addresses some of the arguments that have been put forth favoring censorship. He dismisses the largest objection against censorship by simply stating that he supposes those favoring censorship would not wish to prohibit true art or literature.

Addressing the argument that pornography promotes or leads to socially harmful attitudes and behaviors (the incitment to rape theory), he points out that the harm from pornography would probably be a long-range effect, and would aid in altering our basic attitudes towards sex. Most feminists would probably want to restate that view emphasizing how pornography shapes and reinforces attitudes of misogyny.

The author, while citing no studies or statistics, seems to conclude that pornography does not produce anti-social behavior; further, "normal" heterosexual pornography can ward off anti-social impulses. Berger thus believes that pornography can lessen anxiety and guilt over sex.

While this article may provide useful theories for opposing censorship of erotica, it provides no answers for the type of pornography which "too often involves male violence, aggression or dominance against women."

214.

Byerly, G. and R. Rubin.

      1980.   PORNOGRAPHY: THE CONFLICT OVER SEXUALLY EXPLICIT MATERIALS IN THE UNITED STATES. AN ANNOTATED BIBLIOGRAPHY. New York: Garland Publishing Company.

This excellent collection of primarily recently published items in pornography examines books and dissertations, psychological articles, sociological articles, philosophical and popular articles, government documents, legal articles, and court cases. The authors' special area of emphasis is the reports of the President's Commission on Obscenity and Pornography. The book offers a sharply-focused bibliography on the conflict over pornography in the United States, providing a good balance of perspectives in this highly controversial area.

215. Delacoste, F. and F. Newman. (eds.)

      1981.   FIGHT BACK: FEMINIST RESISTANCE TO MALE VIOLENCE. Minneapolis, Minn.: Cleis Press.

This book was intended as a tool of active resistance to patriarchal violence. It contains a comprehensive directory for crisis centers, support services and resource organizations.

It explores all levels of violence against women through the use of personal stories, essays and possible actions women can take to actively oppose pornography. The book discusses ways women can handle pornography in advertising, as well as

pornographic literature, magazines and movies. It offers ideas
about how to effectively deal with pornography and possible
solutions for handling pornography in local neighborhoods.

216. Diamond, I.

1980.   "Pornography and Repression: A Reconsidera-
tion." SIGNS. 5(4):686-701.

This paper presents a history of the anti-pornography
movement. Feminist ideologies of Millett, Morgan, Dworkin,
Brownmiller, Russell, and Willis are discussed. The <u>what</u> of porn
is not sex, but power and violence. The <u>who</u> of concern are no
longer male consumers and artists, but women. This paper refutes
the findings of the 1970 United States Pornography Commission,
which states that pornography is harmless. It discusses new data
now being collected by Donnerstein, Hallan, Feshbach, and other
social scientists. Diamond believes that recognition of the
institutionalized sex hierarchy, where men are in a dominant
position, provides an explanation of why women are victims in the
pornographic and the real world. She goes on to state that
pornography may be a reaffirmation of male control, especially
for men who have lost control over their lives in the capitalist
system.

217. Donnerstein, E.

1980.   "Aggressive Erotica and Violence Against
Women." JOURNAL OF PERSONALITY AND SOCIAL
PSYCHOLOGY. 39(2):269-277.

To examine the effects of aggressive-erotic stimuli on male
aggression toward females, 120 male subjects were angered or
treated in a neutral, erotic, or aggressive-erotic film. They
were then given an opportunity to aggress against the male or
female via the delivery of electric shock. Results indicated that
the aggressive-erotic film was effective in increasing aggression
overall, and that it produced the highest increase in aggression
against the female. Even nonangered subjects showed an increase
in aggression toward the female after viewing the aggressive-
erotic film. Donnerstein suggests that the association of the
female with the film victim may have contributed to the
aggression directed toward her.

218. Donnerstein, E. and G. Barrett.

1978.   "Effects of Erotic Stimulation on Male
Aggression Toward Females." JOURNAL OF
PERSONALITY AND SOCIAL PSYCHOLOGY. 36(2):180-
188.

This paper examines past research on male aggression and
erotica in relation to male anger and the level of sexual arousal

elicited by the film. Seventy-two male undergraduates participated in the study. Donnerstein and Barrett conclude that the effects of erotic materials on aggression towards males and females seem to be similar whether subjects are angered or not, and whether the erotic stimuli are mildly or highly arousing. Erotic films were found to increase aggression overall. Furthermore, results for physiological arousal suggests that aggression was possibly inhibited for subjects exposed to an erotic film and paired with a female.

219. Dworkin, A.

        1981.   PORNOGRAPHY, MEN POSSESSING WOMEN. New York:
                    G.P. Putnam's Sons.

        The book's theme is the power of men in pornography. It is about the meaning of what is shown in pornography; it does not discuss what should or should not be shown.
        Dworkin points out that the pornography industry is larger than the record and film industries combined. She does not differentiate between pornography and erotica, inasmuch as she holds that erotica is in the male culture, a subcategory of pornography--"the graphic depiction of whores."
        The various strains of male power--the power of self, physical power over and against others, power of terror, power of naming, power of owning, power of money, and power of sex--are intrinsic to both the substance and production of pornography.
        Robin Morgan says about this book that, although not easy to read, it should be fully comprehended if we are to survive and change our reality.

220. Dworkin, A.

        1981.   "Pornography's 'Exquisite Voluteers'." MS.
                    9(9):65-66.

        Andrea Dworkin discusses the ideologies present in pornographic images of women of color in bondage. She examines the historical experience of forcible rape for Jewish women in Nazi Germany and Black women in America, and states that force is not acknowledged as such when used against the racially or sexually despised. For example, the Jewish woman in a concentration camp was blamed for her own victimization by the simultaneously-applied male ideologies of madonna and whore. This despised victim has given contemporary mass sexuality its distinctly sadistic character. Dworkin contends that masochism has become synonomous with femininity, as manifested in normal women.

221. Eysenck, H.J. and D.K.B. Nias.

        1978.   SEX, VIOLENCE, AND THE MEDIA. New York:
                    St. Martins Press.

This book addresses the question whether watching scenes of violence or open sex in the media is likely to cause people to become more violent or to develop distorted views of sexuality. The authors believe that we can learn a great deal from existing research on this question by sorting out reliable studies from careless work.

Results show that repeated exposure to violence increases the chance of the viewer acting violently. With the general issue of sex, study results are more complex. In some instances, open portrayal of sex can be beneficial and may reduce aggression; other kinds of sexual portrayals appear to increase aggression.

The authors conclude that portrayal of sex and violence in the media have an affect on our attitudes and behavior; although such effects are variable. Because of these variables, it is clearly impossible to come up with universally acceptable recommendations. In their favor, the authors attempt to avoid simple answers.

222. Faust, B.

1980.   WOMEN, SEX, AND PORNOGRAPHY: A CONTROVERSIAL AND UNIQUE STUDY. New York: Macmillan Publishing Company.

Beatrice Faust examines women's "turn-ons" and how they differ from men's. Subjects that sexually define men and women such as touching, fantasy, strip shows, pin-ups, aggression, rape, and orgasm are explored.

Some of the questions discussed in revealing detail are: (1)what is the truth about mother love--is it an erotic experience? (2)what is a genuine pornography of women? (3)if men and women are the same, why does pornography turn men on and women off? (4)will the turnabout fad of male strippers become the instant arousal for women that it is for men?

A large difference between male and female eroticism is how women respond to touch, sound, smell, romance, and the nature of the relationships, while men are aroused by what they see -- people, situations and pictures.

This book is a must in the study of pornography and women.

223. Fisher, W. and D. Byrne.

1978.   "Sex Differences in Response to Erotica? Love Versus Lust." JOURNAL OF PERSONALITY AND SOCIAL PSYCHOLOGY. 36(2):117-128.

In this research, Fisher and Byrne examine gender differences to varying erotic themes. In study number one, 30 male and 32 female undergraduate students at Purdue viewed erotic films with themes depicting either love or lust or casual sex (a chance sexual encounter). In study number two, 36 married couples viewed the same films. In both studies, men and women alike were more sexually aroused by the casual sex theme than by those involving love or lust. Fisher and Byrne assert that males and females experience similar physiological responses to erotic stimuli.

224. Fuchs, J.

1980.   "Female Eroticism in the Second Sex." FEMINIST STUDIES. 6(2):304-314.

In this paper, JoAnn P. Fuchs examines Simone de Beauvoir's analysis of eroticism in THE SECOND SEX. Fuchs contends that while THE SECOND SEX displays Simone de Beauvoir's own unique vision and sensitivity about the woman's condition, it fails to go beyond cultural stereotypes of woman's eroticism, and, instead, articulates the message of the patriarchal culture. Fuchs calls for further study to begin where de Beauvoir left off. This would include a description of female eroticism, a description of women's special sensuality and a comprehension of the relationship of sex to the human consciousness. Fuchs asserts that women's victimization in patriarchal society includes an elaborate system of silences constructed against the simple facts of her existence, which ignores her manner of being and invalidates her experience. She discusses the need to create precise, essential and fundamental descriptions to inform these "silences" surrounding all aspects of female human existence.

225. Garry, A.

1978.   "Pornography and Respect for Women." SOCIAL THEORY AND PRACTICE. 4(4):395-421.

This article does not address whether pornography should be censored or not. Instead, it presents an objection to pornography on moral grounds. When pornography degrades people it is morally objectionable, Garry asserts. For example, movies that convey the idea that all women want to be raped are morally wrong because this is degrading to women.

The author discusses Susan Brownmiller's view that pornography provides a model for sexually calloused behavior among men and for a numbing effect on the rest of us. She also presents a study of college men discussed by the Presidential Commission on Obsenity and Pornography, which concluded that the fear of pornography leading to the loss of respect for women is an unwarranted fear. Garry rejects this thesis categorically.

She also addresses the possibility of pornography existing in a non-sexist society and presents some ideas for non-sexist pornography that shows equality between sexual partners.

226. Gastic, R. I.

> 1976.   "The Moral Right of the Majority to Restrict
> Obscenity and Pornography Through Law."
> ETHICS. 86(3):231-240.

Gastic's essay argues in favor of censorship of pornography, which he defines as "the use of language or images relating to the body, violence, or sex that exceeds the bounds of propriety that a significant part of the public finds appropriate."
He points to the recommendations of the National Commission on the Causes and Prevention of Violence which assert that violence in the media warrants state control. The Commission on Obscenity and Pornography, contrariwise, recommended decontrol of sexually explicit materials. Gastic fails to make the connection, though, that what may be dangerous in pornography is the violence not the sexual images. His article provides some arguments about the rights of the majority in a society to form laws and customs. Many of his arguments, however, seem to leave the feeling that sexual images should be hidden from view.

227. Gibbons, F.

> 1978.   "Sexual Standards and Reactions to
> Pornography: Enhancing Behavioral Consistency
> Through Self-Focused Attention." JOURNAL OF
> PERSONALITY AND SOCIAL PSYCHOLOGY. 36(9):976-
> 987.

The attitudes toward erotica of 52 male and 51 female undergraduates in three studies were measured to determine the behavioral effect of self-focusing. The relationship between pretested standards (sex guilt) and reactions to sexual literature was weak in the non-self aware condition, but considerably stronger for the self-focused subjects. The results suggest that focusing attention upon the self tends to inhibit behaviors that are inconsistent with personal attitudes or standards.

228. Goldstein, M.J. and H.S. Kant.

> 1973.   PORNOGRAPHY AND SEXUAL DEVIANCE. Berkeley and
> Los Angeles, Ca.: University of California
> Press.

This book is a report of a research program on pornography that focuses not only on erotic materials, but also on the sexual histories of the persons that were part of the research.
The persons studied were from four groups: persons known to be extensive users of pornography; convicted rapists and child-molesters; a group of persons seeking sex change operations, gay men or lesbians; and a control group.
Much of the data used in the book was derived from research

completed for the U.S. Commission on Pornography and Obscenity, for which this book represents a pilot study.

229. Goodman, P.

1970.   "Pornography, Art and Censorship." Pages 42-
             60 in PERSPECTIVES ON PORNOGRAPHY. New York:
             St. Martins Press.

In discussing censorship. Paul Goodman asserts that we are faced with the dilemmas of a society in transition. We cannot make good law or good sense without sociological and psychological analysis. Not only do we have conflicting data from psychologists as to whether viewing sado-masochism can or cannot cause sex crimes, but also we have the controversy as to whether censorship itself could create a need for sadistic pornography sold at a criminal profit.
In the essay, Goodman argues that there is innocent and useful pornography which should not be censored, and, if censored, could create the harmful type of pornography that it aims to eliminate. Social change in the direction of permissiveness and practical approval, the author contends, integrates sexual expression with ordinary activity of our lives. This will lessen the need to combine sex with degradation, punishment and violence.

230. Gray, S.H.

1982.   "Exposure to Pornography and Aggression
             Toward Women: The Case of the Angry Male.
             SOCIAL PROBLEMS. 29(4):387-398.

This paper presents an overview of research since 1970 into the effects of pornography on men's treatment of and underlying attitudes toward women. While there is little evidence that exposure to hardcore pornography produces aggressive behavior in typical men, aggression in "already angered men" is increased by exposure to such materials. "Deep anger" is a product of psycho-sexual development, and is a greater social problem than pornography, particularly in men who are unable to resolve their anger or to distinguish it from sexual arousal and control over women. The feminist-libertarian controversy over pornography will not be resolved by this article, but the argument regarding the use of pornography by angry men suggests that such so-called "inoffensive material" may be highly volatile for an unknown number of males.

231. Griffin, S.

    1981.   PORNOGRAPHY AND SILENCE: CULTURES REVENGE
                     AGAINST NATURE. New York: Harper and Row,
                     Publishers.

A definitive work on the analysis of pornography, Griffin's
book is highly theoretical. Using a variety of pornographic films
and books, she clarifies the objectification of women in
pornography. The crux of pornography is essentially that the
women who are viewed are denied the reality of the actual user.
Although a pornographer tries to make women the object, she is
actually a mirror of the male who creates the images.
    She discusses at length the effects of pornography and
violence against society as a whole. The book offers insights
into violence perpetuated against women in the "porn" industry
from the days of Marquis de Sade in the 1700's to the current
ordeals of Linda Lovelace.

232. Hatfield, E., S. Sprecher and J. Traupman.

    1978.   "Men's and Women's Reactions to Sexually
                     Explicit Films: A Serendipitous Finding."
                     ARCHIVES OF SEXUAL BEHAVIOR. 7(6):583-592.

Five hundred and ninety-two male and female college students
in an introductory human sexuality class at the University of
Wisconsin were tested for their responses to sexually explicit
films. Reactions were tested via the Byrne-Sheffield Feeling
Scale and Griffitts Physiological Arousal Scale. Researchers
concluded that men and women did not differ in how easily they
become aroused by sexually explicit films. Students were "turned
off" watching someone of the same sex masturbate, and "turned on"
by watching someone of the opposite sex engaged in the same
activity. Reasons given for this phenomena were that (1)the
students may have identified with people of their own sex on the
screen. Many of these students think that masturbation is wrong,
and (2)in fantasy, many students have imagined themselves to be
sexually involved with the person masturbating.

233. Kallan, R. and R. Brooks.

    1974.   "The Playmate of the Month: Naked But Nice."
                     JOURNAL OF POPULAR CULTURE. Fall:328-335.

This article examines from a surprisingly critical
perspective the legitimization of the Playmate of the Month
section in Playboy magazine. Kallan notes that two themes of the
Playmate section attempt to persuade in seemingly opposite
directions. On the one hand, the editors insisted on an available
stereotype; a Playmate could be found by almost anyone, an
ordinary woman. Yet the Playmate was much brighter, generally
better educated, especially respectful of her parents, and an

individualist involved with hobbies, pets, and political issues, attributes that make her superior to most women. She was at once ordinary and superior. These disparate themes converged: conferring approval on her nudity. The first theme suggests that she is not a freak; the second implies that she is a remarkable young woman, deserving the reader's respect.

234. Kirkendall, L., G. Allen, A. Ellis, and H. Colton.

1978. "Sex Magazines and Feminism." HUMANIST. 38(6):44-52.

In a series of essays, the authors argue that pornography helps people understand their own sexuality. "I doubt that viewing sexual pornography produces an increase in sex crimes, just as I doubt that simply viewing violence on television causes violent crime," states one author. Gina Allen, another contributor who takes an opposing view , says that pornography represents violence against women masquerading as sex. She asserts that the Bible is the grandfather of pornography. In the Bible, violence is wed to sex and sex to guilt. Ellis believes that publishing legitimate sex education materials in sensationalist sex magazines facilitates sex education, thereby denigrating the exploitative and nonhumanistic nature of these magazines. Helen Colton equates pornography with the public's depiction of sexuality, and considers the movement against it to be a tidal wave of attempted repression. Overall, these essays depict the liberal attitude about pornography so forcefully opposed by feminists.

235. Lederer, L. (ed.)

1980. TAKE BACK THE NIGHT: WOMEN ON PORNOGRAPHY. New York: William Morrow and Co., Inc.

This collection of current essays (dating 1975 to 1980) examines pornography and its effects on women from a feminist perspective. The introduction by Lederer presents information on the escalation of violence in pornography, and shows how the increase of violence in the mass media contributes to the acceptability of violent acts against women as normal behavior. As Adrienne Rich points out in the afterword, this book offers new facts and insights into the problems of pornography. Rich also points out that this book helps us to peel back the layers of false consciousness and makes visible the interconnectedness of misogynist aspects of our society.

The book provides current, excellent and well-rounded information on pornography with contributions from many well-known feminist writers. Lederer, who is founder of "Women Against Violence in Pornography and the Media," has gathered together in a single volume most of the highly controversial issues in the emergent field of pornography.

236. Linden, R.R., D.R. Pagano, D.E.H. Russell, and S.L. Star.
(eds.)

    1982.   AGAINST SADOMASOCHISM: A RADICAL FEMINIST
                   ANALYSIS. East Palo Alto, Ca.: Frog in the
                   Well, Publishers.

This collection of essays focuses on sadomasochism,
exploring such areas as the history of sadism, sadomasochism, and
liberal, traditional and sadomasochism elements in the feminist
movement.
    The book points out that sadomasochism must be questioned,
regardless of apparent consensuality. "The psychological reality
of consensual sadomasochism is so abstracted from actual social
and historical conditions that shape human relationships and
erotic desire as to be virtually meaningless," the authors
insist. For example, lesbian sadomasochism stems from a sexual
ideology that is patriarchal and non-liberating. For this reason,
feminists must oppose sadomasochism as a delusion and threat to
feminist ideology.

237. Love, R., L. Sloan and M. Schmidt.

    1976.   "Viewing Pornography and Sex Guilt: The
                   Priggish, the Prudent and the Profligate."
                   JOURNAL OF CONSULTING CLINICAL PSYCHOLOGY.
                   44(4):624-629.

Growing out of research supported by the Commission on
Obscenity and Pornography, this study investigated the
relationship between guilt feelings toward sex and voluntary
exposure to erotic stimuli. Testing the hypothesis that persons
who advocate suppression of sexually oriented material are often
suppressing their own feelings about sex, the authors recorded
the amount of time 35 male undergraduate students spent viewing
and rating photographic slides of varying erotic contents. On the
basis of their scores on the Mosher's Forced Choice-Guilt
Inventory, a curvilinear viewing pattern was exhibited by the
moderate-sex guilt group. The viewing time for high-sex guilt
subjects unexpectedly did not increase significantly, whereas the
viewing time for the low-sex guilt group increased linearly as a
function of increasing pornographic content. These results are
consistent with a predicted defensive response on the part of the
high-sex guilt subjects.

238. Malamuth, N.M. and B. Spinner.

    1980.   "A Longitudinal Content Analysis of Sexual
                   Violence in the Best Selling Erotic
                   Magazines." JOURNAL OF SEX RESEARCH.
                   16(3):226-237.

In this research, two raters, one male and one female,

examined all issues of PLAYBOY and PENTHOUSE, January 1973 to
December 1977. While their ratings for pictorial violence were
very close, less agreement was found on comics. Pictorially-
violent sexuality was found to increase over the five years, as
analyzed both in absolute numbers and as a percent of the total
number of pictures. The results are discussed within the context
of empirical research and suggest the possibility that sexually-
violent stimuli may contribute to a "cultural climate" promoting
sexist ideology.

239. Michaelson, P.

        1980.   "How to Make the World Safe for Pornography."
                     Pages 147-160 in THE NEW EROTICISM. New York:
                     Random House.

    "The PLAYBOY ethos is fundamentally the capitalist ethos,"
according to Michaelson, who examines PLAYBOY magazine. More than
any other pop-culture phenomenon, PLAYBOY has been responsible
for changing sex from a dirty joke into "entertainment served up
with humor, sophistication, and spice."
    The author examines the "PLAYBOY empire" from the 1950s,
including not only the magazine itself, but also the Playboy
clubs, hotels, jazz festivals, late night television, and other
features of an organization whose most distinguished achievement
has been profits.
    The PLAYBOY Playmate is not a woman at all, the author
states, but an erotic art object, a fantasy by the photographer's
air brush and the image of the sketch writer. "She does not
function, she is." The picture in the magazine is forever young,
not completely human, because it is an objectification. PLAYBOY
seems not to care, however, about the problems it may create
for women involved in real human relationships with men.

240. Morgan, R.

        1978.   "Theory and Practice: Pornography and Rape."
                     Pages 163-169 in GOING TOO FAR. New York:
                     Random House.

    As Morgan states, "pornography is a theory, and rape is a
practice," a message in both rape and pornography that says that
women need to know their place. The pornographic industry
articulates and encourages this male fantasy of rape.
    The dangers of censorship, though, is that in all likelihood
it would begin with books such as OUR BODIES, OURSELVES, rather
than with violent "porn" films. The important work against
pornography needs to be done by women, inasmuch as feminists
cannot trust the male-controlled judiciary system to handle the
problem.
    Morgan's essay encourages women to stop being victims of the
"theory of rape." A powerful essay, Morgan wants women to be less
concerned about our embarrassment, and more centered on being

free as women.

241. Muedeking, G.D.

1977.   "Pornography And Society." Pages 463-502 in
             E. Sagarin and F. Montanino (eds). DEVIANCE:
             VOLUNTARY ACTORS IN A HOSTILE WORLD. New
             York: Scott, Foresman, and Company.

The sudden explosion of interest in pornographic materials
in the United States has led to attempts to explain how this
cultural development has succeeded. The author indicates the
following reasons for this phenomenon: growth in international
media communication, especially among Western countries;
liberalization of laws of production and distribution;
questioning of sexual roles and norms with a resulting lack of
standard guidelines for judging what is appropriate and
inappropriate in individual lifestyles; indeterminacy of the
obscenity laws and the near impossibility of enforcement; and
finally, the inability of important social institutions, such as
the family and church, to preserve traditional regulations
concerning sexual behavior. Public concern over pornography is
unlikely to alter the increasingly early exposure to information
and portrayals of sex. "The suppression of sex is associated with
normal sexual development," the author insists. Muedeking
emphasizes frequent and massive sex education. He does not,
however, make the necessary distinction between erotica
(enhancement of sensual pleasure and sexual identity) and
pornography (the portrayal of exploitation and violence, usually
against women and children). What this author fails to emphasize
is that "hardcore" pornography remains a massive onslaught
against the integrity of women's bodies, and a violation of the
relational, affectionate mode of sexual relating.

242. Palmer, C.

1979.   "Pornographic Comics: A Content Analysis."
             JOURNAL OF SEX RESEARCH. 15(4):282-298.

This research was undertaken to document the nature of the
pornographic themes found in a collection of pornographic comics,
called "eight pagers," produced between 1930 and 1940, using
content analysis. The study of eight newspapers provides some
historical background into the subject of pornography as a multi-
million dollar industry during the Great Depression. In these
comics, females were depicted as similar to males in carnal
appetite and sexual aggression. Male chauvinism was apparent in
many of the comics, and male fantasies were equally displayed and
fulfilled. Numerous behaviors were considered legally or morally
deviant, but the comics also showed normative sexuality by
concentrating on monogamous, heterosexual behavior. Finally, the
article discusses taxonomical, linguistic and methodological
problems involved in studying pornographic comics.

100

243. Payton, J.

    1979.   "Child Pornography Legislation." JOURNAL OF
             FAMILY LAW. 17(3):505-544.

    This article critically examines legislation against the
framework of constitutional restrictions and limitations   of
enforcement that have been enacted to curb the alarming growth of
child pornography in the United States. The author offers a
reasoned analysis, rather than dwell on isolated incidences of
the nature of child pornography. Existing law consists of (1)a
federal law requiring that material be obscene before it is
suppressed; (2)state legislation which ranges from a narrower
application than the federal law to statutes banning the
publication and sale of all materials depicting child
pornography; (3)the holdings of two federal courts that statutes
to be enforced must comply with Supreme Court guidelines on
obscenity. The author calls for citizen involvement to insure the
enforcement of obscenity laws. The States, through licensing
laws, inspection, and supervision of boarding schools, camps,
group homes, etc., should move against the source of supply of
child pornography.

244. Pincus, S. and L.K. Waters.

    1976.   "Effects of Age Restrictions and Pornographic
             Content on Desirability of Reading Material."
             PSYCHOLOGICAL REPORTS. 38:943-947.

    This study evaluated reading materials for 96 women and 96
men under 21 years of age. The purpose of the study was to find
if imposing restrictions on the sale or purchase of pornographic
materials actually increases the desirability of the materials.
The effect that restriction of pornographic materials may have on
the intended receiver is an area of study that has been
neglected, when considering control of pornographic materials.
    The study found that age restrictions had a significant
effect with higher ratings when the subjects were told the book
was restricted, even when no explicit pornographic content was
indicated. When the book was shown to be pornographic, there were
no differences between books that were restricted and those that
were nonrestricted. The study supports the theory that when a
commodity is restricted, there will be an increase in the
desirability of the material and an increase in an effort to
obtain it.

101

245. Pollack, F.

    1970.   "A Trip Around the Halfworld." Pages 170-195 in PERSPECTIVES IN PORNOGRAPHY. New York: St. Martin's Press.

    Pollack feels one of the problems with finding a solution to the controversial issues of pornography and censorship is that we have failed to define obscenity satisfactorily. One of the areas he explores is the often obscene messages the general public gets through advertisements. He points to many examples among them: "Does she or dosn't she?;" "It's not how long you make it, it's how you make it long;" and an advertisement for a railroad stating "to come with us is the only way to come." This he feels is part of the obscenity acceptable in a capitalist society.

    He also analyzes what he identifies as mainstream pornography that deals with sadism. He refers to the stories of Mickey Spillane as sadism disguised as masculine virtue and potency. The message society gets from the media is that violence is more of a virtue than a vice.

246. Rich, A.

    1980.   "Afterword." Pages 313-320 in L. Lederer (ed.) TAKE BACK THE NIGHT. New York: William Morrow and Co., Inc.

    Adrienne Rich comments that TAKE BACK THE NIGHT is a sort of a "microcosm of the American feminist movement as it stands at the beginning of the 1980's." Rich found that the ideas of the book coalesced into a work that is "vastly more than the sum of its parts." As Rich points out, TAKE BACK THE NIGHT pictures a progression of political consciousness, all the way from an acceptance of status quo to a probing and radical skepticism concerning woman's exploited role in society. She reiterates that each selection in the volume stresses that pornography is not sex or eros, but an exercise in the objectification of the female. This, in turn, sets the stage for women's degradation and exploitation. The very confrontation of the patriarchy of pornography is a radicalizing experience for feminists. The author issues a call to action to combat the pornographer, who not only defines women in the slave context, but threatens to exploit her as a result of this other-imposed label.

247. Rist, R.C. (ed.)

    1975.   THE PORNOGRAPHY CONTROVERSY: CHANGING MORAL STANDARDS IN AMERICAN LIFE. New Brunswick, N.J.: Transaction Books.

    The philosophical or theoretical level and the pragmatic or operational level of the pornography controversy are debated in this book. The philosophical level pertains to the notions of what is or what is not moral, the rights of a person in society and parameters of civil democracy.

The pragmatic level is concerned with the use of force to contain and possibly censor cultural expression, the enactment of law and what constitutes pornography. The book is divided into four parts: "Some Theoretical Concerns," "Pornography and Dilemmas of Morality," "Pornography and Dilemmas of Law," and "Pornography and Social Science Research."

To quote the editor, "The legal, moral, cultural, and social dilemmas that face those who would define, deplore, defend, or control the use and distribution of sexually explicit material in American society are fully explored in these essays."

248. Rushdoony, R.J.

1974.   THE POLITICS OF PORNOGRAPHY. New York: Arlington House Publishers.

Pornography is a pseudo-religious expression of people who hold a perverted theory of humankind and the universe, according to the author, and explicit sex in pornography is only part of the message.

Reviewing the writings of de Sade to show how today's pornography is a logical development of hedonistic impulses, the book puts forth the views that violence is basic to pornography; porn is an escape from reality that perverts the young; porn is an essential part of the New Left; legislation alone can not stop pornography; and churches often unwittingly promote pornography.

Pornographers aim to change society and profit in the process; for example, witness singles-housing complexes, PLAYBOY, and homosexual movements (all of which shatter the values of Christian civilization, according to Rushdoony).

While this book is definitely NOT a feminist analysis of pornography, it offers a "moral majority" argument that liberals strongly oppose; that is, the refusal of liberals to confront the highly negative impact of pornography for women and society.

249. Russell D. and S. Griffin.

1978.   "On Pornography: Two Feminist Perspectives." CHRYSALIS. 4:11-19.

A feminist perspective on pornography, the first perspective by Russell, refutes the "crude," inadequate and male-biased research of the government's Commission on Obscenity and Pornography with recent research findings about the effects of media violence. There is an erroneous equation of erotica and explicit sexual materials with pornography. Many porn models are runaways or children who have been coerced (even sold) into involvement. All are vulnerable to physical abuse. Pornography is the objectification of women's bodies and this objectification is an essential element of rape. The First Amendment issue, raised so readily in discussions about banning pornography, suggests that a political ploy is being used to confuse and intimidate. Russell proposes laws banning pornography and calls for grassroot involvement on a community level to restrict pornography. Susan Griffin offers a second perspective; discussing a chapter from her book, PORNOGRAPHY AND SILENCE (included in this bibliography).

250. See, C.

    1974.   BLUE MONEY. New York: David McKay Co., Inc.

BLUE MONEY, subtitled PORNOGRAPHY AND THE PORNOGRAPHERS, is an intimate look at the two-billion dollar fantasy industry. The author describes her book as a collection of verbal portraits of the people who have made their fortunes in the pornographic industry. Her method of research was "mainly hanging around." She spent between two and three years in the formal research and writing of the book and was involved in the industry for several years prior to the actual research.
    Portraits of a movie magnate, businessman, and an attorney, whose job it is to keep the porn producers out of jail, reveal the business-side of the industry. Additionally, she interviewed the stars working in these films, as well as performers in the live sex shows. Although the article presents some interesting insights into the world of pornography, the author seems to treat pornography as casually as the people working in the industry. The chapter on Linda Lovelace, written prior to her leaving Chuck Traynor, makes one doubt the authenticity of the portraits of some others presented. For example, Linda Lovelace is presented as a woman looking up to her "Svengahli," rather than a terrified and tortured woman, a view later given by Linda Lovelace.

251. Smith, D.

    1976.   "The Social Content of Pornography." JOURNAL
             OF COMMUNICATION. 26(1):16-23.

The study presented in this paper tries to answer questions about "adults only" fiction paperbacks which are accessible to the general public. It does not deal with the materials available only through adult bookstores or mail order houses.
    The questions the paper tries to answer are: What is the content of "adults only" fiction? How much sex is in these books? What kind of sex? What else other than sex is in the books? What plots or themes dominate, if any?
    According to Smith, the data from 1967 to 1974 reflect a clear rise in explicit sexual content of books available to the general public. The books were rated according to the proportion of pages devoted to physical sex episodes. The greater the number of pages devoted to sexual activity, the higher the index number. The index went from .29 in 1967 to .63 in 1974. By comparison, books such as FEAR OF FLYING or PORTNOY'S COMPLAINT (which are mass marketed) seldom have an index rating higher than .05.

Little change is evident in the presentation of sex roles, the nature of sex or the relationship of men and women. "Almost defiantly, it remains a man's world," as the dominant theme in these books is machismo.

252. Sontag, S.

> 1970.   "The Pornographic Imagination." Pages 131-169
>   in D.A. Hughes (ed.) PERSPECTIVES ON
>   PORNOGRAPHY. New York: St. Martin's Press.

This essay discusses pornography in literature. Sontag asserts that pornography should be considered a psychological phenomenon and an item in social history, but, in addition, a convention within the arts. Can pornography be considered literature, she asks?

Much of the essay has to do with her analysis of the book THE STORY OF O, which, Sontag argues, is a highly literary book as well as an erotic book, contrary to many detractors who see little merit in it.

253. Steiner, G.

> 1970.   "Night Words: Human Privacy and High
>   Pornography." Pages 120-132 in THE NEW
>   EROTICISM. New York: Random House.

Steiner inquires: Is there any science fiction pornography? Does human imagination have something new to add to the repertory of erotica? The answers are not promising. The inescapable monotony of pornography is obvious once everything has been tried. "If one tries to narrate every mode of sexual pleasure and pain... the variables are surprisingly few."

The author's concern is that pornographers do our imagining for us. He believes that the danger lies not in censorship, but in the fact that "our dreams are marketed wholesale" by the pornographer. The standardization of sexuality, whether through controlled license or compelled puritanism, accompanies totalitarian politics, Steiner concludes.

254. Stolvig, B.

> 1980.   "Pornography in Sweden: A Feminist's
>   Perspective." Pages 86-90 in L. Lederer (ed.)
>   TAKE BACK THE NIGHT. New York: William Morrow
>   and Co., Inc.

Laura Lederer explores pornography in Sweden by interviewing Swedish feminist writer Britta Stolvig. Consumption of pornography is widespread in Sweden with about 30 million copies of pornographic magazines being sold annually in a country with a population of only four million males. Third world children as well as grotesques are said to be favorite subjects of Swedish pornography. Stolvig expresses concern that sexual behavior has become overly liberal in Sweden even to the point where the women's movement has no clear-cut definition of rape. Especially disturbing to Stolvig is the appearance in the behavior of small boys of degrading attitudes toward their female playmates. Stolvig enumerates various anti-pornographic activities currently promoted by Swedish women.

255. Teish, L.

      1980.   "A Quiet Subversion." Pages 115-118 in L. Lederer (ed.) TAKE BACK THE NIGHT. New York: William Morrow and Co., Inc.

    Teish reveals in "A QUIET SUBVERSION" that pornography continues to present degrading images of the Black woman, counteracting the Black movement's emphasis on cultural recognition and heightened self-image. This pornography is diametrically opposed to the image of the Black Women's Liberation Movement, and in some sense, pornography acts to subvert the movement. Along with prostitution and state control over reproduction, pornography works against women's true interests and liberation.

256. Tynan, K.

      1970.   "Dirty Books Can Stay." Pages 133-146 in THE NEW EROTICISM. New York: Random House.

    This is a well-written article for the case of noncensorship. Hardcore pornography has a simple and localized purpose, Tynan argues, to produce an erection. Although he somewhat oversimplifies the use of pornography, Tynan identifies some benefits of being able to read sexually explicit materials. For example, pornography enables us to realize that we are not alone in our sexual practices if we stray from the missionary position. Pornography also serves a purpose for men geographically cut-off from women.
    The real or potential damage to women by pornography is not addressed, nor is the issue of violence in pornography. The forces for opposing censorship will have to take into account the violence issue before they convince feminists.

257. U.S. Commission on Obscenity and Pornography.

      1970.   THE REPORT OF THE COMMISSION ON OBSCENITY AND PORNOGRAPHY. Washington, D.C.: U.S. Government Printing Office. (Superintendent of Documents).

    This 646-page report is the government study that resulted

in the controversial recommendation of decontrolling sexually explicit materials. The Commission concludes that the public does not need to feel apprehensive over the use of obscene or pornographic materials, as members were unable to find evidence of pornography causing a lack of respect toward women.

The report is divided into four parts: overview of findings, recommendations of the Commission, reports of the panels, and separate statements of the Commission members.

258. Yeamans, R.

     1980.   "A Political-Legal Analysis of Pornography." Pages 248-251 in L. Lederer (ed.) TAKE BACK THE NIGHT. New York: William Morrow and Co., Inc.

Any use of the media which equates sex with violence, Yeamans defines as pornography. As an attorney, the author proposes that neither the liberal nor the conservative views concerning pornography as "free speech" are acceptable. She offers a third approach to the problem by focusing upon the intimate connection between sex and violence. Police practices which furnish protection of life and limb are cited to bolster Yeamans' contention that the courts must be made to take a legal position to stop this incitement by pornography of violence with women as targets. The rights of media owners who produce pornography are in direct conflict with women who are abused by the consumers of pornography. "The privately-owned media are creating and exacerbating a social problem," the author pleads. Soliciting persons to commit crimes is regulated; why shouldn't pornography? Yeamans likens the pornography issue to that of segregation in the schools, where a long period of education and organization were needed to create a social climate that would induce courts to reexamine the issue.

C. Rape

259. Bode, J.

        1978.   FIGHTING BACK: HOW TO COPE WITH THE MEDICAL,
                     EMOTIONAL, AND LEGAL CONSEQUENCES OF RAPE.
                     New York: Macmillan Publishing Company.

    The author, beginning with her own rape experience and its
traumatic consequences, examines various aspects of rape as it
affects women. Illustrating several case histories of rape (in
the victims' own words), Janet Bode lays to rest the many myths
which have misrepresented the crime. As she probes the emotional
and physical aftermath of rape, Bode indicates what women
experience from the initial shock, to the shame, fear, and long-
lasting anxiety that rape often provokes.
    Ms. Bode discusses medical treatment, such as the initial
examination for V.D. and pregnancy, police procedures and legal
proceedings. This includes what to expect if charges are filed,
as well as revisions of the rape law that are taking place
throughout the United States.

260. Brownmiller, S.

        1975.   AGAINST OUR WILL: MEN, WOMEN AND RAPE. New
                     York: Simon and Schuster.

    Brownmiller's comprehensive work on rape examines this crime
as an anti-woman act with the largest proportion of material
centered around male heterosexuals and the normal patterns of
male violence. In this analysis of the causes and consequences of
rape, Brownmiller points out that rape is exclusively a male
invention (and not a female-precipitated crime) that both
expresses inequality and prevents equality of the sexes. The
hidden currents of male-female relationships, Brownmiller holds,
are based ultimately upon male power and coercion. But dominance
is also a male-on-male strategy. This is expressed most
dramatically in war situations, wherein rape of the women of a
conquered nation becomes symbolic of the total power of the
conquerors over formerly dominant rulers. Writing from a feminist
perspective, Brownmiller offers an uncompromising thesis: men
maintain their power through violence, a now-familiar theme in
feminist interpretations of pornography.
    The book presents one of the strongest statements against
current legal practices, which treat rape as the victim's
problem, not a system problem. Case studies, historical documents
and a polished writing style make this a fascinating, if
tormented, study of women's victimization.

261. Burgess, A.W. and L.L. Holmstrom.

       1974.   RAPE: VICTIMS OF CRISIS. Bowie, Maryland: Robert J. Brady Company.

     Using the illustrations of several case histories of both rape victims and rapists, the authors provide information on the victims' needs, offenders' motivations and the institutional problems in dealing with rape. The study has five parts: Section one concerns a new view of rape, while the second section is about the reactions to rape. Part three covers the community reaction to rape, while the fourth and fifth sections focus on effective crisis intervention and counseling for the victims.

262. Chappell, D., G. Geis, S. Schafer, and L. Siegel.

       1978.   "Forcible Rape: A Comparative Study of
        *   Offenses Known to the Police in Boston and Los Angeles." Pages 107-122 in J. M. Henslin and E. Sagarin (eds). THE SOCIOLOGY OF SEX. New York: Schocken Books.

     Culture and ecological contexts, the authors conclude, make a significant difference in the rates of forcible rape, even when holding constant the variations in criteria for arrest and police reporting. The authors compare two cities to make this conclusion. For instance, Los Angeles has a more permissive sexual milieu than Boston, yet has higher rates of forcible rape and different patterns of contact (e.g. higher incidence of stranger rapists, concentration of weekend rape incidents, multiple offenders, and minority offenders). The fact that Los Angeles has a higher proportion of minorities, tends to be more anonymous and has dispersed populations, rather than concentrated populations in well-established neighborhoods, all account for the higher incidence of forcible rape in that city as compared with Boston.

263. Edwards, S.

       1981.   FEMALE SEXUALITY AND THE LAW: A STUDY OF CONSTRUCTS OF FEMALE SEXUALITY AS THEY INFORM STATUTE AND LEGAL PROCEDURE. Oxford, England: Martin Robertson.

     This historical analysis examines conceptions of femininity and female sexuality as these have shaped law and the legal process. Edwards focuses on nineteenth-century England and the proliferation of sex offense statutes and procedural rules that have become contemporary law. Edwards' initial premise is that the law is an arena for controlling female sexuality. The analysis has three parts. In part one, Edwards identifies the historical paradox that has defined women. Women were regarded as incapable of actively violating sexual prescriptions. At the same time, they were seen as precipitating or otherwise contributing to their victimization. This paradoxical definition of female sexuality came to manifest itself in the specialized focus of statutory and case law. Part two focuses on the role of gynecological theories which reinforce this female paradox. Female biology, as a central causal factor, implies that female sexuality is both normal and pathological. The framework developed in earlier chapters is used to evaluate the legal response to sex offenses in part three. The paradoxical conception of women, gynecological determinism, victim precipitation, and suspicion regarding the credibility of female complainants converge in what Edwards refers to as the routine management of "discretion." In the case of rape, a crime defined in terms of protecting the sexually passive female from the active male, the procedural emphasis is not to determine the guilt or innocence of the assailant, but of the complainant. Thus, it is women's character and sexual experience that are on trial for the crime of rape.

264. Gager, N. and C. Schurr.

     1976.   SEXUAL ASSAULT: CONFRONTING RAPE IN AMERICA. New York: Grosset and Dunlap.

In this comprehensive study, the authors explore some controversial and difficult aspects of rape. These center around six questions: (1)why can the defendent's attorney use details of the victim's personal life as evidence against the credibility of her statements? (2)why is corroboration of the victim's testimony required in most states? (3)why are rape cases the only ones in our courts that reverse the rights of the victim and the accused, with the victim forced to prove her innocence? (4)why are wives not permitted to charge their husbands with rape in most states? (5)what can be done to prevent rape? (6)what can we do to ease the pain when it happens to women?
According to Gager and Schurr, the hope for a humane and intelligent understanding of the rapist and restitution for the victim depends on a change in cultural and institutional perspectives on rape. It is through education of not only the public, but also of the police and the medical and legal establishments that America as a whole will be able to confront rape and its cruel aftermath.

265. Holmstrom, L.L. and A.W. Burgess.

     1978.   THE VICTIM OF RAPE:INSTITUTIONAL REACTIONS. New York: John Wiley and Sons.

This is an in-depth study of how rape victims confront and endure the legal process and how our institutions respond to the crime of rape. Using direct on-the-scene reports, personal interviews and case histories, the authors document the rape victim's plight. Included in the book are several tables that present the research findings in easily understood numerical terms and discussions on changes now taking place. This book uses an interdisciplinary approach to explore the ways in which constructive changes can be implemented into our criminal justice system and medical bureaucracies and professions.

266. Medea, A. and K. Thompson.

1974.   AGAINST RAPE. New York: Farrar, Straus, and Giroux.

In ten descriptive chapters, the authors discuss rape, using a number of perspectives. What is rape, why do men rape women and who is the rapist are three of the questions examined. The different types of rapes, social patterns, rape patterns, precautions and preventions, and the movement against rape are also investigated.

The appendix contains a survey on rape for 1972-1973, with significant statistics on all facets of this crime, as well as a partial list of rape crisis centers and other anti-rape groups throughout the United States. With this book, Andrea Medea and Kathleen Thompson have made a significant contribution in the continuous feminist struggle against rape.

267. Sanders, W.B.

1980.   RAPE AND WOMEN'S IDENTITY. New York: Sage Publications.

The author refutes many of the myths surrounding the crime of rape and provides some new conclusions on rape and its consequences by emphasizing the victim. He also examines the socially assigned roles both the police and the victim adopt, how each present themselves, how they interact with one another, and the implications of these self presentations for both low enforcement and for women's treatment following rape.

268. Schwendinger, J. and H. Schwendinger.

1981.   "Rape, Sexual Inequality, and Levels of Violence." CRIME AND SOCIAL JUSTICE. 16(winter):3-31.

In this comparative rape study, the authors reject as empirically and politically unsound the natural-law theory of rape. This theory holds rape to be inherent in men, not to variations of economic-political structure. Subsequent feminist outrage that has followed such a notion has been easily channeled into law-and-order policies that have had little or no impact on reducing violent crimes, including rape. Instead, a structural

theory of rape provides a foundation for political action.
Drawing on four tribes--the Mbuti, Lovedu, Mpondo, and Baganda
societies-- the authors demonstrate that male violence (the
behavioral basis for rape) varies by certain structural features:
individual male ownership of private property, domestication of
women's labor, an economy based on production for exchange,
social class relations, and sexual discrimination in every sphere
of life. In a word, the greater the general social inequality,
the higher the levels of male violence and female discrimination.
Capitalism, which fosters high levels of social inequality and
violence, is then examined in terms of the "fetishism of
violence," which tends to be expressed sexually against both
women and men. Rape becomes a male strategy for manipulating and
controlling women. But this does not mean that all males are
inherently violent, or that violence is due to the so-called
"beastial" nature of men. Feminists made rape a symbol for all
the social harms generated by sexual inequality. The official
response has contributed to further repression of political
dissent, rather than to prevent this violent crime, which has
actually increased, especially in racially oppressed communities.

269. Weis, K. and S.S. Borges.

    1973.   "Victimology and Rape: The Case of the
             Legitimate Victim." ISSUES IN CRIMINOLOGY.
             8(2):71-115.

    The authors provide a sociological perspective on the victim
of rape, examining how society, through its representatives, turn
the victim of rape into the criminal. By now a well-rehearsed
argument in the feminist literature, this study does an excellent
job of summarizing the legal and human problems associated with
the traditional criminal justice interpretations.

VIII

Crimes of Women

A. General

270. Adler, F.

    1977.   "Interaction Between Women's Emancipation and Female Criminality -- A Cross-Cultural Perspective. INTERNATIONAL JOURNAL OF CRIMINOLOGY AND PENOLOGY. 5(2):101-112.

    This article describes the increase in criminality by women and links it to the changed social conditions brought about by women's demands for equality. Data from other nations reflect the American experience, that as the social and economic disparity between the sexes decreases, there is a correlative increase in female criminality. Women have moved beyond the categories of prostitution, shoplifting and an occasional husband poisoning, the article points out. Statistics show that crimes by women in nearly every category have doubled and tripled in the past decade. This changing situation, according to the author, will require an adjustment in the definition of delinquency, formerly considered a phenomenon restricted to males.

271. Adler, F.

    1975.   SISTERS IN CRIME. New York: McGraw-Hill Book Company.

    The book offers a psychosocial perspective through which female criminal behavior can be understood to be a natural extension of normal female behavior, as both a product and producer of the larger forces of social change. The author proposes to document the extent and nature of the changing pattern of female crime in America. With the information available, Adler plots the course of rising crime rates and projects the future direction of female crime. An important concern throughout the book is that women are indeed committing more crimes than ever before, and these crimes involve a greater degree of violence, and, even in prison, the "new female criminal" exhibits a hitherto unmatched pugnacity. The author's thesis is supported with a variety of statistical data; some of which is highly questionable.

272. Adler, F. and R.J. Simon.

1979.   THE CRIMINOLOGY OF DEVIANT WOMEN. Boston:
           Houghton Mifflin Company.

     This text is a collection of essays on women in crime. It
deals with significant contemporary issues in female criminology
and their solution by the criminal justice system, offering
historical, cross-cultural and theoretical approaches. The types
of crimes women commit, the treatment they receive in the courts
and their behavior and adjustment in prison is given special
emphasis. Rates and types of deviance are examined in selections
by Ward, Simon and Nagel, and Weitzman. Some of the pieces are
speculative, raising more questions than providing answers. This
is an important text since it was written at the end of the
seventies, the decade of the women's movement, which first opened
up these issues to scholarly attention.

273. Bertrand, M.

     1967.   SELF IMAGE AND REPRESENTATIONS OF FEMALE
                OFFENDERS: A CONTRIBUTION TO THE STUDY OF
                WOMEN'S IMAGE IN SOME SOCIETIES. Doctoral
                Dissertation, University of California,
                Berkeley.

     Criminological findings are presented as indexes of
differentiation between the sexes and as a lead to women's image.
This work is developed on the theoretical framework that in male-
dominated societies women are subject to a pattern of
instrumentality. This deprives them of perceiving themselves as
agents and makes them victims and objects. According to the
author, it also deprives society of the will to sanction
effectively, especially when women commit illegal acts. The
author states that the values and expectations to which women are
subjected should be reflected in social representations, such as
laws, criminal sex ratios and sentencing practices. A literature
survey on sex ratios is given in the introduction. The treatment
of female offenders is discussed, and the state of female
criminality and juvenile delinquency in France, Canada, Belgium,
and the United States is analyzed statistically. In dealing with
the self-image of female offenders, the author examines the
probability of instances in which women see themselves as
different from men according to the agent-object model of
inquiry. Tables, graphs, test questionnaires and statistical
analyses are included.

274. Bowker, L.H. (ed.)

     1981.   WOMEN AND CRIME IN AMERICA. New York:
                Macmillan Publishing Company, Inc.

     This set of articles offers a balanced overview of the role
of women as criminals, victims and offenders in the criminal

justice system. The book includes theoretical articles and reports of fieldwork surveys and experiments, emphasizing throughout the necessity to take a value-committed stance when discussing the victimization of the innocent and powerless. Articles by Carol Smart, Rita Simon, Peggy Giordano, et. al. help to clarify the true figure of female crime in America. Rape and wife-beating, usually eliminated in standard criminology readers, is well represented here. This is a good supplementary text for criminology courses, and should be a valuable asset to a women's studies library.

275. Bowker, L.H.

      1978.   WOMEN, CRIME, AND THE CRIMINAL JUSTICE
                 SYSTEM. Lexington, Ma.: Lexington Books.

      Criminal justice administrators, instructors in women's studies courses, activists in the women's movement, and anyone interested in sexual equality will find something of interest in this book. It illuminates the multiple relationships between women, criminal behavior and the criminal justice system. It attempts to answer such questions as: (1)What kind of crimes do women commit? (2)What are the trends in the incidence of female crime in the United States and around the world? (3)Why are there differences between the crimes perpetrated by men and those committed by women? (4)Are women commonly the victims of crime, particularly violent crime? (5)Is "the new female criminal" a fact or a myth? (6)How are female criminals and victims treated by practitioners in the criminal justice system? (7)Why do women enter into a life of crime? A strong statement by the author asserts: "The criminal justice system, a behemoth dominated by men and male ways of looking at the world, represents the most formal development of cross-sex social controls in human society." This general theme is carried throughout the book.

276. Crites, L. (ed.)

      1976.   THE FEMALE OFFENDER. Lexington, Ma.:
                 Lexington Books.

      This edited collection of studies presents a realistic picture of female offenders. It recognizes that, although in some respects, women have been treated more leniently within the system, the so-called "pedestal factor" has seldom worked to the advantage of women in the criminal justice system. This anthology of works includes the excellent study by Jennifer James on the motivations for entrance into prostitution. Contrary to popular belief, prostitution is an institutionalized occupational choice resulting from the same motivations that persuade other individuals to choose legitimate careers. This is the basis for the argument made by James and others that prostitution should be decriminalized.

277. Datesman, S.K. and F.R. Scarpitti. (eds.)

1980.   WOMEN AND CRIME AND JUSTICE. New York: Oxford
             University Press.

The book analyzes the extent and nature of female crime in
the United States: its sociological and anthropological causes,
its patterning, the way society deals with female crime in its
system of justice, and the relationship of women's criminality to
the women's movement.
    Roughly one-third of the fourteen essays are written by the
editors, attesting to their research involvement. The authors
have provided a concise introduction to each of the five
sections. WOMEN AND CRIME AND JUSTICE may well prove to be the
philosophical manifesto for sociological research in this
important area.

278. Davis, N.J. and B. Anderson.

        1982.   "Gender, Crime, and the Sociology of
                     Knowledge: Uncovering Ideological Biases in
                     an Academic Tradition." In R.B. Smith and
                     P.K. Manning (eds.) AN INTRODUCTION TO SOCIAL
                     RESEARCH. Handbook of Social Science Methods,
                     Vol. One.   New York: Ballinger Publishing
                     Company.

This study examines representative criminology textbooks
from 1918 through 1975 to assess the typical portrayal of sex
roles. Among the twenty texts examined, most lacked sociological
grounding, and were not written in an explanatory mode. Non-
logical and unsubstantiated assertions about sex-related traits
and acts were common, as were non-rational assumptions about the
general nature of men and women. Negative gender identification
exists for both males and females, but men are more likely than
women to receive negative evaluations from criminology text
writers. On the whole, women are invisible in criminology, except
for highly publicized cases, as most texts did not treat the
female criminal or victim in sociological terms. The paper
concludes that the sexist bias in criminology textbooks should be
balanced with a "perspectivist" approach. This uses a sociology
for the oppressed that would employ the knower's point of view.

279. Henson, S.D.

        1980.   "Female As Totem, Female As Taboo." Pages 67-
                     80 in E. Sagarin (ed.) TABOOS IN CRIMINOLOGY.
                     Beverly Hills: Sage Publications.

The reluctance of criminologists to examine the relationship
between feminism and increased female crime strongly suggests
that female crime is a taboo topic. This taboo-like constraint
operates to confuse and undermine serious inquiry. Granted that
the women's movement is largely comprised of middle- and upper-

116

class women, while offenders are primarily drawn from working-class groups, it is still the case that the feminist movement contributes to female crime in a number of ways. For example, it expands women's career opportunities, hence more openings for deviance and crime, and encourages the breakdown of inhibitions toward aggressive behavior. Law enforcement officials, too, may respond to liberated versions of women, affecting arrest and prosecution rates. The author rejects the victim status of women created by some feminists and calls for a less defensive analysis of the manifold varieties of female behavior. The author ignores, though, the growing body of literature on the social control of women, when she asserts that "women have not been and are not now victims of male oppression."

280. Jones, A.

      1980.   WOMEN WHO KILL. New York: Holt, Rinehart, and Winston.

    The focus of this book is on fear: the fears of men, who even as they shape society are desperately afraid of women, and so have fashioned a world in which women come and go only into "certain rooms;" and the fears of those women, who finding the rooms too narrow and the doors still locked, lie in wait or react in deviant ways. Written from an uncompromising feminist viewpoint, the author states that the story of women who kill is the larger story of women. The book consists of a series of studies, mainly historical, which approaches the subject of women who murder from different perspectives. The intention is to dispel some false notions and to examine the connections among women, society and killing. One of the studies cited is the Borden patricide case because of its broad concerns with social control and intergenerational conflict.

281. Klein, D.

      1976.   "The Etiology of Female Crime: A Review of the Literature." Pages 5-31 in L. Crites (ed.) THE FEMALE OFFENDER. Lexington, Ma.: D. C. Heath and Company.

    This article states that most of what has been written up to this point is based on assumptions that are sexist, racist and classist; assumptions that have served to maintain a repressive ideology with its extensive apparatus of control.
    Klein states we need a new research on women and crime, one that has feminist roots and a radical orientation. "It is necessary to understand the assumptions made by the traditional writers and break away from them."

282. Knudson, B.

      1974.   CAREER PATTERNS OF FEMALE MISDEMEANANT
                 OFFENDERS. Michigan: University Microfilms,
                 Inc.

     Critically examining female misdemeanant offenders, this
study reviews the relevant literature, drawing on a number of
directly or tangentially-related streams in criminology and
sociological materials. The author argues that existing data are
empirically weak; and emphasizes that, instead, what is needed
are alternative theoretical formulations for exploring women and
crime issues. Employing a typological or "charting" approach into
new research territory, the author presents some divergent
findings, and sketches some implications of the data in terms of
the pragmatic problems involved in decisions concerning the lives
of women who commit minor crimes.

283. Leonard, E.B.

      1982.   WOMEN, CRIME, AND SOCIETY: A CRITIQUE OF
                 THEORETICAL CRIMINOLOGY. New York: Longman.

     Leonard examines the existing field of literature pertaining
to women and crime, including statistics regarding feminine
crime, problems linked to current methods and the treatment of
women by the criminal justice system. Numerous sociological
theories are analyzed with special emphasis regarding their
application for women. The concluding chapter, "Toward a Feminist
Theory of Crime," presents a nonsexist theory of crime. An
extensive bibliography concludes this timely book.

284. Simon, R.J.

      1975.   WOMEN AND CRIME. Lexington, Mass.: Lexington
                 Books.

     This book describes the extent and type of female
involvement in crime in the United States. Simon bases her
selection of material and overall presentation on the notion that
female offenders suffer from lack of research attention.
     The author presents two opposing positions--one school of
criminology perceives women as victims of male oppression and
societal indifference; while the other proposes that women
offenders are more cunning and crafty than men, hence they use
the chivalry of the male legal system to avoid arrest, conviction
and imprisonment. Simon rejects the chivalry argument, because it
denies the reality of women offenders' experiences in the
criminal justice system. This includes increasing arrest rates
and incarceration nearly equal to men for similar offenses.

285. Smart, C.

1977.   WOMEN, CRIME, AND CRIMINOLOGY: A FEMINIST
         CRITIQUE. London: Routledge and Kegan Paul.

Smart offers this study as a beginning attempt to develop a
new direction in the study of female criminology, especially in
challenging the current argument that women's emancipation is
responsible for the increase of criminal activity among women.
Much of the increase should be interpreted as representing
changes in the social control over women.
Traditional studies have for long remained unchallenged in
their sexist interpretations of women's crime. For example, W.I.
Thomas (1923) insisted on the biologically determined inferior
status for women, not only in conventional society, but also in
the "world" of crime and delinquency. Such thinking contributes
to stereotypical categories that bear little relationship to
women's experiences. While Smart provides a critical
interpretation of criminology, she fails to formulate an
alternative perspective. Despite the shortcomings, this is a
well-recommended book.

286. Sparrow, G.

1970.   WOMEN WHO MURDER. New York: Abelard-Schuman.

An overly subjective analysis of why and what kinds of women
murder prompts the author to state that sex is the prime motive
for women who murder. A stupid woman would not be a successful
murderer, the author says, but he fails to provide adequate
support for this assertion. "Should convicted women murderers be
hanged?" The answer is "yes" in theory, but "no" in practice. The
author finds it offensive to hang a woman, but suggests that it
might be appropriate to hang a man. He rejects those who make no
distinctions between men and women when it comes to the ultimate
penalty of the law. This book is an example of the pre-feminist
mode of interpreting female crime. Overloaded with stock phrases
and simplistic solutions, the book will hopefully be replaced
with a more intellectually astute analysis of a much-abused
topic.

B. Female Delinquency

287. Brenzel, B.

1980. "Domestication as Reform: A Study of the Socialization of Wayward Girls, 1856-1905." HARVARD EDUCATIONAL REVIEW. 50:196-213.

Barbara Brenzel examines nineteenth-century juvenile reform policies by telling the story of Lancaster, a progressive reform school for girls in Massachusetts. Analyzing the efforts of reformers to socialize poor girls, many of whom were immigrants, she discribes the contradictory dual-purposes underlying these policies--fear and benevolence. The discussion of Lancaster illustrates how particular policies and programs for potentially deviant girls reflected ninteenth-century thought about reform, childhood poverty and especially the role of women in society.

In the first period (1790-1870), female penal units outwardly resembled male penitentiaries in many respects, although their inmates usually received inferior care. During the second stage (1870-1930), strenuous and often successful efforts were made to establish an entirely new type of prison, the women's reformatory. Here, women would receive care more appropriate to their "feminine" nature. Yet by legitimating differential justice, the reformatories in fact institutionalized a tradition of providing care that from our current perspective was inherently unequal. In the third stage (1930-present), the women's prison system continued to evolve in ways which perpetrated the older traditions of inferior treatment.

The women's prison system is not a small scale replica of the male prison system. In fact, the women's prison system differs radically from the male system on a number of dimensions, including historical development, administrative structures, some of its disciplinary techniques, and the experiences of its inmates. These differences refute the popular view of "the" prison system as a monolith structure with a single history.

288. Crow, R. and G. McCarthy. (eds.)

1982. TEENAGE WOMEN IN THE JUVENILE JUSTICE SYSTEM: CHANGING VALUES. Tucson, Arizona: New Directions for Young Women.

In twenty-four selections, experts in the fields of juvenile justice and women's studies, public policy makers, and social activists describe the operation of juvenile laws, courts and social services as they affect teenage females. The articles reveal the societal bias and attitudes toward women that have had a profound impact on the legal system and on the lives of young women. They also spell out a variety of alternatives that can bring about positive changes in the condition of an oppressed group too long neglected in our society.

289. Davidson, S. (ed.)

1982.   JUSTICE FOR YOUNG WOMEN: A CLOSE-UP ON CRITICAL ISSUES. Tucson, Arizona: New Directions for Young Women.

This anthology illuminates the conditions which lead girls into the juvenile justice system, as well as the sexist bias which pervades that system. Here are well documented articles on teenage prostitution; the realities of incest; the historic background of reform schools; new trends in research on young female offenders; strategies for overcoming the inequitable treatment of young women; and a rare first-person account by a youthful female offender. Reforms in the treatment of young women in the justice system can use this study as a foundation.

290. Mennel, R.M.

1973.   THORNS AND THISTLES: JUVENILE DELINQUENCY IN THE UNITED STATES, 1825-1940. Hanover, N.H.: University Press of New England.

Mennel offers an historical overview of the official response to juvenile delinquency in the United States. The first organized efforts to treat juvenile delinquency as a distinct social problem centered around the establishing of refuge houses in New York, Boston, and Philadelphia during the 1820's. This movement was a "milestone in the shift from family-centered discipline to institutional treatment administered by society," and was motivated by the growing social awareness that family discipline was no longer sufficient to control the numbers of neglected and abandoned children living in the larger seacoast cities. The founders of this movement were concerned with the need to remove children from jails and teach them the value of thrift, honesty and individual responsibility.

The proliferation of reform schools from 1850 to 1890 dramatized the failure of houses of refuge to prevent the growth of juvenile delinquency. Philanthropists and their followers who created the reform schools as a more efficient control system for youth held very different views on the causes and cures of juvenile delinquency than earlier houses of refuge.

The number and variety of reform schools for boys and girls multiplied during the later nineteenth century, but so did the severity of institutional problems. The origin of the juvenile court may be more clearly understood within the context of the deficient structure of the "child saving" philanthropy of the Chicago reform schools. Thus, construction of the Juvenile Court was an attempt to reassert the right of the state to assume parental power over delinquent children, which the increasingly

121

violent and exploitative nature of reform schools seemed to be incapable of fulfilling. The courts were supposed to treat each child individually, studying their particular psychic and social needs. Class and sex biases blinded reformers, however, to the limitations of their reform doctrine which persists today.

291. Platt, A.M.

1977.   THE CHILD SAVERS. Chicago: The University of Chicago Press, (revised).

Anthony Platt provides a provocative, historical perspective on THE "CHILD SAVERS," movement of the late 1800's and early 1900's. First published in 1969, the second edition (1977) has been enlarged and includes the author's critical analysis of the first edition.

In the new introduction, Platt critiques the book's theoretical perspective by relating its assumptions to developments in criminological theory in the late 1960's, as well as drawing upon recent historical interpretations of the Progressive era. Platt's original introduction sets the tone for perspectives on the origins of delinquency and provides a review of juvenile justice--a part of a general movement directed toward removing adolescents from the criminal law process and creating special programs for delinquent, dependent and neglected children. This occurred for both boys and girls. This book addresses the origins and structure of the child-saving movement in the United States. Specifically, it focuses on the child-saving movement in Chicago, wherein the State of Illinois originated the first juvenile court in 1899. The author makes no specific distinction between male or female delinquency, nor was this the intent of this study. However, Platt does provide an important historical account of the preemptive force behind the child-saving movement, that of women leaders.

Some of the women had tremendous political and economic clout, all of the women had "role clout." Women were considered the "natural caretakers for all children." The child-saving movement in Chicago was mobilized through the efforts of a group of feminist reformers who helped to pass special laws for juveniles and create new institutions for their reformation. Child-saving, however, was a reputable task for any woman who wanted to extend her housekeeping functions into the community without denying anti-feminist stereotypes of women's nature and place.

The laws and institutions created by the women of the child-saving era have been a motivating force in the current laws and institutional responses to females' delinquent behavior.

122

292. Reeves, M.

    1929.   TRAINING SCHOOLS FOR DELINQUENT GIRLS. New
               York: Russell Sage Foundation.

    The first detailed study on 57 institutions for delinquent
girls was sponsored by the Department of Child Helping of the
Russell Sage Foundation, completed in 1924.
    One of the purposes of this early study was to provide data
in order to set standards for such schools. "Only through an
intensive study of the practices to be avoided, as well as those
to be followed," could minimal standards be set, the author
points out. All aspects of these schools are examined from the
physical and psychological care of the inmates to the physical
settings and structure.
    Social control of wayward girls, while less ruthless than
for boys, incorporated many of the same concepts of treatment,
care and training. The goal for both boys and girls committed to
state institutions, the book clarifies, is to tighten the
industrial reins around America's working class youth.

293. Schlossman, S. and S. Wallach.

    1978.   "The Crime of Precocious Sexuality: Female
               Juvenile Delinquency in the Progressive Era."
               HARVARD EDUCATIONAL REVIEW. 48:65-94.

    The juvenile justice system's discrimination against poor
and minority children has been well documented, but the system's
discrimination on the basis of gender has been less widely
recognized. Drawing on neglected court records and secondary
sources, Schlossman and Wallach show how girls bore a
disproportionate share of the burden of juvenile justice in the
Progressive era. The authors note that during the Progressive era
female juvenile delinquents often received more severe
punishments than males, even though boys usually were charged
with more serious crimes. The authors conclude that the
discriminatory treatment of female delinquents in the early
twentieth century resulted from racial prejudice, new theories of
adolescents and Progressive era movements aimed to purify
society.

294. Thomas, W.I.

    1923.   THE UNADJUSTED GIRL. Boston: Little, Brown
               and Co.

    This early work on female delinquency is fairly progressive
for its era, while still embodying many of the ideas about
restrictive sex that characterized the Victorian era. Although
female delinquency in this context was generally believed to be
sexual in nature, this is spoken of only indirectly, emphasizing
the social and emotional aspects of female sexual behavior, often

as a way of excusing it. For example, a girl's devotion to her pimp is seen as springing from the same "instinct" which keeps a wife faithful to her husband; in a word, the female virtues of "loyalty, endurance, and self-sacrifice."

The book has five chapters: The Wishes, Regulation of the Wishes, The Individualization of Behavior, The Demoralization of Girls, Social Agencies, and The Measurement of Social Influences. Human wishes, a central theme, is further delineated by the following typology: desire for new experiences, the desire for security, the desire for response (appreciation), and the desire for recognition. Only within the context of the satisfaction or the lack of satisfaction of these needs can female delinquency be understood, Thomas insists.

In a chapter on the "demoralization of girls," Thomas states, "the girl cannot be said to fall, because she has never risen. She is not immoral, because this implies the loss of morality, but a-moral -- never having a moral code." For Thomas and other early sociologists lower-class manners and morals bring about the unfitting behavior. Sexual passions do not play an important part in female behavior; rather sex is a tool or means to the end of economic support and achieving other social and psychological needs. Perhaps the strongest feature of Thomas' work on female delinquency is his recognition of the importance of social organization and its prior influence in shaping young women's lives.

295. Vedder, C.B. and D.B. Somerville.

    1970.   THE DELINQUENT GIRL. Springfield, Illinois: Charles C. Thomas Publishing Co.

Statistical and sociological studies reveal that the proportion of women to men has been steadily increasing in the population, in the labor market, in the control of wealth, in the commission of crime, and in a similar fashion, in reported female delinquency. As Vedder and Somerville point out, research on delinquents has been primarily limited to males. Using Illinois as a representative situation, the authors examine the dynamics of female delinquency as behavior quite distinct from males who misbehave.

The Illinois Youth Commission's list of major offenses leading to the commitment of youthful females, in order of frequency, are: running away, incorrigibility, sex delinquency, probation violation, and truancy. These categories are most often referred to as the "big five" reasons, leading to incarceration of this population in Illinois. The authors' analysis includes a comparative study between the states to determine how practices in Illinois compare with those in other states.

The authors provide a sensitive portrayal of the delinquent girl through presenting case histories of girls involved in specific offenses, as well as several self-reported case studies that depict the incidences leading to commitment.

C. Prostitution

296. Baizerman, M., K. Thompson, K. Stafford-White, and "An Old, Young Friend."

       1979.   "Adolescent Prostitution." CHILDREN TODAY. Sept./Oct.:20-4.

This article examines juvenile prostitution in the Twin Cities area of Minneapolis-St. Paul, Minnesota. The authors provide a brief history of juvenile prostitution, and then examine the sexual, birth control, and working practices of juvenile prostitutes in this area, as well as that of the pimps. Factors which can lead to prostitution are delineated, and the important issues of love and prostitution are explored. The final section consists of the authors' recommendations for preventing prostitution among juveniles. The authors view efforts directed at pimps and johns as wasting time; instead, intervention should concentrate on the girls, both before and after their entrance into the profession.

297. Boyer, J.

       1982.   "Once a Whore, Always a Whore: Implications of Sexual Esteem for Counseling." CHANGE: INTERDISCIPLINARY JOURNAL OF CHILDREN. 5(3):14-6.

Basing her conclusions on the study by Jennifer James and Seattle-based studies (1977 to 1982), Ms. Boyer explores the past experience of both male and female juvenile prostitutes, comparing them to a control group of non-sexually labelled delinquents. Most research on prostitution has limited itself to such factors as neglect and economics, ignoring the role of sexual self-esteem. This study indicates early loss of self-esteem through such experience as rape, incest, molestation, and coercion of first intercourse to be primary indicators of later sexual deviance. If youth service personnel are going to overcome the defeat and apathy expressed by so many young prostitutes in the phrase "once a whore, always a whore," they must deal directly with their client's sexual self-esteem and labelling.

298. Boyer, D. and J. James.

    1978.   "Easy Money: Adolescent Involvement in
                Prostitution." In K. Weisberg (ed.) WOMEN AND
                THE LAW: THE INTERDISCIPLINARY PERSPECTIVE.
                Cambridge: Scheukman.

    Previous research on prostitution has focused on familial
abuse, and economic factors without looking at the perceived or
forced loss of a woman's self-esteem as a contributing factor to
the life of prostitution. Sex role confusion prevails in the
background of many women offenders, involving the internalization
of a deviant sexual self-concept. In this chapter, the authors
discuss reasons why some women choose prostitution or become
locked into a deviant female identity when others do not.

299. Boyer, D. and J. James.

    1982.   INTERVENTION WITH FEMALE PROSTITUTES.
                University of Washington, Department of
                Psychiatry and Behavioral Sciences.

    It is a fact that women involved in prostitution will
probably continue their involvement without intervention, as well
as other criminal activities such as drugs and alcohol. This
makes it important that health care and criminal justice
professionals, who see these women on a regular basis, develop an
effective intervention approach if they are to help these women,
The authors provide a conceptual framework for intervention,
beginning with a theory of sexual labelling that provides a
framework for understanding involvement in prostitution.
Intervention guidelines are provided, dealing with the
therapist's interaction with the client prostitute, as well as
three barriers to positive change: negative self-image, informal
labelling and societal reaction.

300. Brown, M.E.

    1979.   "Teenage Prostitution." ADOLESCENCE.
                14(56):665-80.

    This article addresses the problems faced by female teenage
prostitutes. The author covers precipitating conditions,
including alienation from family, parental abuse, education,
change, and employment. This article also addresses the entrance
into prostitution, including such variables as financial needs,
adventure, delinquent associates, institutionalization, perceived
powerlessness, sexual promiscuity, occupational history, drug use
and abuse, and running away. Treatment at the hands of the
juvenile justice system is explored.

                            126

301.

1981. "Child Exploitation." DIRECTIONS Newsletter, New Directions for Young Women, National Female Advocacy Project.

This newsletter focuses on prostitution in the Portland, Multnomah County area in Oregon. The newsletter examines background data on the girls and boys involved, and discusses the programs available to them. Some information is provided on differential law enforcement of male and female prostitutes.

302. Davis, N.J.

1978. "Prostitution: Identity, Career and Legal-Economic Enterprise." Pp. 195-222 in J.M. Henslin and E. Sagarin (eds). THE SOCIOLOGY OF SEX. New York: Schocken Books.

This study has two parts. The first considers the movement into prostitution by analyzing the stages of drift into the first act of prostitution, then turns to transitional deviance and finally looks at professionalization. Motives are examined for each stage and reveal sharp differences between the younger, experiential phase and the latter professional stage where sex is an occupation, not adventure or "fun." Based on a jail sample of thirty prostitutes from correctional institutions in Minnesota, the article shows how hustler norms that reinforce the deviant identity include a strong money motive, hostility to clients and a counter-morality -- motives that neutralize the heavy social stigma. Part two takes a structural view of the "working girl" and explores changes in prostitution over a ten year period in Portland, Oregon. Occupational reorganization involves disguised sex selling and "house prostitution" -- party girls, call girls, sauna baths, massage parlors and legal bordellos. While ostensibly changed, the reorganized structure retains many traditional features of sex stratification, including ruthless exploitation by managers, clients, police, and other sex sellers.

303. Deisher, R., G. Robinson and D. Boyer.

ADOLESCENT FEMALE AND MALE PROSTITUTION. Unpublished paper, University of Washington, Seattle, Wa. 98195.

This paper considers the process of involvement in prostitution, the typical background histories which can lead to involvement, and various negative effects of the process of becoming a prostitute. Characteristics of both male and female prostitution are highlighted; their similarities and differences. The authors conclude with practical suggestions for intervention by physicians with this problematic population.

304. Gagnon, J.H. and W. Simon. (eds.)

    1967.   SEXUAL DEVIANCE. New York: Harper and Row, Inc.

In their introduction to this collection of essays, the editors assert that there are a relatively large number of forms of sexual deviance, and distinguish among three categories: first, "normal deviance," such as premarital coitus; second, "pathological deviance," such as incest, sexual contact with children, exhibitionism, voyeurism and assault offenses; and third, female prostitution and male and female homosexuality. It is homosexuality and prostitution that are mainly treated in this volume. In addition, there are illuminating essays on sexuality in the child and adolescent, as well as the history and contemporary forms of prostitution. One article considers the sex seller's risk of exposure to drugs, alcohol and venereal disease. Especially interesting from a feminist viewpoint is a paper on the prostitute's self-image and system of values. Interviews with sexual deviants elicited candid, informative responses.

305. Goetze, J.

    1982.   "Mean Streets: A Mother's Perspective." NORTHWEST MAGAZINE. Sunday October 17, 1982.

This article explores a mother's reaction to her daughter's entrance into prostitution. She discusses her daughter's background (middle class), her entrance into the profession, and her efforts to get her out of prostitution. In addition, the author talks about the role of the pimp in persuading and keeping girls in prostitution.

306. Gray, D.

    1973.   "Turning Out: A Study in Teenage Prostitution." URBAN LIFE AND CULTURE. 1:401-425.

This article is based on data from the author's study of teenage prostitutes, aged 17-19, in the Seattle area. The main thrust of this study centers around social control theory. The author sees prostitution as occurring due to the breakdown or lack of ties with conventional social order as a result of social and emotional deprivation in the family lives of these girls, academic failure and frustration at school, and boredom and dissatisfaction with the world of legitimate work. These factors, along with early sexual experience and contacts with a person "in the life," lead many girls to prostitution.

307. Hallman, T. Jr.

   1982.   "Mean Streets: The Enduring World of Portland
                Prostitution." NORTHWEST MAGAZINE. Sunday
                October 17, 1982.

    This article examines prostitution in Portland, Oregon,
focusing on the police point of view. Their enforcement practices
do not work, and they know it, leading to a great deal of
frustration on their part, as well as feelings of powerlessness.
Officers seem to desire change, one way or another, as at present
their enforcement is little more than a temporary response to a
poor law.

308. James, J.

   1980.   "Self-Destructive Behavior and Adaptive
                Strategies in Female Prostitution. Pp.311-359
                in N.L. Farberow (ed.) THE MANY FACES OF
                SUICIDE: INDIRECT SELF-DESTRUCTIVE BEHAVIOR.
                New York: McGraw-Hill.

    James contends that prostitution is a traditional variation
of the female sex role. Once seen as abnormal and destructive to
society and the individual prostitute, prostitution should more
appropriately be viewed as an aspect of, not a contradiction to,
the female sex role. The lifestyle of female streetwalkers reveal
its utility as an "alternative, survival-promoting adaptation,"
and as a "self protective reaction to the legal harassment of the
profession." Often the prostitute is without alternative
resources. Early labeling as a "whore" and a lifestyle and
subculture that offered little measure of place and status (i.e.
lack of normal peer group and family) leads to perception of
loss. This intensifies self-destructive behavior (e.g. drug
abuse, coercion by pimps, exposure to legal harassment). Until
prostitutes age, the deviant lifestyle, which promises money,
adventure, independence, and peer group involvement, tends to
blind her to the self-destructiveness of her situation.

309. James, J.

   1977.   "Prostitutes and Prostitution." Pp.368-423 in
                E. Sagarin and F. Montanino (eds). DEVIANTS:
                VOLUNTARY ACTORS IN A HOSTILE WORLD. New
                York: Scott, Foresman, and Company.

    In this excellent overview of the social status and
lifestyle of prostitutes, James reviews the existing knowledge
base and proposes a new theoretical direction. Women are
prostitutes for two reasons: "The primary cause of women becoming
prostitutes is the supply and demand equation that grows out of
the sexual socialization process." This involves sex as a

commodity. "The secondary cause of women becoming prostitutes are those circumstances that lead them to make the shift from subtle sexual sale to overt prostitution." These involve a variety of troubles, usually associated with the family and peer relations. The functions of prostitution are also enlarged from earlier studies, which neglected such customer motivations as "special services," male bonding and therapy. The pimp and the customer are shown to play significant, if not primary, roles in structuring prostitution as an "attractive occupational option for many women."

310. James, J. and N.J. Davis.

      1982.   "Contingencies in Female Sex Role Deviance." HUMAN ORGANIZATION.

    The question in this research on 136 street prostitutes and 133 non-prostitute offenders entailed: What are some typical contingencies that occur in the course of female sexual development that contribute to a devalued self and facilitate the movement into adult sexual deviance? Exploring the association between adult female prostitution and juvenile experiences (specifically home life, sexual experience and criminal involvement), the authors show how prostitutes' juvenile social and sexual histories vary from non-prostitute offenders. Such contingencies as parental departure, withdrawal from high school, unsatisfactory or non-normative sexual experiences, pregnancy, drug use, and a juvenile record have a cumulative negative impact that contributes to a devalued self and the subsequent "drift" or "slide" into prostitution. Prostitutes also learn the advantages of being a prostitute--independence, glamour amd excitement--that often outweigh the loss of status in the majority culture.

311. James, J., N.J. Davis and P. Vitaliano.

      1982.   "Female Sexual Deviance: A Theoretical and Empirical Analysis." DEVIANT BEHAVIOR: AN INTERDISCIPLINARY JOURNAL. 3:175-95.

    Societal analysis of sex role typing, attribution theory in social psychology and reaction theory in the sociology of deviance provide theoretical convergences that enable the authors to focus on career contingencies in the drift toward deviance. This paper applies these concepts to a theory of sexual labelling by identifying six early sexual experiences that are empirically shown to shape deviant sexuality in adult women. The responses to a standardized protocol were obtained for two large samples of deviant adult women. The results are based on extensive analysis that controlled for race and economic status while an adolescent. The findings reinforce previous conjectures and hypotheses about the influential factors in the drift toward female sexual deviance.

312. James, J. and J. Meyerding.

> 1977.   "Early Sexual Experience and Prostitution."
> AMERICAN JOURNAL OF PSYCHIATRY. 134(12):1381-
> 1384.

The authors examined the results of research on "normal"
women and prostitutes, comparing several aspects of their early
sexual experience. The prostitutes held in common many negative
experiences not found or found less often in other populations of
"normal" women, such as incest and/or coerced sex, intercourse at
a young age, and few or no meaningful relationships with men.
Living in a society which values women for their sexuality, these
women discovered that sex could be used to gain status, even if
it is negatively labelled by the larger society. A woman who
views herself as "debased" or "spoiled" sexually may see
prostitution as the only viable alternative for status left open
to her.

313. James, J. and P. Vitaliano.

> FACTORS IN THE DRIFT TOWARDS FEMALE SEX ROLE
> DEVIANCE. Unpublished paper, University of
> Washington, Department of Psychiatry and
> Behavioral Sciences, Seattle, Wa. 98195.

Drawing on data from their comprehensive study in Seattle
under a grant from the National Institute on Mental Health, this
paper examines the association between adult female prostitution
and juvenile home life, early intercourse, pregnancy "wastage"
(stillbirths, abortions, and miscarriages), and criminal
involvement. Unlike most prostitution research which focuses
solely on such factors as early neglect and economic impetus, the
authors examine how the previously stated factors may effect a
young woman's self-concept and identification with the
traditional female role, bringing about a "drift" into sex role
deviance. The authors' data found a significant association
between these negative experiences and prostitution, which they
link to an eventual perceived loss of a positive feminine role
during adolescence and its possible effect on identification as a
prostitute.

314. Khalaf, S.

> 1965.   PROSTITUTION IN A CHANGING SOCIETY. Beirut:
> Khayats.

This book describes a sociological study conducted by the
author on legal prostitution in Beirut, Lebanon. The author
interviewed many of Beirut's prostitutes and provides findings on
such areas as background data, factors leading to prostitution,
what life is like in the red light district, and future plans of

the women involved. Although dated in some of its attitudes, the book does have some sound information, and includes the author's questionnaire.

315. McInery, V.

    1982.   "Mean Streets: The View From the Other Side of the Street." NORTHWEST MAGAZINE. Sunday, October 17, 1982.

    In this article, the author reports on her interview with two Portland, Oregon prostitutes, examining their family background, entrance into prostitution, their life within it, and their future plans.

316. Sandford, J.

    1975.   PROSTITUTES. London: Morrison and Gibb, Ltd.

    This book covers many areas of the prostitution business, identifying four areas: female prostitution, male prostitution (small), "the tease and other forms of sexploitation," and the "tamer shores of sexploitation." The section on females discusses a range of sex selling from streetwalkers to brothels, with a large section on why women sell sex and men buy it. A section on "schoolgirl prostitutes" is also included.

317. Silbert, M.H. and A.M. Pines.

    1981.   "Occupational Hazards of Street Prostitutes." CRIMINAL JUSTICE AND BEHAVIOR. 8(4):395-399.

    This study represents the first major attempt to investigate various forms of victimization of street prostitutes, both on and off the job. Two hundred juvenile and adult female prostitutes in the San Francisco area were interviewed, all reporting high levels of victimization. Physical abuse, by both customers and pimps, customer rape, forced perversions, nonpayment, robbery, clients going beyond the prostitution contract, and unfair split of payment with pimps were all reported. These events go unreported because the women tend to blame themselves for their victimization, and because they believe the police will not do anything for them even if they report.

318. Urban and Rural Systems Associates.

    1982.   TESTIMONY BEFORE THE SUBCOMMITTEE ON JUVENILE JUSTICE OF THE SENATE JUDICIARY COMMITTEE, JULY 21, 1982. U.R.S.A., East Office, 1221 Connecticut Avenue N.W., Washington, D.C. 20036.

The Urban and Rural Systems Associates is a social policy research firm, awarded a contract by the Youth Development Bureau to study adolescent prostitution, with a special focus on adolescent male prostitution. This testimony briefly describes the main findings of URSA's two year national study regarding both male and female prostitution, identifies three types of adolescent male prostitutes, and delineates intervention strategies.

319. Vitaliano, P. and J. James.

> DEVIANT FEMALE SEXUALITY: SOME ADOLESCENT AND ADULT CORRELATES. Unpublished paper, University of Washington, Department of Psychiatry and Behavioral Sciences, Seattle, Washington 98195.

In their paper, the authors compare differences between prostitutes and other female offenders. Several researchers have discussed the association between negative sexual experiences in female adolescence, low self-image, and a subsequent life-style as an adult. In this sample, negative sexual experiences in adolescence occurred significantly more often in the sample of prostitutes (N=152) than that of general women offenders (N=117). The authors suggest that therapists involved with adolescents whose self-image has been damaged by negative sexual experiences explore the implications of these findings.

320. Walkowitz, J.R.

> 1980.   "The Politics of Prostitution." SIGNS: JOURNAL OF WOMEN IN CULTURE AND SOCIETY. 6(1):123-135.

Historical precedents for the current feminist attack on commercial sex has its roots in earlier feminist campaigns against male vice and the double standard. Prostitution, pornography, white slavery, and homosexuality were all viewed as manifestations of male sexual license, moral campaigns which the author considers "self defeating." Yet she concedes that these crusades mobilized over prostitution helped to define and construct sexuality in the nineteenth century. They also delineated the relations in which public intervention and definitions of deviance would develop. A century ago, feminists were ambivalent about commercialized sex, and prostitution today remains an uncomfortable reminder to the middle class feminists of their own absorption in moral supremacy.
On the whole, anti-vice crusades in the nineteenth century merely diverted feminists anger into repressive campaigns. This had little effect in controlling men or corporate interests whose goals were antithetical to the values and ideals of feminism.

321. Walkowitz, J.R.

1980.   PROSTITUTION AND VICTORIAN SOCIETY: WOMEN,
CLASS, AND THE STATE. Cambridge: Cambridge
University Press.

The Contagious Diseases Act of mid-Victorian England opened
up to public discourse a massive documentation about the lives
and actions of prostitutes. This revealed important social and
political developments. For example, the rise of the
institutional state, the emergence of the women's movement,
changing social and sexual mores, and the problems of state
intervention, and deviance were all related to the development of
a medical apparatus charged with policing "sexually deviant"
women. Once considered part of the working class population,
under the impact of these Acts, prostitutes became an outcast
group. This well-documented analysis makes a major contribution
to women's history, working class history, and the social history
of medicine and politics.

322. Worlock, M.

1982.   COMMUNITY TASK FORCE ON PROSTITUTION: FINAL
REPORT AND RECOMMENDATIONS. Portland, Oregon,
April 1982.

As a Final Report, the paper begins with background
information on the Task Force and ends with an appendix of Task
Force members and resource persons involved with research or
prevention and control of prostitution that the Task Force drew
upon. The report is broken into two components, Juvenile and
Adult Prostitution in Portland in 1981. Areas studied are:
background data, causes for involvement in prostitution, law
enforcement data, impact on the community, existing resources and
lack thereof, and recommendations involving setting up Project
Luck, a federally-funded program, to link social service
organizations in the Portland area to better serve the needs of
runaways and juvenile prostitutes.

IX

Divorce, Separation and Widowhood

323. Anspach, D.F.

>   1976.   "Kinship and Divorce." JOURNAL OF MARRIAGE
>   AND THE FAMILY. 38(2):323-330.

This article investigates the impact of divorce and remarriage on women's kinship ties. All of the women studied had one or more minor children. Married, divorced, and remarried women were interviewed and compared. Two major findings are reported. First, divorced or remarried women are unlikely to contact or receive help from their former husband's kin. But remarried women are integrated into the current spouse's kinship network. Second, the kinship ties of divorced women are imbalanced because there is no sharing of kinship ties with non-relatives.

324. Arling, G.

>   1976.   "The Elderly Widow and Her Family, Neighbors,
>   and Friends." JOURNAL OF MARRIAGE AND THE
>   FAMILY. 38(4):757-768.

Arling found that the morale and personal satisfaction level is more satisfying when widows associate with their friends. Because parents and children share a lifetime of family interaction, they sometimes find it difficult to "truly share" experiences. Widows usually show concern for their children and vice-versa, but satisfying personal relationships with children are seldom possible. Friendship groups help boost the widow's morale. Research in this area should stipulate which status and income groups are most likely to seek personal relationships outside kinship structures.

325. Barrett, C.J.

>   1981.   "Intimacy in Widowhood." PSYCHOLOGY OF WOMEN
>   QUARTERLY. 5(3):473-487.

Widow's intimate relationships are studied in this research by Barrett. She looks at three types of people with whom widows have close ties, and the effects these people have on the widows. First friends, then family and finally "others" (i.e. associates) are discussed. Also considered is the widow's "relationship" with her dead spouse, and the implications of this for adjustment in widowhood.

326. Brown, P. and R. Manela.

> 1978. "Changing Family Roles: Women and Divorce."
> JOURNAL OF DIVORCE. 1(4):315-328.

Brown discovered that women with "traditional" sex role attitudes were more vulnerable to psychological stress and low self-esteem during divorce. It was found that women whose attitudes towards sex roles were nontraditional (or became nontraditional during the divorce) experienced positive feelings about themselves and their lifestyles, and were also able to take steps toward personal growth. It is apparent that a woman's attitude toward the roles of the sexes plays an integral part in her successful coping with divorce.

327. Brown, P., L. Perry, and E. Harburg.

> 1977. "Sex Role Attitudes and Psychological Outcomes for Black and White Women Experiencing Marital Dissolution." JOURNAL OF MARRIAGE AND THE FAMILY. 39(3):549-561.

The study topic--a comparison between black and white women going through the divorce process--involves interviewing women twice; once when they began the divorce process and again four months later to determine if attitude changes had occurred. Despite racial differences, the women did not differentiate in two significant areas: First, in their traditional sex-role attitudes, and second, in a change from traditional to nontraditional attitudes over time. Where differences between races did occur is in: (1)their psychological outcomes, based on attitudes, (2)the level of self-esteem, and (3)their marital satisfaction. Causes for these differences are ethnic-related and also attributed to orientation to traditional roles.

328. Colletta, N.D.

> 1979. "Support Systems After Divorce: Incident and Impact." JOURNAL OF MARRIAGE AND THE FAMILY. 41(4):837-846.

This article summarizes a study that compared the support systems of married and divorced mothers. It was designed to show the impact of support systems on the single-parent family and on its ability to function. The research, conducted in 1976 and 1977, showed that families under stress need strong support systems, and that the mother must be satisfied with the support she receives. If the support systems are lacking and/or if the mother is not satisfied with them, then her relationships with her children may become very restricted and harsh.

329. Corcoran, M.

1979.   "The Economic Consequences of Marital Dissolution for Women in the Middle Years." SEX ROLES. 5(3):343-353.

What is the economic status of divorced women? The author finds that women's economic status is greatly reduced due to changes in their marital status. This change occurred even though women took steps to combat their loss of income. Lack of alternatives for women who find themselves without a husband and with little income is the chief difficulty. Research is needed that would address this problematic area to discern possibilities and solutions to economic loss.

330. Granvold, D., L. Pedler, and S. Schellie.

1979.   "A Study of Sex Role Expectancy and Female Post-Divorce Adjustment." JOURNAL OF DIVORCE. 2(4):383-393.

These researchers identified factors that were significantly related to women's adjustment after divorce. The subjects were women who had been divorced or separated in the past five years and who had not remarried; all of the women were white. The research employed a four part questionnaire. Findings showed that older women and women who had been married longer were more "self-accepting," and were better adjusted to their lives after divorce. Two predominant factors causing divorce were (1)lack of communication, and (2)conflicts about family responsibility.

331. Gurak, D.T. and D. Gillian.

1977.   "The Remarriage Market: Factors Influencing the Selection of Second Husbands." JOURNAL OF DIVORCE. 3(2):161-173.

The factors that influence remarriage of divorced women involve (1)the woman's age at separation, (2)whether or not she had children and (3)her educational level. The authors examined these conditions in terms of two outcomes: (1)the interval between divorce and the probability of remarriage, and (2)the selectivity of those that remarry. It was shown that constraints affected the possibility of remarriage; women who had children, or who were older or had more than a high school education were less likely to remarry. Not enough data was gathered, however, to control for confounding variables (i.e. having a good job).

332. Halem, L.C.

1982.   SEPARATED AND DIVORCED WOMEN. Westport,
             Connecticut: Greenwood Press.

This book explores the dilemmas and triumphs of divorce and
separation. It focuses on middle-class American women with
custody of dependent children, using extensive questionnaire
data, numerous open-ended interviews, and in a unique experiment,
role-playing the life of a recently separated woman. The result
is an in-depth examination of the legal, economic, social, and
psychological implications of marital dissolution.

Halem constructs her analysis of middle-class divorce around
her own real-life experiences. Assuming the identity of "Sheila
Ash," a fictitious women separated from her husband, the author
checked legal services, applied for jobs, investigated day-care
centers, and looked for places to live (with children and a dog).
During the course of this five year exploration, "Sheila" also
examined a wide range of community services available for
separated and divorced people and their children in a suburban
town (called "Westside" by the author). Augmenting her personal
discoveries with the thoughts and feelings of more than fifty
female interviewees (and a lesser number of men), Halem explores
various aspects of separation and divorce, from child care and
relations with the ex-spouse, to the problems of forging a new
economic and social identity.

333. Harvey, C.D. and H.M. Bahr.

1974.   "Widowhood, Morale, and Affiliation." JOURNAL
             OF MARRIAGE AND THE FAMILY. 36(1):97-106.

Widowed and married people from five nations (United States,
Italy, United Kingdom, Germany, and Mexico) were examined to
compare attitudes and affiliative ties. Neither "self" theory or
"role" theory perspectives adequately explain the differences
between widows and those who were married. Socioeconomic status
is the major factor with lower-income widows experiencing the
greatest negative impact. Among poor widows, there are more
negative attitudes and fewer affiliative ties.

334. Houseknecht, S.K. and G.B. Spanier.

1980.   "Marital Disruption and Higher Education
             Among Women in the United States."
             SOCIOLOGICAL QUARTERLY. 21(3):375-389.

With this study, Houseknecht and Spanier show the reason
that women with five or more years of college education have such
a high incidence of marital disruption, when compared to women
with four years of college training. Three variables were found
to have the greatest impact if the women were (1)non-white,
(2)employed and/or (3)earning a high income. If these variables

138

were present, divorce or separation were likely. Finally, the article suggests four possible reasons for this relationship: (1)insecure male identities and women's sense of status loss, (2)female economic independence, (3)female career commitment, and (4)non-shared social support systems.

335. Lopata, H.Z.

        1981.   "Widowhood and Husband Sanctification."
                   JOURNAL OF MARRIAGE AND THE FAMILY.
                   43(2):439-450.

        Lopata studied Chicago area widows to see why many idolize their late husbands. Age, education and race have an impact upon how the dead husband is viewed. Older, white or highly educated women appear to erase their husband's faults after his death. This may lead to over-idealization of the dead spouse, and subsequently non-coping behavior as widows.

336. Lopata, H.Z.

        1979.   WOMEN AS WIDOWS. New York: Elsevier.

        Widows in the Chicago area were the basis for Lopata's book. She first discusses their characteristics (age, birthplace, education) and then discusses income level. Support systems are critically examined, and reasons indicated why widows fail to use such supports. The final chapters detail descriptive profiles of various types of widows.

337. Lopata, H.Z.

        1973.   WIDOWHOOD IN AN AMERICAN CITY. Cambridge,
                   Mass.: Schenkman Publishing Company.

        American, urban widows who are 50 years or older provide the focus of this book. Her basic conclusion is that widows "re-enter" society differently due to their place in the modern social system. Types of urban widows range from the "self-initiating" woman to the "social isolate." Some widows quickly adjust to widowhood, while others never do, depending on their social and economic status.

338. Lopata, H.Z. and H.P. Brehm.

        1982.   WIDOWHOOD. New York: Praeger Publishers.

        Discussing the economic and social circumstances of widows and orphans, the authors propose that the needs of this group are not being met by present policies. Examining the effects of existing policies, such as the Social Security Act and survivor benefits, the authors conclude that problem definition, program development and program implementation do not correspond with one another, contributing to their inadequacy as guidelines for policy. They conclude that future policy should address these issues, as well as issues of maximum family limitations and income inadequacy, as well as helping widowed homemakers to re-enter the world of work.

339. Morgan, L.A.

    1981.   "Economic Change at Mid-Life Widowhood: A Longitudinal Analysis." JOURNAL OF MARRIAGE AND THE FAMILY. 43(4):899-907.

Morgan points out that there are three major issues about economic change due to widowhood. The first is that there is a marked difference between income for married and widowed women; widowed women have lower incomes. Second, when comparing personal income levels of women before and after the death of husbands, there is "minimal" change. And third, although dollar amounts of income may not change, the source of income does.

340. Mueller, C.W. and H. Pope.

    1980.   "Divorce and Female Remarriage Mobility: Data on Marriage Matches After Divorce for White Women." SOCIAL FORCES. 58(3):726-738.

Mueller and Pope's study of female mobility after remarriage compares the occupational status of women's first and second husbands to discover if their mobility is upward, downward or static. The women in this study were all white and were in their second marriage after the first had ended by annulment or divorce. Although the researchers measured mobility according to the husband's job, it was the status of the women that was the important predictor of mobility.

The authors suggest that courtship is an "exchange." This means that marriage partners view each other in terms of "equal worth," and exchange their status in marriage according to this perception. The study concluded that one half of the women were upwardly mobile while the other half maintained their status quo.

341. Norton, A.J.

    1980.   "The Influence of Divorce on Traditional Life-Cycle Measures." JOURNAL OF MARRIAGE AND THE FAMILY. 42(1):63-69.

This report compares women's life-cycles within their families and the likelihood of divorce by studying traditional families that break-up through marital dissolution. The research was restricted to women who were mothers born between 1900 and

1959. Three categories of women were compared: (1)those married once, and who were still married, (2)those married once and divorced, and (3)those married once and who were now in their second marriage. It was discovered that the family "life-cycle" process seems to differentially affect the likelihood of divorce at different stages.

342. Paskowicz, P.

    1982.   ABSENTEE MOTHERS. Paradise, Ca.: Universe Books.

Mothers who do not live with their children provoke strong societal censure, and often stereotyped as irresponsible, self-centered, unloving, and/or promiscuous. In exploring this sensitive, almost taboo subject of the "absentee mother," the author reveals the deep anguish and social reality behind these mothers' decisions. Based on interviews with one hundred mothers living apart from their children, Paskowicz concludes that the absentee mother is typically a woman who married very young, was psychologically unprepared for motherhood, and discovered that she was unable to cope with the often unrealistic expectations of mothering that were self and other imposed.

The decision to give up custody is rarely a choice. More commonly, the mother confronts unbearable psychological pressure, fearing that she will experience a mental breakdown, abuse her children or commit suicide. For other women, dissolving their marriage, but anxious to keep their children, the husband's threat to withhold child support or to exert physical intimidation may weaken her resolve.

For absentee mothers, isolation, loneliness, depression, and guilt commonly accompany the mother-child separation. For some women, the enforced rejection of their children reanimates emotional deprivation experienced during their own childhood. Paskowicz attributes strict religious upbringing and the patriarchal family (and subsequent husband-dominated marriage) as causal agents in setting the stage for later psychological problems for these women.

343. Peterson, J.A. and M.L. Briley.

    1977.   WIDOWS AND WIDOWHOOD: A CREATIVE APPROACH TO BEING ALONE. Piscataway, New Jersey: New Century.

Through the experiences of numerous individuals, the reader is led through the trauma that those who lose a husband or wife experience. The authors describe how women work through the grief and the making of a new life, including new roles and statuses that must be assumed. Financial advice, as well as a helpful chapter concerning the diversity of sexual lifestyles available to widows, are included.

344. Spicer, J.W. and G.D. Hampe.

  1975.   "Kinship Interaction After Divorce." JOURNAL
            OF MARRIAGE AND THE FAMILY. 37(1):113-119.

    Divorced women and men were interviewed to discern the
similarities and differences of kinship interaction. Because
divorce drastically changes a person's life, and because females
are a "critical link" in the kinship network, women typically
have more contact with consanguines and affines after a divorce
than men. Finally, it was shown that kin contact is primarily
along child-parent lines.

345. Thornton, A.

  1978.   "Marital Instability Differentials and
            Interactions: Insights from Multivariate
            Contingency Table Analysis." SOCIOLOGY AND
            SOCIAL RESEARCH. 62(4):572-595.

    Thornton studied the marital dissolution of women using
several factors as variables. He discovered that both non-white
women and women who marry young have higher dissolution rates
than others. In addition, he found that Baptists and
Fundamentalists have higher instability rates in marriage than
other religious groups. The relationship between divorce and
education is contingent on race with low educated, non-white
women having higher divorce rates.

X

Lesbianism

346. Abbott, S. and B. Love.

1972.   SAPPHO WAS A RIGHT-ON WOMAN: A LIBERATED VIEW
OF LESBIANISM. New York: Stein and Day.

The plight of the female homosexual in society is explored
by two feminist lesbians. The authors relate the struggle
experienced by gay feminists who are part of the women's
liberation movement. The issues and conflicts inherent in the
lesbian community are examined as well as societal sanctions
levied against gays.

The book is divided into two parts: first, "what it was
like," and the second, describing "living in the future." The
authors describe the personal cost paid by lesbians for their
sexual orientation; how they cope with guilt that often manifests
itself in frustration, anxiety, dispair, and suicide; and their
struggle to hide their sexual preference in a straight society by
passing themselves as straights to employers, family and friends.
Although sanctuaries are often limited, some lesbians find
companionship in gay bars and gay organizations, while others
lead a life of isolation. The final chapter emphasizes the
necessity for the individual lesbian to achieve self acceptance,
and advises how this can be done through the process of
consciousness raising and leading a self-fulfilling life.

347. Albro, J. and C. Tully.

1979.   "A Study of Lesbian Lifestyles in Homosexual
Micro-Culture and the Heterosexual Macro-
Culture. JOURNAL OF HOMOSEXUALITY. 4(4):331-
334.

In this study, 91 lesbians were interviewed with the
majority being white, middle class, urban, young, and well
educated. Readers are cautioned that the sample may be biased.
This middle class population of lesbians probably differ in
unknown ways from minority or poor lesbians.

Focusing on lesbian lifestyles and their interaction in both
the homosexual subculture and the heterosexual macro-culture, the
authors designed the questionnaire to identify significant
features in their present relationships (either positive or
negative). Responses to an "openness scale" are also noted.

The research revealed that, although lesbians seek
acceptance by the culture in which they reside and worry about
the criminality of their sexual preference, it is only in

isolated circumstances (among relatives or at work) that they masquerade as heterosexuals to gain approval. On the whole, these lesbians did not feel accepted in the heterosexual world, so they turned to the "homosexual micro-culture for their social life and support system."

348. Bell, A.P. and M.S. Weinberg.

      1978.   HOMOSEXUALITIES: A STUDY OF DIVERSITY AMONG MEN AND WOMEN. New York: Simon and Schuster.

The culmination of a plan, originally conceived by Dr. Alfred Kinsey, HOMOSEXUALITIES contain much of the research that he initiated. This lengthy volume is organized into five parts with each section's findings being divided between male and female respondents. (1) The "Introduction" includes the rationale for the study as well as the methods of research. (2) "Dimensions of Sexual Experience" includes the homosexual-heterosexual continuum, overtness, level of sexual activity, cruising, sexual partnerships, sex appeal, sexual techniques, level of sexual interest, sexual problems, acceptance of homosexuality and a typology of sexual experience. (3) "Social Adjustment" includes work, religiousness, politics, marriage, friendships, social activities, and social difficulties. (4) "Psychological Adjustment" includes a review of earlier studies on the differences of psychological adjustment between homosexuals and heterosexuals as well as the results of their findings on "various measures of psychological adjustment." (5) A concluding overview expresses the hope that this research will enable homosexuals to better understand themselves as well as foster greater understanding of homosexuality by heterosexuals.

Earlier studies tended to concentrate primarily on the similarities among homosexuals, often assuming that an individual's sexual preference prescribed his or her behavior in all other aspects. It was also assumed that all homosexuals were alike, and that it was valid to compare them as a totality to a heterosexual population. Bell and Weinberg's work is a departure from these earlier studies with their greater emphasis on the diversity within the homosexual population, especially the variation in lifestyles between men and women.

349. Bell, A.P. and M.S. Weinberg. (eds.)

      1972.   HOMOSEXUALITY: AN ANNOTATED BIBLIOGRAPHY. New York: Harper and Row.

This often cited bibliography includes 1265 items in 550 pages. Published in 1972, the book reviews books and articles written between 1940 and 1968. Special emphasis is placed on the fields of psychology, psychiatry and sociology. Areas excluded are biography, autobiography, literary works, all popular magazines, except SEXOLOGY, and most general books on homosexuality.

The volume is divided into three parts: (1)physiological considerations, including etiology and treatments; (2)psychological considerations, including etiology and treatments; and (3)sociological considerations, having to do with the homosexual community: social and demographic aspects, homosexuality in history, non-western societies and special settings, societal attitudes toward homosexuality, and homosexuality and the law. Each of the sub-categories contains a male and female component.

The book concludes with an extensive listing of other bibliographies and dictionaries. Both an author and subject index occupy the final pages.

350. Bell, A.P., M.S. Weinberg, and S. Hammersmith.

1981.   SEXUAL PREFERENCES: ITS DEVELOPMENT IN MEN AND WOMEN. Bloomington, Indiana: Indiana University Press.

Based on 1500 interviews of both heterosexuals and homosexuals, Bell, Weinberg and Hammersmith explore the question of how sexual preference is developed in men and women. Theories concerning the etiology of homosexuality are discussed along with the relationship of parents, peers and life experiences. Findings reveal that "childhood gender nonconformity appears to have been very much involved in the process by which some respondents came to be homosexual and others came to be heterosexual."

351. Bell, A.P., M.S. Weinberg, and S. Hammersmith.

1981.   SEXUAL PREFERENCE: ITS DEVELOPMENT IN MEN AND WOMEN: STATISTICAL APPENDIX. Bloomington, Ind.: Indiana University Press.

A companion to SEXUAL PREFERENCE: ITS DEVELOPMENT IN MEN AND WOMEN, this volume includes supplemental data collected in interviews, including responses to over 500 questions pertaining to social and sexual histories.

The book has four parts: Part I includes both interview questions and responses by interviewees; Part II and Part III have the data concerning white males and white females; and Part IV contains diagrams and statistics pertinent to "specific types of homosexual men and women."

352. Cotton, W.L.

1975.   "Social and Sexual Relationships of Lesbians." JOURNAL OF SEX RESEARCH. 11(2):139-148.

Using 30 white middle-class female homosexuals as subjects, Cotton examines the characteristics of lesbian relationships; the socioeconomic status of lesbian lovers and friends; a comparison between the fidelity and longevity of male vs. female homosexuals; and the presence or absence of the "incest taboo." He also examines the similarities and differences in the patterns of social interaction among male and female homosexuals.

Findings indicate that lesbian social interaction closely approximates heterosexual females with much activity centered around the home, often with the accompaniment of another lesbian couple. As with nongay women, lesbians often associate in cliques, tending to socialize with a small group of close friends. Promiscuity was low with evidence of a high degree of fidelity. Differences in socioeconomic status were minimal with a close matching of age, race and ethnicity (age being the most common difference). Egalitarian relationships tended to be the norm with most women working and sharing expenses equally. Among both female and male homosexuals, observing the "incest taboo" was important with the majority seldom having sex with close friends.

353. Hall, M.

1978.   "Lesbian Families: Cultural and Clinical Issues." SOCIAL WORK. 23:380-394.

Because social workers are seeing an increasing number of lesbian clients in their practices, Hall suggests that issues surrounding the counseling of women involved in alternative lifestyles should be addressed by practitioners serving this population. The author admonishes workers to explore their level of understanding of the lesbian subculture; to make a self-appraisal concerning their acceptance of lesbians on both an emotional and intellectual level; and to acquaint themselves about the roles and multifaceted problems lesbians encounter.

The author highlights the situations lesbians cope with in their parental roles, including adoption procedures, custody struggles, judicial prejudice, friction between lovers and children, special problems concerning their male children, and how to communicate "coming out of the closet" to children. Social workers are urged by the author to both advocate for the lesbian family in court and become more knowledgeable about the special problems encountered by women who must endure a deviant status in the homophobic society in which they and their children live.

354. Hedblom, J.H.

1972.   "The Female Homosexual: Social and Attitudinal Dimensions." Pages 31-64 in Joseph A. McCaffrey (ed.) THE HOMOSEXUAL DIALECTIC. Englewood Cliffs, N.J.: Prentice-Hall, Inc.

The author utilizes observational as well as survey techniques in his attempt to apply the scientific approach to a study of lesbian lifestyles and vocations. Examining the lesbian "subculture," the author finds that it strongly reflects a female orientation that is shared with heterosexual women but not by heterosexual men.

Three theoretical explanations about the etiology of homosexuality are examined: (1) the medical model with its pathological emphasis on the physiological and psychological goals of curability; (2) the family interaction model with an emphasis on the part familial roles play in contributing to homosexuality; and (3) a combination of both the medical and family interaction models.

Socialization among lesbians is described, including dating patterns, entertainment, living arrangements, entrance and integration into the gay community, and positive and negative relations with the heterosexual world.

355. Hopkins, J.

1969.   "The Lesbian Personality." BRITISH JOURNAL OF PSYCHIATRY. 115(529):1433-1436.

This early article in lesbian research supports the hypothesis that no primary or secondary personality factors were found to be statistically significant in differences between lesbian and heterosexual women. Utilizing Cattell's 16-PF test on two groups of women (24 lesbian and 24 heterosexual) who showed no psychotic disorders, investigators found that lesbians tended to be more independent, resilient, reserved, dominant, bohemian, and self-sufficient than heterosexual females. The study rejected the traditional interpretation of lesbian women as neurotic and misfits.

356. Katz, J. (ed.)

1975.   GAY AMERICAN HISTORY: LESBIANS AND GAY MEN IN THE U.S.A.: A DOCUMENTARY. New York: Thomas Y. Crowell Company.

Katz traces the changing character of the homophile movement through its historical development. The history of both male and female homosexuality is delineated through documents. Oral histories, gathered through taped interviews, focus on individuals who have been important to gay American history.

Four hundred years of homosexual history is reflected in this collection, much of which has remained hidden until recently. These documents, reprinted in the original, and free from editing and interpretation, were chosen to reflect a diachronic study of gay American history.

Katz's exhaustive research contributes to the growing lesbian literature. Unlike many books on homosexuality, GAY AMERICAN HISTORY endeavors to devote equal treatment to lesbians and gay men with an emphasis placed on materials that reflect significant issues of the feminist movement. Section III offers the "underside" of history in: "Passing Women: 1782-1920," including articles such as "Two Amazons in the Union Army" and "Marriages Between Women."

357. Kirkpatrick, M. and C. Smith.

>1981.   "Lesbian Mothers and Their Children: A Comparative Survey." AMERICAN JOURNAL OF ORTHOPSYCHIATRY. 51(3):545-551.

Research on the differences between children living with a lesbian mother versus living with a heterosexual mother was conducted on forty children ranging in age from five to twelve. Results indicated few differences between the two groups of mothers with their explanation for divorce being the only variable that was dissimilar. For example, lesbian women cited lack of psychological intimacy, while nonlesbians reported multiple reasons, such as substance abuse by the husband, involvement with other women, and so forth. The authors found an "unexpectedly high percentage" of these children experiencing emotional difficulties. There were, however, no differences between the two groups of children in either incidence of pathology or gender role development.

358. Klaich, D.

>1974.   WOMEN PLUS WOMEN: ATTITUDES TOWARD LESBIANISM. New York: Simon and Schuster.

This book includes interviews of two lesbians, a writer and a teacher, revealing their attitudes and feelings as they cope with various developmental tasks over their life cycles. Klaich exposes many of the myths concerning lesbians, some of which have their origins in the pre-Freudian era when lesbianism was considered to be a disease rather than a crime or sin. The historical perspective offered by Klaich provides a counter-balance to Freud's psychoanalytical theories of lesbianism. Social service practitioners can especially benefit from the first hand interviews.

359. Lewin, E. and A. Lyons.

>1982.   "Everything in its Place: The Coexistence of Lesbianism and Motherhood." Pages 249-273 in W. Paul, J.D. Weinrich, J.C. Gonsiorek, and M.E. Hotvedt (eds.) HOMOSEXUALITY: SOCIAL, PSYCHOLOGICAL, AND BIOLOGICAL ISSUES. Beverly Hills, Ca.: Sage Publications.

This chapter summarizes the findings from a study conducted in the San Francisco Bay area, between 1977 and 1979, which focused on the way both lesbians and heterosexual single mothers

adapt to their environmental problems.
The authors emphasize that there are many similarities between heterosexual women and lesbians in their perception of the motherhood role as this impinges on their lives. This includes the support they receive from kin, friendships, both casual and intimate, as well as their relationships with ex-husbands.

360. Lewis, K.G.

1980.   "Children of Lesbians: Their Point of View."
         SOCIAL WORK. 25(3):198-203.

Karen Lewis interviewed twenty-one children (ten males and eleven females) of lesbian mothers. Subjects represented eight families and an age span from nine to twenty-six years. Problems that were identified concerned the children's working through the acceptance of the mother's new lifestyle, the children's interaction with the mother's lover, as well as issues concerning their own sexuality. Interviews with the children revealed that the receiving of love and security was the most critical ingredient for a child's survival regardless of the sexual preference of the mother.

361. Loewenstein, S.F.

1980.   "Understanding Lesbian Women." SOCIAL
         CASEWORK: THE JOURNAL OF CONTEMPORARY SOCIAL
         WORK. 61(1):29-38.

Loewenstein's article for social workers has the explicit goal of educating the field about the nature of lesbians and their problems, many of which can be attributed to stereotyping and discrimination. Beginning with a definition of homosexuality in general, and lesbianism in particular, the author draws on extensive research findings to characterize the lesbian relationship as well as the roles that lesbians play within familial contexts as daughters and mothers.
Loewenstein takes the "value-laden perspective" that social workers must take sides, be sensitive to the problems of lesbians and treat them like any other individual who needs help. She quotes Dorothy Riddle: "Lesbian women need to be accepted and affirmed--rather than being tolerated or feared or treated as invisible."

362. Marmor, J. (ed.)

1980.   HOMOSEXUAL BEHAVIOR: A MODERN REAPPRAISAL.
         New York: Basic Books, Inc.

Marmor's collection of articles by scholars in the field of sexuality prompted Evelyn Hooker to write: "Although there is a plethora of books on homosexuality, none of them can be compared with this one in the breadth and depth of its presentation of the many faceted aspects of this controversial subject." Each of the three sections of the book are devoted to a different perspective concerning homosexuality: "The View of the Social Sciences," "The View of the Biological Sciences" and "The View of the Clinician." Of special interest are chapter 8, "Lesbians and Their Worlds;" chapter 15, "Clinical Aspects of Female Homosexuality;" and, chapter 20, "Psychodynamic Psychotherapy of Female Homosexuals."

The epilogue, "Homosexuality and the Issue of Mental Illness," recounts the American Psychiatric Association's decision to remove homosexuality from its listed designation as a "sociopathic personality disturbance." Marmor, past president of the APA, stresses the social control aspect of social labeling of variant behavior, contending that "the labeling of homosexual behavior as a psychopathological disorder, or 'perversion,' however honestly believed, is an example of defining normality in terms of adjustment to social conventions." Bibliographic information concludes each chapter.

363. Martin, D. and P. Lyon.

1972.   LESBIAN/WOMAN. San Francisco: Glide Publications.

Longtime supporters of the homophile movement, Lyon and Martin have written a personal account, describing the day-to-day experiences of the lesbian. Issues such as coping with various roles, including parenting and family attitudes, gaining self acceptance and liberation while progressing through the "coming out" process, are discussed. The writers expose myths and stereotypes concerning lesbians. Various lesbian lifestyles are presented, including the complications that arise in a black-white relationship.

Concluding chapters trace the theories and accompanying treatments of "sexual inversion" as a sin, a crime and a disease, as well as the role of the church and courts in the stigmatizing process that lesbians experience.

364. Martin, D. and P. Lyon.

1972.   "Lesbians are Mothers Too." Pages 131-163 in LESBIAN/WOMAN. San Francisco, Ca.: Glide Publications.

Martin and Lyon challenge stereotypes of lesbians, arguing that these women, like their heterosexual counterparts, have the same needs for love and security for themselves and their children. Published in 1972, this book illustrates some of the progress made by lesbian mothers in their ability to lead a more open lifestyle, as well as to obtain their parental rights in the judicial system.

365. Masters, W.H. and V.E. Johnson.

 1979.   HOMOSEXUALITY IN PERSPECTIVE. Boston: Little,
          Brown and Company.

     Masters and Johnson, pioneers in the study of heterosexual
function and dysfunction, have shifted their research focus to
homosexuality. In addition to examining the sexual response of
homosexuality, a comparison is also drawn between homosexual and
heterosexual functioning. Treatment of homosexual dysfunction is
investigated with new information concerning the physiology of
homosexual response. Myths surrounding sexual interaction between
homosexual couples are also dispelled.
     The book is divided into two sections: the first, a
preclinical study in which the authors compare the sexual
responses of 91 homosexuals to a control group of 57 heterosexual
couples. The second part discusses a program tailored to the
treatment of homosexual dysfunction, as well as help for those
seeking to establish a heterosexual orientation.
     In order to obtain a broader spectrum of sexual behavior,
research on ambisexuals is included that compares the fantasy
patterns of homosexual, ambisexual and heterosexual males and
females.
     Masters' and Johnson's research indicates that there is no
appreciable difference in physiological response to sexual
stimulation between heterosexual men and homosexual men or
between heterosexual women and homosexual women. While
heterosexuals are afforded greater variety in sexual stimulation
techniques than homosexuals, they are hampered by certain
cultural beliefs, i.e. assuming that the male is a sex expert
and, more importantly, a lack of curiosity concerning his/her
sexual partner. Handicapping the heterosexual couple further is
the lack of communication concerning preferences in sexual
techniques, a phenomenon seldom found in homosexual
relationships.

366. Oberstone, A. and H. Sukoneck.

 1976.   "Psychological Adjustment and Lifestyle of
          Single Lesbians and Single Heterosexual
          Women." PSYCHOLOGY OF WOMEN QUARTERLY.
          1(2):172-188.

     This article is based on a doctoral dissertation and
utilizes the Minnesota Multiphasic Personality Inventory,
M.M.P.I., to interview 25 homosexual and 25 heterosexual women,
20 to 45 years of age. Both groups are equally matched in age,
marital status, education, and occupational levels.
     Heterosexual and homosexual lifestyles are explored as well
as individual psychological adjustments. Research shows that
homosexuals and heterosexuals have similar lifestyles, but there
are variations within each category of sexual preference. The
authors challenge obsolete myths about lesbians, including those
of promiscuity, "butch/femme" roles, poor work records, excessive

drinking, and suicide.

Oberstone and Sukoneck conclude that "lesbians and heterosexual women are comparable in terms of their psychological adjustments and similar in the dimensions of lifestyles that were tested." The authors point to the similar socialization process experienced by all women in our culture as the plausible explanation for this similarity.

367. Parker, W.

    1977.   HOMOSEXUALITY BIBLIOGRAPHY: SUPPLEMENT, 1970-1975. Metuchen, N.J.: The Scarecrow Press, Inc.

Two volumes are offered and organized in a similar style with the numerous headings designated by type of publication. The author surveys information relating to homosexuality from a wide variety of sources, including pamphlets, documents, theses, dissertations, books (non-fiction), articles in newspapers, specialized journals, literature, and the media. Special attention is paid to court cases and laws affecting homosexuals. An extensive author and subject index is included, the latter devoting a page of citations to female homosexuals.

368. Ponse, B.

    1978.   IDENTITIES IN THE LESBIAN WORLD: THE SOCIAL CONSTRUCTION OF SELF. Westport, Connecticut: Greenwood Press.

Research for this book was based on three years of fieldwork, including extensive interviews with seventy-five gay women ranging in age from sixteen to seventy-six. Most of the subjects were white and middle class, and had some college background. Ponse moves from micro-to-macro levels of analysis as she examines the role of the lesbian as an individual and her interaction with both the gay and straight communities. Labeling theory and self-labeling are also examined in an effort to explain identity construction.

The pejorative effects of traditional psychological theories are stressed, as well as the pressures of societal institutions in the forming of a lesbian's self identity. In this context, the author explores the role of secrecy, stigma and the pressures to join either the straight or gay community that lesbian women experience. In an effort towards destigmatization, Ponse endeavors to dispel the notion that lesbians are sick, and that homosexuality is pathological. Rather, she presents lesbianism as an authentic, viable lifestyle.

369. Potter, S.J. and T.E. Darty.

1981. "Social Work and the Invisible Minority: An Exploration of Lesbianism." SOCIAL WORK. 26(3):187-198.

In this article, Potter and Darty propose three objectives: (1)define lesbianism and examine some of the anti-lesbian myths; (2)explore areas of discrimination experienced by lesbians, such as housing, employment, education, and child custody; (3)instruct social workers in ways to better serve their lesbian clients (for instance, it is important for them to know that studies show that lesbian mothers are not much different from heterosexual single mothers).

The article encourages agencies to hire staff, regardless of their sexual preference, and argues that rather than counseling women to give up lesbianism for a heterosexual orientation, social service professionals would be more productive by helping clients acquire needed social services.

370. Raphael, S.M. and M.K. Robinson.

1980. "The Older Lesbian: Love Relationships and Friendship Patterns." ALTERNATIVE LIFESTYLES. 3(2):207-229.

Authors Raphael and Robinson explore the phenomenon of intimacy and aging, while focusing on a long neglected population, the older lesbian. These women reveal diversity in ethnicity, religious affiliation, previous coupling relationships, educational backgrounds, and working experiences.

The in-depth interviews explore the following topics: (1)attitudes toward and preparations for aging; (2)kinship and friendship networks; (3)friends and lovers; and (4)identity and community. As these titles suggest, special attention is given to love relationships and friendship patterns that are further elaborated with numerous quotes from the research subjects.

Misconceptions about lesbian lifestyles and relationships are explored. There is little evidence to substantiate the notion that older homosexual women lead lives of lonely desperation. Rather, the research indicates that these women preferred serial monogamy with sexuality playing an important role in their lives. Preference for partners of similar age, and the establishment of strong friendship ties were common experiences. The advent of gay liberation has strengthened the support system afforded these women. The authors conclude that there are now "positive role models for future age cohorts of older women who are seeking non-traditional supports and living arrangements in later life."

371. Reiss, B.F., J. Safer, and W. Yotive.

        1974.   "Psychological Test Data on Female
                    Homosexuality: A Review of the Literature."
                    JOURNAL OF HOMOSEXUALITY. 1(1):71-85.

    The authors present projective and non-projective test
findings on lesbians, challenging the assumption that
homosexuality is a pathology whose manifestations in both males
and females emanates from a "similar dynamic origin."
    The article discusses projective tests used in earlier
homosexual research, beginning with studies by Fromm and Elonen
(1951), who conducted the first study of homosexuals utilizing
projective tests. Next, the authors describe the Rorschach and
Draw-A-Person tests by Armon (1960), the first statistical
attempt to validate the psychoanalytic approach to lesbian
psychology on a substantial population. This is then compared to
Hooker's studies on male homosexuals.
    Further studies include Hopkins' (1969,1970) research, which
is described as the "most comprehensive study of lesbians," and
Gundlach's and Reiss' (1968,1973) work, which matched homosexual
and heterosexual women to determine the degree of "field
independence and dependence."
    Non-projective studies generally indicated a far better
adjusted female homosexual. Freedman's research (1967), further
suggests that lesbian subjects were better adjusted
psychologically than the controls.
    The authors' are cautious about generalizations, noting the
limitations of comparing projective and non-projective testing,
and the lack of reliable replications. Finding a truly
representative lesbian population may be an impossibility, they
conclude, further restricting the validity of the research on
lesbians.

372. Rosen, D.H.

        1974.   LESBIANISM: A STUDY OF FEMALE HOMOSEXUALITY.
                    Springfield, Illinois: Charles C. Thomas.

    Lesbianism is presented as a "way of life" rather than a
pathology. Part I surveys both the patient and nonpatient-
centered studies concerning lesbians. Part II, "Lesbian Research
Study," is a descriptive study to ascertain the characteristics
of lesbians based on responses to questionnaires distributed to
26 women belonging to the Daughters of Bilitis. Data include
demographic features, as well as check lists to describe feminine
versus masculine characteristics. Tables summarize the results,
and individual case histories are also included. In Part III,
"Female Homosexuality as a Way of Life," Rosen draws on such
experts as Kinsey, Szasz and Cory to reinforce his contention
that lesbianism is a lifestyle rather than a sickness.
    Other chapters address cultural factors, etiology,
psychiatric treatment, the future of lesbianism, and the need for
further research. The book includes a foreword by Evelyn Hooker,

a bibliography and index.

373. Schafer, S.

1976.   "Sexual and Social Problems of Lesbians." THE
           JOURNAL OF SEX RESEARCH. 12(1):50-69.

This study, conducted by the Institute for Sex Research at
the University of Hamburg, includes 150 lesbians ranging in ages
from 18 to 40. The three phases of "coming out" are described as
well as the loneliness and isolation that lesbians experience
during the "coming out" process.

Research reveals that many lesbians experience numerous
heterosexual experiences during adolescence, indicating that
females may be generally socialized to participate in
heterosexual relationships (gay males participate in far less
heterosexual activity than lesbians).

Respondents reported experiencing a conflict between their
homosexual feelings and society's expectation of a heterosexual
norm. Solutions to this dilemma include: (1)denying one's
homosexuality, as in becoming sexually abstinent or participating
in an unsatisfactory heterosexual experience; (2)leading a double
life, which is the most common adaptive practice; (3)openly
acknowledging one's homosexuality, an adaptation for half of the
sample.

Two-fifths of those studied indicated an ambivalent attitude
towards confessing their homosexuality with many opting for
selective honesty concerning their sexual orientation. While a
large number of these lesbians sought counseling, they reported
receiving inadequate treatment.

XI

Mental Illness

374. Bart, P.B.

1972.   "Depression in Middle-Aged Women." READINGS
          ON THE PSYCHOLOGY OF WOMEN. J. M. Bardwick
          (ed.) New York: Harper and Row. Pp.134-142.

This is a study of depressed middle-aged women that draws a
direct relationship between the treatment received within a
society by its minority members (in this case, aging women) and
the measurement of a nation's humanity. The article focuses on
the importance of roles, stressing how women's roles both link
them to society and lead to mental illness. A parallel is drawn
between the roles women perform in society, their relationship to
these roles and the degree of depression experienced by women
during middle age.
     Bart attributes middle-age depression to loss of esteem due
to the lack of important roles, rather than to the hormonal
changes of menopause.

375. Bruch, H.

1978.   THE GOLDEN CAGE: THE ENIGMA OF ANOREXIA
          NERVOSA. Cambridge: Harvard University Press.

Anorexia Nervosa --the fasting disease-- is occurring at a
rapidly rising rate. Dr. Bruch brilliantly traces through case
studies inquiring why this affliction befalls the "young, rich
and beautiful." In their search for selfhood, anorexic youngsters
(who are mainly young women) will not accept anything that the
world has to offer. Too much has been expected of them in the
matter of appearance, good behavior and academic achievement.
     This volume treats family life extensively, since the
development of anorexia nervosa is so closely related to abnormal
patterns of family interaction. All anorexics, according to Dr.
Bruch, are so involved with their families that they have failed
to achieve a sense of independence. The task of psychotherapy in
anorexia is to help a patient in her search for self-directed
identity by evoking an awareness of her feelings and needs.
Therapy is an attempt to repair the perceived conviction of
incompetence.

376. Chessler, P.

1973.   "A Word About Mental Health and Women."
MENTAL HEALTH. 57(3):5-7.

Chessler examines three aspects of the mental health
profession and its relation to women that include: what the
profession does to women, how it perceives women and how the
profession has taught women to perceive themselves. Dr. Chessler
also outlines five major clinical biases and discusses the ways
these prejudices affect women's mental health care.

377. Chessler, P.

1972.   WOMEN AND MADNESS. New York: Doubleday and
Co.

Female psychology and the increasing number of women who see
themselves as neurotic or psychotic and who seek psychiatric help
and/or hospitalization are the main concerns of Phyllis
Chessler's book. The author focuses on the basic psychological
dimensions of female personality in Western culture, which
promote private therapy, mental hospitals and patient careers.
Empirical data on sixty women are presented, as well as an
analysis of the nation's mental illness statistics from 1950 to
1969. Chessler raises some critical issues, among which is the
practice of sexual exploitation of patients by their therapists.

378. Crisp, A.H.

1980.   ANOREXIA NERVOSA: LET ME BE. New York: Grune
and Stratton.

This volume offers a thorough treatment of the starvation
disease, found especially among adolescent women. It covers the
physical, behavioral and experiential features of the condition,
as well as providing a history of fasting and the variants of
anorexia nervosa. The prevalance and incidence of the disease is
more widespread than observers once believed. A background to the
disorder may hinge on childhood bodily growth. Thus, the book
describes the sense of self in terms of body weight, volume and
shape. Finally, it includes personal accounts of people who have
had anorexia nervosa, as well as four accounts by parents.
The author, a psychiatrist, sees the disease as a
maturational crisis, usually beginning in family relationships.
In other words, helping the patient also requires helping the
parents. The author suggests that anorexics practice projective
art and design their own clothing for effective therapy. The book
includes paintings by patients of their families, feelings and
views of treatment. Like many books of this genre, it is strongly
patient-centered.

379. Farina, A. and H.D. Hagelauer.

1975.   "Sex and Mental Illness: The Generosity of
Women." JOURNAL OF CONSULTING AND CLINICAL
PSYCHOLOGY. 43(1):122-125.

This article examines four studies that focus on whether or
not having a previous history of mental illness will affect
possible employment opportunities. In one of the studies, clerks
in large department stores were asked if, in their opinion, a
person seeking employment with a history of mental illness will
be less desirable than a person without such a history. The
results of this study, included under the section of statistical
methodology, concludes that there is no relationship, either
positive or negative between a history of mental illness and
desirability. Rather, the most important characteristic in
securing employment is that of the overall demeanor of the
applicant. Most interestingly, women interviewees accorded full
acceptance of the ex-mental patient, while men strongly rejected
the same applicant. The authors assert that the results of their
study refuted the popular belief that both men and women equally
reject ex-mental patients.

379A.Grunebaum, H. et al.

1975.   MENTALLY ILL MOTHERS AND THEIR CHILDREN.
Chicago: University of Chicago Press.

In 1960, Dr. Grunebaum, then a senior psychiatrist at the
Massachusetts Mental Health Center, suggested that a young mother
on his ward consider caring for her mentally-ill child while in
the hospital. In this book, Dr. Grunebaum and his colleagues
(J.L. Weiss, B.J. Cohler, C.R. Hartman, and D.H. Gallant) break
new ground as well as invite further exploration into the matter
of joint hospital admission of mothers and their children.
The authors' aims include: (1)describing the administrative,
diagnostic and interpersonal considerations for planning a joint
admission; (2)providing a review of postpartum emotional
disorders; (3)reporting a pilot investigation of the development
of joint admission children; (4)delineating a framework for
mother-oriented nursing care; and (5)presenting a detailed
analysis of the relations between this nursing process and
outcome.
It is the explicit hope of these authors that this book will
enlighten psychiatrists, psychiatric nurses and other
professionals who have a practical or research interest in
psychopathology, as well as general readers concerned with
institutional change.

380. Guttentag, M., S. Salasin, and D. Belle. (eds.)

    1980.   THE MENTAL HEALTH OF WOMEN. New York: Academic Press.

    In an effort to answer one broad question: What is the state of mental health of women in this country, and how does it differ from the mental health of men, the authors put together a combination of data on women's experiences of mental health problems. The focus is on the theoretical analysis of the significance of women's mental illness patterns, as well as therapy and policy issues. The book emphasizes the depressive syndrome, and includes the thinking of some of the leading thinkers on depression in women. The data on women's mental health are impressive, and derive from several types of treatment facilities and programs.

381. LaTorre, R.A.

    1975.   "Gender and Age." JOURNAL OF CONSULTING AND CLINICAL PSYCHOLOGY. 43(1):97-98.

    This study investigates attitudes toward the mentally ill as a function of the perceived gender of the mentally ill patient. Two case histories were presented to 108 students who were asked to respond to the cases on the basis of certain guidelines: the severity of the mental illness, general deficiencies, ability to be the patient's friend, degree of the psychiatric intervention needed, and probable outcome of psychotherapy. Results of the study showed that students viewing women as schizophrenic patients judged them to be more severely ill than males. Women were also considered to be more difficult to accept as a friend than were men. As women were judged to be more severely ill than males, they were similarly believed to need more psychiatric intervention. Women were also expected to achieve greater adjustment through therapy than men. Young schizophrenic men were rated less severely ill than either young or old schizophrenic women. These findings point to underlying cultural assumptions about sex roles that may distort therapists' perceptions about gender and mental illness.

382. Leonard, L.S.

    1982.   THE WOUNDED WOMAN: HEALING THE FATHER-DAUGHTER RELATIONSHIP. Athens, Ohio: Ohio University Press.

    THE WOUNDED WOMAN explores the psychological and spiritual conflicts of women who have had injured relationships with their fathers, either with the personal father or the symbolic "patriarchal father," or both.
    The author, a Jungian analyst, explores the various self-destructive life patterns that result from this wounding. She

uses examples from her own life, her therapeutic work with women clients, and examples from dreams, fairy tales, myths, films, and literature. The book is both a personal revelation of the author's struggle to transform her own wounded relationship with her father as well as a psychological analysis of the universal struggles modern women face to find an affirmative, creative way of being in the world.

THE WOUNDED WOMAN speaks to men too, for men are also wounded in their relation to femininity. Rather than suspicious, distrustful relationships between men and women, the author believes that by understanding the father-daughter wound and through the work of psychological transformation, it is possible to achieve fruitful, caring relationships between men and women and between fathers and daughters. This would entail relationships which honor both the mutuality and uniqueness of the sexes.

383. Lewis, H.B.

    1976.   PSYCHIC WAR IN MEN AND WOMEN. New York: New
             York University Press.

    Because an exploitative society injures the two sexes differently, the type and content of mental disorders vary. Men experience contradictions between being "tough and tender" and learn to deny feelings in order to succeed; their orientation is rational. Women respond to the conflict between the need to be loved and autonomy by an over investment in feelings. Their psychic orientation is emotional. And while men develop "crazy ideas"-- obsessional neurosis and schizophrenia-- women suffer from depression, a reaction to the failure of others to respond adequately to the woman's emotional needs. The author questions P. Chessler's data (WOMEN AND MADNESS), which asserts that women are more likely than men to be schizophrenic, inasmuch as statistics show that only recently are women "catching up" with male schizophrenic rates. Block urges that mental health requires changing the exploitative institutions and structuring non-aggressive relationships as a viable approach.

384. May, R.

    1972.   "Black and Impotent: The Life of Mercedes."
             in R. May: POWER AND INNOCENCE: A SEARCH FOR
             THE SOURCES OF VIOLENCE. New York:
             W.W.Norton. Pp.81-99.

    The theory that violence is pervasive in many persons and resides beneath overt passivity and apathy is explored in this case history of a black woman's psychoanalysis. The woman's inability to feel and express anger resulted in her inability to bear children and caused her to dream of violent actions against people close to her. The author presents cultural, racial and sexual ramifications of minority oppression. On the whole, there are overdrawn generalizations based on a single case.

385. Palmer, R.L.

1981.   ANOREXIA NERVOSA. New York: Penguin Books.

Psychiatrist R.L. Palmer examines anorexia nervosa, the condition suffered by increasingly alarming numbers of adolescents and young women. The author discusses its causes, symptoms and treatment and provides advice and information for anorexics, their families and professionals.

386. Paykel, E.S., M. Weissman, B.A. Prusoff, and C.M. Tonks.

1971.   "Dimensions of Social Adjustment in Depressed Women." THE JOURNAL OF NERVOUS AND MENTAL DISEASE. 152(3):158-172.

This is a study of forty depressed female patients and forty normal women from the general population using a semistructured interview scale that measured social adjustment. Ratings were made on 48 items covering a wide spectrum of discrete behaviors, interpersonal relationships and satisfactions. The study dimensions provided an alternative framework for describing social maladjustment of depressed patients. In addition, the research used observations of pattern change and examination of treatment effect in the study of medication and psychotherapy.

387. Reich, T. and G. Winokur.

1970.   "Postpartum Psychoses in Patients with Manic Depressive Disease." THE JOURNAL OF NERVOUS AND MENTAL DISEASE. 151(1):60-68.

Based on a consecutive series of 61 manic-depressive patients (including a group of twenty bipolar manic-depressive mothers and twenty female relatives who had children and an episodic affective disorder), the authors examine the postpartum state. During the risk period of 15 to 80 years and, especially, during the childbearing years, the frequency of postpartum breakdowns were significantly greater than the frequency of nonpuerperal episodes. Of the patient group, postpartum episodes followed 30 percent of all births among 41 percent of the female family members with children and an affective disorder. These rates are much higher than the general population's rates. After the first episode of manic-depressive illness, the postpartum illness rates rose to 50 percent in the patient group and 25 percent in the family group. This suggests that careful observation and early treatment are indicated.

388. Reiff, R.

1974.   "The Control of Knowledge: The Power of the
             Helping Professionals." JOURNAL OF APPLIED
             BEHAVIORAL SCIENCE. 10(3):451-461.

Reiff contends that the basis of professional power is not
knowledge itself but the control of knowledge. Historically, the
helping professions have been licensed to define who is ill,
needy or deviant and who is entitled to help. It is argued that
while the helping professions have a vested interest in
maintaining a commodity concept of services, the nature of
service policies deprives clients of their consumer rights. To
reduce the power of the helping professions, the community would
have to break up their monopolistic control. If professional
institutions, such as the educational system, were compelled to
share their power with society, it would inevitably result in the
democratization of knowledge.

389.

1975.   "Report of the Task Force on Sex Bias and Sex
             Role Stereotyping in Psychotherapeutic Prac-
             tice." AMERICAN PSYCHOLOGIST. 30(12):1169-
             1174.

In 1974, the American Psychological Association established
a task force to examine the nature and extent of sex bias and
sex-role stereotyping in the profession, especially as it affects
the treatment of women. The task force found that, in general,
practitioners fostered traditional sex roles among women. There
was also a bias in expectations and devaluation of women. The
sexist language of the profession was also noted. Use of women as
sex objects was apparent, i.e., seduction of female patients.
While the widespread sexist bias is seen as detrimental to women,
the task force suggests changes which would eliminate these
problems in the profession. Among these changes are more
extensive and enlightened education for practitioners, students
and the lay public.

390. Rosenkrantz, P., S. Vogel, H. Bee, and I.P. Broverman.

1968.   "Sex Role Stereotypes and Self-Concepts Among
             College Students." JOURNAL OF CUNSULTING AND
             CLINICAL PSYCHOLOGY. 32(3):287-295.

Sex role stereotyping is well documented in this society,
these writers emphasize, and go on to explain the dimensions of
these stereotypes and how they function to enforce the dominant
prejudices of the social order. For example, this culture tends
to place much greater value upon those traits deemed as masculine
than those thought of as being feminine. Self concepts of men and
women are differentially affected. The findings indicate that:

(1) despite changes in the historical position of women, sex role stereotypes continue to exist; (2) these stereotypes reflect similar prejudices, regardless of social status; (3) the sex roles of both men and women are highly defined and extremely rigid; and, (4) women tend to view their position as having less social value than men to the society at large. This background helps to explain the pervasive obstacles to equality women confront.

391. Scarf, M.

    1980.   UNFINISHED BUSINESS: PRESSURE POINTS IN THE LIVES OF WOMEN. Garden City, New York: Doubleday and Company, Inc.

Using case studies of women as illustrations, Scarf shows the physical and psychological pressure points over six decades of a woman's life beginning with adolescence. A large portion of this book deals with the identification and treatment for depression, one of the leading afflictions of women. Examples of various forms of depression Scarf examines are self-starvation, under-or-oversleeping, hypersexuality, frigidity, menopausal depression, and nervous breakdown. The message of this book is that correctly understood, analyzed and treated, most of the unhappiness and distress in women's lives can be comprehended and resolved.

392. Seiden, A.M.

    1976.   "An Overview: Research on the Psychology of Women." AMERICAN JOURNAL OF PSYCHIATRY. 133(10):1111-1112.

In this report, the author examines recent research on the psychiatric clinical treatment of women. The report reveals that much of this research is on schizophrenia. Therapists were often found to foster traditional, stereotypical assumptions of sex roles. Sexual involvement with patients, while admittedly rare, was also noted. Seiden concludes from her research that there is much room for improvement within the profession, especially regarding the treatment of women.

393. Vigersky, R.A. (ed.)

    1977.   ANOREXIA NERVOSA. New York: Raven Press Books.

This collection of essays concerns what some observers have called the "fasting disease," which is on the rise among adolescent girls. The articles are divided into three sections. Section one covers psychological antecedents of anorexia nervosa; a typical anorexic; measurement of body image in anorexia;

pretreatment predictors of weight change in anorexia; pretreatment evaluation; and the long-term prognosis in anorexia. Section two includes an examination of the concept of satiety; extra-hypothalamic controls of feeling; satiety in monkeys; food intake, fatness and reproductive ability; thyroid hormone metabolism in prolonged experimental starvation in man; and studies of testosterone metabolism in anorexia. Section three includes the general management of anorexia nervosa and difficulties in assessing the efficacy of treatment; behavior modification in anorexia; clinical and metabolic observations in a successful treatment plan; and the outcome of anorexia nervosa. This stimulating book should be of interest for both physicians and informed readers.

394. Weissman, M.M.

> 1972.   "The Depressed Woman as a Mother." SOCIAL
> PSYCHIATRY. 7:98-108.

The writer examines maternal role performance in a group of clinically acutely-depressed women and compares them with matched normal controls. The depressed women were significantly more impaired than controls, including diminished emotional involvement, ruptured communication, disaffection, increased hostility, and resentment. Examining these disturbances within the context of the family life cycle from post partum to the empty nest, the specific mother-child problems were observed to vary with the stages of the life cycle. Depressed mothers of infants were helpless in caring for their children, over-concerned or directly hostile, conditions which laid the ground-work for future problems with the child. Among mothers of school age children, impairments included irritation, uninvolvement and intolerance of children's noise and activity. The most severe problems, though, tended to occur among adolescents who reacted to the mother's hostility and withdrawal with serious deviant behavior. The researchers emphasize that early and intensive treatment of the depressed mother can facilitate major preventive work for the entire family.

395. Weissman, M.M. and E.S. Paykel.

> 1974.   THE DEPRESSED WOMAN: A STUDY OF SOCIAL
> RELATIONSHIPS. Chicago: The University of
> Chicago Press.

Responding to the growing public interest in the problem of female depression, the authors deal mainly with one significant aspect of despondency, namely, social adjustment, which has received relatively little study. They describe the social and family life of 40 women who were acutely depressed and their after-recovery period. The authors then compared these women with 40 of their psychiatrically-normal neighbors. The book details the lives of these 80 women with charts and tables, delineating such matters as work performance and family attachment. Not content to merely offer symptoms of depression, the authors clearly show the experiences of depressed people in their everyday lives.

The research is significant for many audiences: public officials, and citizens involved in the development of public policy related to health and social services, researchers in mental health and psychiatry, and in the social and behavioral sciences, and mental health practitioners involved in the care and treatment of patients.

396. Belle, D.

1982.   LIVES IN STRESS: WOMEN AND DEPRESSION.
Beverly Hills: Sage Publications.

Capturing the focal point of this volume, the foreword, written by Jessie Bernard, draws the parallel between the "feminization of poverty" and the etiology of depression in women. LIVES OF STRESS evolved from research conducted for the Stress and Families Project funded by the National Institute of Mental Health. Endeavoring to understand both the causes of depression in poor women as well as the consequences of this malady on their individual as well as family life, numerous intensive interviews were conducted with 43 women (average age 30 years) and their families. In addition, five self-reporting scales were utilized to measure depression, anxiety, self-esteem, and mastery.

This work, divided into six parts, includes: In Part I, "The Introduction," Belle provides the background and structure of the study, including "Research Methods and Sample Characteristics;" Part II, "The Ecology of Poverty," consists of three articles that focus on various aspects of respondent's lives, past and present, and how this impinges on their mental health; Part III, "Women and Society," includes articles related to societal institutions and how they impinge on women and their families; Part IV, "Relationships," explores the multiple interactions between the women interviewed, their friends, relatives, men in their lives, and children; Part V, "Well-Being," is devoted to the way women cope and their mental and physical health and treatment; and Part VI, "Conclusion," is comprised of a follow-up on the families together with summaries of the study.

Belle concludes that "seen in the context of human lives, depression appears an almost unavoidable response to an environment that allows women little control over most of the important things in life and little hope that life will improve." Several strategies for protecting the mental health of low-income mothers are presented.

397. Coles, R. and J.H. Coles.

1978.   WOMEN OF CRISIS. New York: Dell Publishing Co.

The biographical portraits of five women, who, as children,

were described as "children of crisis," grew into womanhood to become women of crisis, as described in the Coles' book. Ruth (a migrant worker), Hannah (a housewife from Harlon County), Teresa (a Chicana resident in a barrio), Lorna (an Eskimo woman), and Helen (a maid), tell their struggles, hopes and fears as they deal with the daily issues of sex, race and class within their own families as well as the "outside" world. None of the women considered themselves feminists, yet the Coles found that each recognized the constraints and demands imposed on them by virtue of their sex.

398. Fishman, W.K.

    1982.   THE NEW RIGHT: UNRAVELING THE OPPOSITION TO
             WOMEN'S EQUALITY. New York: Praeger
             Publishers, Inc.

    The author has collected information on the interconnections within the "New Right," the people and institutions linking such groups as the Moral Majority, Gun Owners of America, the National Right-to-Life Commissions, Conservative Digest, and the Republican Party. She considers the "New Right" to be not so much a new phenomenon as it is a new political force to be dealt with, and discusses why it has suddenly become so politically visible, as well as why it seems to focus so heavily on family and reproductive issues. Fishman argues that the "New Right" is only a repetition of a previous "solution" to economic crisis, i.e. get women out of the labor force and thus lessen competition by sending them back to the home. As the fiscal crisis deepens, this solution will become increasingly appealing to many politicians and citizens, the author concludes.

399. Iglitzin, L.B.

    1977.   "A Case Study in Patriarchal Politics: Women
             on Welfare." Pages 96-112 in M. Githens and
             J. L. Presage. A PORTRAIT OF MARGINALITY. New
             York: Longman.

    The institution of public welfare reflects society's image of the proper role of women, creating a double bind for AFDC women. Welfare encourages "feminine" stereotyping by encouraging the support of the wife-mother ideal, that enforces an outdated morality. This promotes a "women's-work" orientation, and pits women against other women, as well as inculcating feelings of apathy and powerlessness. Breaking out of the mold requires that public welfare agencies need to stop reinforcing attitudes of submissiveness, suppliance, dependence, and passivity among their clients, and to cease the channeling of women into low-paying, menial "women's work" jobs.

400. Peterson, J.

    1974.   ESCAPE FROM POVERTY: OCCUPATIONAL AND
               ECONOMIC MOBILITY AMONG URBAN BLACKS.
               Chicago: University of Chicago Press.

    James Peterson has made a significant contribution to the
mobility literature with this book in two ways. First, the book
fills a void in the literature in that it emphasizes the social
mobility of urban blacks as a significant phenomenon in its own
right. Secondly, by including a careful examination of working
women and the role their income contribution makes to the
mobility pattern of the urban poor, he has broadened the scope
and definition of mobility.
    Chapters two and three form the center of the book, wherein
Peterson presents his data and findings on occupational and
income mobility of black men and women.

401. Rousseau, A.

    1981.   SHOPPING BAG LADIES: HOMELESS WOMEN SPEAK
               ABOUT THEIR LIVES. New York: The Pilgrim
               Press.

    Photographs and interviews for this essay were gathered by
Rousseau while she served as a volunteer in a program serving
shopping-bag ladies. These women are characterized as indigent
females who have either given up on the welfare system or who are
unable to qualify for state support; or in a few instances, are
too proud to receive aid. They choose instead to make their own
way on the streets.
    A literature review reveals that while "skid-row" males were
often the topics of study, poor elderly women who lived on the
street were neglected and ignored. Treated as a "sociological
mystery," these women were seldom studied and rarely offered
help. Findings indicate that the few agencies that serve
indigents were much more helpful to poor men than to poor women.

402. West, G.

    1981.   THE NATIONAL WELFARE RIGHTS ORGANIZATION: THE
               SOCIAL PROTEST OF POOR WOMEN.   New York:
               Praeger Publishers, Inc.

    This book examines the factors that led to the rise of the
National Welfare Rights Organization in 1966. This was the first
national protest movement of welfare women for reforming the
welfare system and establishing a guaranteed income for the poor
based on need. The author's thesis is that both organizational
and political conflicts led to the development of the welfare-
rights movement, especially the increasingly hostile political
climate toward the welfare poor. She also demonstrates how the
organization functioned across class lines as a mobilizing
instrument that linked white and black women.

XIII

Singles

403. Bahr, H. and G. Garrett.

     1976.   WOMEN ALONE: THE DISAFFILIATION OF URBAN
              FEMALES. Toronto: D. C. Heath and Company.

     This important sociological study, based on empirical data
gathered from the Columbia Bowery Project in New York City (1963-
1970), focuses on the themes of homelessness and disaffiliation
among urban females. Utilizing a life-history interview, the
relationship between disaffiliation and age is addressed with an
emphasis on the specific problems of housing, health, loneliness
and isolation, neighborhood environment, personal frustrations,
income, and daily activities. The study design focused on the
area of undersocialization, anomie, generational retreat,
marginality, social mobility, and disengagement. One significant
finding is that patterns of affiliation and lifetime profiles are
related to the variables of employment, family, voluntary
associations, and the church.
     The social characteristics and drinking patterns of two
female populations (independent and institutionalized homeless
women) are examined, followed by a comparison between homeless
men and homeless women, that underscores the unequal treatment
accorded females in a treatment setting. Bahr and Garrett
conclude by censuring societal failure to provide adequate
services to disadvantaged women.

404. Cargan, L. and M. Melko.

     1982.   SINGLES: MYTHS AND REALITIES. New York: Sage
              Publishers.

     The authors discuss the myths and misconceptions surrounding
singles in America, dispelling many of the traditional
stereotypes. Gaining their information from an intensive study
conducted in a "small but typical community," they distinguish
between various sub-groupings; the divorced, widowed and never-
married. The authors identified important social distinctions
between the various categories of singles with respect to their
lifestyles, sexual behavior, family background, health, and
happiness.

405. Edwards, M. and E. Hoover.

   1975.   THE CHALLENGE OF BEING SINGLE. Los Angeles:
           J.P. Tarcher, Inc.

   A psychologist, Edwards was the originator of the "Challenge
of Being Single" classes at the University of Southern
California, who now collaborates with Eleanor Hoover on a book
comprised of the findings of thousands of interviews reflecting
the needs and attitudes of single individuals. The authors
explore problems encountered by persons who have a single status,
such as societal pressures, myths and stigmatization, as well as
some practical solutions to such problems as where to find other
singles and guidelines for a fulfilling sex life. The book
concludes with a chapter celebrating the joys of being single
together with a "singles manifesto" aimed at making explicit
single persons' attitudes toward self, others and society.
   While not a sociological treatise on the single status, THE
CHALLENGE OF BEING SINGLE provides positive reading for the
increasing numbers of single women who find themselves with this
status either by choice or by circumstances.

406. Peterson, N.

   1981.   OUR LIVES FOR OURSELVES: WOMEN WHO HAVE NEVER
           MARRIED. New York: G. P. Putnam's Sons.

   "I wonder why Jane never married, she seems like such a nice
person," captures for Peterson the "marital imperative" that, she
argues, permeates our society. Women who have never been legally
married comprise five to seven percent of the female population.
Drawing on a sample of single women, ages 20 to 78, Peterson
discusses various age groups' life experiences, decisions made
and difficulties encountered and surmounted. Issues of sexuality,
stigmatization, reasons for not marrying, aloneness versus
loneliness, and freedom are sensitively explored. The research
reveals women who "closely parallel Bruno Bettelheim's model of
mental health: self-mastery and wholeness, or autonomy."
   Future predictions concerning single women include an
increase in the numbers of never-married women, an increase in
single parenthood and positive changes in laws and regulations
for single women.

407. Staples, R.

   1981.   THE WORLD OF BLACK SINGLES: CHANGING PATTERNS
           OF MALE/FEMALE RELATIONS. New York: Greenwood
           Press.

   This book explores the dating and mating patterns of single,
college-educated, urban black Americans, ages 25 to 45. Issues
examined include sexuality, interracial relationships and

170

friendship patterns. Information was obtained from census data, newspaper records, personal interviews, and a national questionnaire. With this information, the author analyzed the basic problems of black singles in establishing long-lasting family relationships, concluding that many serious marital and family-related problems of educated blacks are linked to their uncritical acceptance of Western European-American standards and definitions of the "good family." The author also includes a detailed bibliography.

408. Weiss, R.

1979.   GOING IT ALONE: THE FAMILY LIFE AND SOCIAL SITUATION OF THE SINGLE PARENT. New York: Basic Books, Inc.

Building on his earlier book, MARITAL SEPARATION, Weiss explores the environment of the single parent, a phenomenon experienced by almost half of the women and children in America. This study is based on an impressive amount of research, including over two hundred single parents, forty children of single parents and a small sample of married couples for comparative purposes.
Divided into four parts, the book describes the process of becoming a single parent, the problems of finances, work and childcare, as well as the relationship with one's own family. Next, the management of the single parent household is discussed, including the three major tasks: income production, home maintanence and childcare. Parenting styles and intrafamily relationships are also considered. The third part explores the relationships that develop outside the family and the networking that builds the much-needed community for the single parent. Finally, Weiss looks at the problems and benefits of being a single parent.

XIV

Suicide

409. Baechler, J.

1975.   "Age and Sex." Pp.284-298 in SUICIDES. New
York: Basic Books, Inc.

Employing a global context, Baechler concludes that men
more often adopt a strategy of power and women adopt one of
dependence. In the context of suicide, this means that more men
than women commit suicide and more women than men attempt
suicide.

410. Burns, M.M.

1980.   "Alcohol Abuse Among Women as Indirect Self-
Destructive Behavior." Pp.220-231 in N.L.
Farberow (ed.) THE MANY FACES OF SUICIDE:
INDIRECT SELF-DESTRUCTIVE BEHAVIOR. New York:
McGraw-Hill.

A review of the alcohol literature, primarily from clinical
data, support the view that alcohol abuse by women is self-
destructive. The reasons for this and implications for indirect
self abuse has not been adequately examined. The author asserts
that alcohol abuse by women is related to woman's situation as a
limiting second-class role: "A social and economic system and
interpersonal relationships within that system...restrict the
development of the full self." This tends to develop the self-
destructive characteristics of "despair, dependency,
helplessness, hopelessness, passivity, and rage." These serve to
initiate and sustain the addictive, destructive use of alcohol.
In turn, alcohol often releases rage and reduced anxiety,
although Burns suggests that the nonspecific anxiety from which
women seek relief is a "chronic existential anxiety." Traditional
roles of parenting and homemaking sustain women for only a
relatively few years, and often produce only meager or negative
self-esteem that may lead to depression. Burns concludes that it
is dissatisfaction with the circumscribed feminine role, as it is
constituted in modern, urban society, that contributes to the
misuse of alcohol and alcohol-related suicide.

411. Hamblin, R.L. and R.B. Jacobsen.

> 1972.   "Suicide and Pseudocide: A Reanalysis of
> Maris's Data." JOURNAL OF HEALTH AND SOCIAL
> BEHAVIOR. 13(1):99-104.

These authors take exception to Maris' theoretical
perspective that holds that the majority of self-destructive
women are engaged in forms of "ego-defensive risk-taking which
may prove fatal but are intended to be problem solving." A
reanalysis of Maris's data on deviant females provides a
reinterpretation of this self-destructive behavior. Utilizing a
more elaborate path analysis failed to support the dominant
psychiatric theory that reactive depression leads to suicide
attempts and ultimately suicides. Instead, depression is
reconceptualized as a defense mechanism, which inhibits suicide
for a female. Suicide attempts are self-therapy, thus the concept
"pseudocide" suggests the extent to which these attempts fail to
lead to suicide. Finally, the path analysis suggests that female
suicide is primarily attributable to weak defenses, particularly
in the case of a female who has pursued a conformist pattern.

412. Kinsinger. J.R.

> 1973.   "Women Who Threaten Suicide: Evidence for an
> Identifiable Personality Type." OMEGA.
> 4(1):73-84.

This article offers a comparison of women who threatened,
but never attempted suicide. Psychological tests were made on two
groups: one group who had attempted suicide and one group each of
nonsuicidal control psychiatric patients and normals. Those who
had attempted suicide and nonsuicidal psychiatric patients were
found to be very similar. However, the women who had a history of
suicide threats, but no attempts, were discriminated from the
other groups by means of the MMPI and Leary Interpersonal Check
List.

413. Maris, R.W.

> 1981.   PATHWAYS TO SUICIDE: A SURVEY OF SELF-
> DESTRUCTIVE BEHAVIORS. Baltimore: The Johns
> Hopkins Press, Ltd.

A random sample gathered from a Chicago populace provides
three hundred cases of successful suicides that are the focus of
Maris's scholarly book on the nature and etiology of this
perplexing phenomenon. The author's theory of "suicidal careers"
is developed in terms of the factors influencing completed
suicides. Such suicides are contrasted and compared to those
persons who attempted suicide or died a natural death.
Chapter 3 is of particular interest to those studying

suicides among women: "The Development of Suicides: Age, Sex and Developmental Stagnation," in which the author identifies the major differences between men and women who commit suicide. "The prevalence of female suicides and female suicide rates both peak between the ages of forty-five and forty-nine. These suicide peaks suggest abortive life-stage transitions centering primarily on work for males and on love, marriage and family for females."

414. Paykel, E.S. and M.N. Dienelt.

   1971.   "Suicide Attempts Following Acute Depression." THE JOURNAL OF NERVOUS AND MENTAL DISEASE. 153(4):234-243.

   This is a follow-up study ten months after the initial study of 187 depressed female patients. Sociodemographic variables, previous history, personality dimensions, and symptom ratings were analyzed to explore predictors of suicide attempts. The study shows there is a significant statistical divergence between the patients who attempted suicide during the follow-up period and the patients who did not attempt suicide. Suicide attempters show significant differences in clinical patterns of neurotic rather than endogenous depression, overt hostility, evidence of a personality disturbance suggestive of character disorder, and a previous history of suicide attempts. The findings are consistent with other descriptions from earlier studies of women who have attempted suicide among the general population.

415. Wallace, S.E.

   1973.   AFTER SUICIDE. New York: John Wiley and Sons.

   Employing a case-study method and a narrative style, Wallace focuses on the written and oral accounts of the experiences of twelve Boston women widowed by suicide. Various coping mechanisms were employed, such as withdrawal, denial of losses and reinvolvement. The reactions of the widow's family and friends were also significant in normalizing the event. The author strives to "understand in each case the influence of the marital relationship on the suicidal act and the effect of that act on the widowed survivor."

XV

Teenage Pregnancy

A. General

416. Abernathy, T.J., Jr., I.E. Robinson, J.O. Balawick, and K. King.

    1979.   "Comparison of the Sexual Attitudes and Behavior of Rural, Suburban and Urban Adolescents." ADOLESCENCE. 14(summer):298-295.

The purpose of this study was to determine whether adolescents from rural, suburban and urban environments differ from one another in their sexual attitudes and behavior. In general those with rural backgrounds prove to be the most conservative and those from the cities to be the most liberal. However, both urban males and females, even though they are more liberal in many of their views than rural youth, are less willing than those with rural backgrounds to grant women the same sexual freedom as men. In addition, suburban females, although not the most permissive in their attitudes, have the highest rate of casual sex.

The findings indicate several conclusions. Permissiveness is not unidimensional; it is possible for those in a group to be the most liberal in some aspects and conservative in others. Also, there is not a perfect relationship between sexual attitudes and behavior. The sexual behavior within a population is a consequence of the way in which the members define it and the meanings they attach to it, rather than a consequence of urban background. There were also qualitative, as well as quantitative differences among the values of adolescents in each of these residential categories.

417. Allen, J.E. and D. Bender.

    1980.   MANAGING TEENAGE PREGNANCY, ACCESS TO ABORTION, CONTRACEPTION, AND SEX EDUCATION. New York: Praeger Publishers, Inc.

The author presents his findings of a two-year study on the ways local communities manage teenage pregnancies. Analyzing data gained from teenagers, service providers, public officials, and community representatives, the book examines current efforts at dealing with teenage sexuality and pregnancy, and distinguishes between communities considered successful versus ineffective in their efforts to manage this social problem. The access of the teens in this study to counseling, abortion, contraceptives, sex education, and pre- and postnatal care are compared with national trends.

418. Bolton, F.G.

1980. THE PREGNANT ADOLESCENT: PROBLEMS OF PREMATURE PARENTHOOD. Beverly Hills, California: Sage Publications.

Using up-to-date research and data from hundreds of studies, the author examines the social problem of teenage pregnancy and its implications for women and their infants, especially the capacity of adolescent mothers to care for and raise children. He identifies important stages where adolescent mothers can be helped to be better mothers, emphasizing the possibility of a cyclical relationship between adolescent parenthood and maltreatment of children. This problem is rarely identified or discussed in most of the relevant literature. Bolton examines several theories which attempt to explain teenage pregnancies, arguing that they result not because society is "out of control," nor because present changes in social mores inevitably result in higher rates of such pregnancies, but rather, that these unplanned pregnancies are due to a complex of social factors. Bolton details the social and personal constraints placed upon young parents and their offspring. The final chapter deals with the creation of social policy for pregnant teens.

419. Cobliner, W.G.

1981. "Prevention of Adolescent Pregnancy: A Developmental Perspective." BIRTH DEFECTS: ORIGINAL ARTICLE SERIES. 17:35-47.

A discrepancy between biological and psychosocial maturation is one of the key elements preventing teenagers from practicing effective birth control. A study of 50 adolescents seeking contraceptive counseling and 143 who had unintentionally conceived, illustrated the role of the family, particularly the mother or the principal caregiver, in facilitating or checking the subjects' progress toward autonomy and responsibility. A systematic study of the entire range of relations between teenagers and their respective principal caregivers is recommended as an approach to preventing a greater majority of unintended teenage pregnancies.

420. Dworkin, R.J. and A.N. Poindexter.

    1980.   "Pregnant Low-Income Teenagers: A Social Structure Model of the Determinants of Abortion-Seeking Behavior." YOUTH AND SOCIETY. 11(3):295-304.

While there has been substantial sociological research on the attitudes of women seeking abortion, few studies have been concerned with teenage abortion. Proposed is a theoretical model to test decisions to abort or to deliver among low-income, pregnant teenage girls. A path model is hypothesized containing seven variables: age, race, religion, education, marital status, number of children, delivery, and abortion-seeking behavior. Using hospital admission interview data, an analysis of 1,341 abortions and 390 deliveries at Houston's Jefferson Davis County Hospital was made. Behavior was most directly affected by the number of children, marital status and age. The tendency to seek abortion is evident among those under age twenty who have not experienced social reinforcement for commitment to having children. Recommendations include a more aggressive sex education program within the regular school curricula.

421. Falk, R.M., M. Gispert and R.H. Bavcom.

    1981.   "Personality Factors Related to Black Teenage Pregnancy and Abortion." PSYCHOLOGY OF WOMEN QUARTERLY. 72(March):283-285.

Forty-eight adolescents who applied for therapeutic abortions were compared with 55 adolescents who planned to have their babies and 67 adolescents who were not pregnant (the control group). All subjects were single, black and aged 15 or 16 years. Controls were the most socialized, followed by those who had applied for abortions and last those girls who planned to have their babies (full term). The full-term girls seemed to experience a void and appeared to be trying to fill it and assume an adult role by having a baby. Those who had applied for abortions did not seem to have the same needs. Girls who became pregnant and described the relationship with the reported father as casual appeared to have more daily problems, lack socialization, be less clear thinking, and have poor self-control. Pregnant girls who had good communication with their mothers showed no differences from girls with poor communication with their mothers.

422. Furstenberg, F.F.

    1980.   "Burdens and Benefits: The Impact of Early Childbearing on the Family." JOURNAL OF SOCIAL ISSUES. 36:64-87.

This study explores the impact of teenage pregnancy and childbearing on the adolescent's family, as well as the amount and type of support extended to the pregnant teenager by the family of origin. The analysis draws on data from a longitudinal study of childbearing teenagers in Baltimore. Also was a series of intensive case studies of adolescents and their families carried out at the Philadelphia Child Guidance Clinic, with nine black, three white and three Hispanic families. Findings reveal that many services are furnished to the young parents. The paper focuses on the family's relations with the father of the child, the division of childcare responsibilities, the effect on the parent's marriage, and the consequences for sibling relations.

423. Hale, D. and E. Vadies.

1977.   "Attitudes of Adolescent Males Toward Abortion, Contraception, and Sexuality." SOCIAL WORK IN HEALTH CARE. 3(2):169-174.

Young males appear to be reassessing their roles in preventing unwanted conception. This article reports the findings of a study of 1,017 young men's attitudes toward pregnancy, family planning and sexuality. A questionnaire was used over a two-year period and administered by the Planned Parenthood Association of the Chicago area. Findings indicate that young men are tending to see the responsibility for contraception more as a dual responsibility than as that of the female alone. Findings also show a strong sentiment against abortion on the part of black teenagers, with the opposite being reported by white teens, who are more likely to favor abortions.

424. Kaplan, H.B., P.B. Smith and A.D. Pokorny.

1979.   "Psychosocial Antecedents of Unwed Motherhood Among Indigent Adolescents." JOURNAL OF YOUTH AND ADOLESCENCE. June:181-207.

A number of hypotheses regarding psychosocial antecedents of unwed childbearing in indigent female adolescents derive from a general theory of deviant behavior. Questionnaire data were obtained in 1971 from 7,618 female seventh-grade students in 18 Houston junior high schools; 82 of these were identified as indigent unwed mothers from the 1971-1976 files of a major clinic. Each was matched with one matched and two random control subjects. Subjects who later became unwed mothers showed lower guilt deflection and higher defenselessness, vulnerability, self-devaluation, self-degradation, contra-normative attitudes, and deviant responses.

425. Kuhn, J.C.

    1982.   "Stress Factors Preceding Postpartum
                Psychosis: A Case Study of an Unwed
                Adolescent." MATERNAL-CHILD NURSING JOURNAL.
                11(2):95-108.

An observational study was conducted to identify the
behavioral stresses of adolescence, pregnancy and illegitimate
conception in a 19-year old girl. The adolescent's pre-natal
stresses included: maternal conflict; struggle for independence,
and peer isolation; fear for the safety of the infant; feelings
of punishment; and fear of loss of control over her body, mind
and environment.

426. Lehrer, S.

    1980.   "Health Risks to Teenage Mothers." U.S.A.
                TODAY. 108(fall):12.

In a survey of 1,200 teenagers, only 48 percent knew that
teenage mothers have more problems during labor than females over
20. Only 25 percent were aware that mothers under the age of 15
are five times more likely to die during childbirth than females
over the age of 20. Only 45 percent knew that mortality is twice
as high among babies born to females under the age of 15 as among
those born to females aged 20-24. A total of 57 girls within the
sample who had been or were pregnant were matched against 57
girls of similar backgrounds who had never been pregnant. Never-
pregnant girls were somewhat better informed than the pregnant
girls about the hazards of pregnancy to their own health and that
of the child. The knowledge difference between the two groups
(who were both surprisingly ignorant of some basic health
factors) was slight. While it would be erroneous to assume that
because the never-pregnant girls were better informed, they kept
from becoming pregnant, it was concluded that information about
the health problems related to teenage pregnancy could serve as
an indication of whether sex education programs are effective.

427. Lewis, C.C.

    1980.   "A Comparison of Minors' and Adults'
                Pregnancy Decision." AMERICAN JOURNAL OF
                ORTHOPSYCHIATRY. 50(3):446-453.

Pregnancy decision-making of legal minors (17 and younger)
and legal adults is compared on the basis of 42 interviews with
women 13-25 years old. Minors were less likely than adults to
anticipate consultation with a professional regarding the
pregnancy, and more likely than adults to perceive decisions
about pregnancy, disposition and contraception as being
"externally" determined. Implications of these differences for
age and pregnancy-decision consequences are considered.

179

428. Mathis, J.L.

1976. "Adolescent Sexuality and Societal Change." AMERICAN JOURNAL OF PSYCHOTHERAPY. 30(3):433-440.

Data is insufficient to assess the reactions of adolescents to social change in terms of the direction or magnitude of actual changes now occurring in sexuality. However, some social changes which are affecting it include: the increasing rate of social change; the threat of human extinction or other disasters; the growing affluence, which among other things makes adolescents useless in society; and the drive toward equal opportunity for all individuals. The lack of close-knit social units or of stable norms reduces tolerances for stress. Adolescents more often than in past decades engage in sexual intercourse, are doing so at earlier ages, are ignoring the double standard, and are more open about their behavior, the author concludes.

429. McKenry, P.C., L.H. Walters and C. Johnson.

1979. "Adolescent Pregnancy: A Review of the Literature." THE FAMILY COORDINATOR. 28(1):17-28.

Various aspects of the increasing problem of adolescent pregnancy are reviewed and analyzed with a focus on the implications for family practitioners. Various explanations of the etiology of adolescent pregnancy are explored, including physiological, psychological, social, and cognitive factors. Medical risks for mother and child are delineated, as well as non-medical risks.

430. Murcott, A.

1980. "The Social Construction of Teenage Pregnancy: A Problem in the Ideologies of Childhood and Reproduction." SOCIOLOGY OF HEALTH AND ILLNESS. 2(1):1-23.

The widely held assumption that "teenage pregnancy" constitutes a social problem, stimulated the writer to explore more deeply neglected aspects of this social construction. It is suggested that ideologies of reproduction fail to regulate teenage intercourse and effective contraceptive use. Sampling 147 females between the ages of 12 and 18, Murcott sought to understand the qualities of the interpersonal relationship of the adolescent dyad. As expected, this dyad is more strongly associated with exposure to pregnancy risk than qualities of either peer or family relationships. However, certain qualities of the dyadic relationship, such as peer contraceptive use and relationship satisfaction, can have a counterbalancing influence on pregnancy risk. A consistent relationship between positive peer influence among those peers that practice regular contraceptive use, can reduce the pregnancy risk considerably.

431. Phipps-Yonas, S.

    1980.   "Teenage Pregnancy and Motherhood: A Review
               of the Literature." AMERICAN JOURNAL OF
               ORTHOPSYCHIATRY. 50(3):403-431.

    This article reviews medical and non-medical studies of
teenage pregnancy and its outcomes, and assesses the state of
current knowledge. It is suggested that while the typical teenage
girl is biologically ready for motherhood, a complex set of
social and psychological variables leads those least well-suited
for the role into becoming teenage parents. The author also
examines the effectiveness of special programs for pregnant
adolescents and their offspring, and offers implications for
policy and prevention.

432. Protinsky, H., M. Sporakowski and P. Atkins.

    1982.   "Identity Formation: Pregnant and Non-
               Pregnant Adolescents." ADOLESCENCE.
               17(spring):73-80.

    In this study, the Ego Identity Scale was administered to 30
pregnant adolescents (age 15-19 years) and 30 non-pregnant
controls to examine contrasts in identity formation. Pregnant
subjects scored significantly lower than non-pregnant subjects,
indicating a greater level of identity confusion. Pregnant
subjects tended toward role fixation, while control subjects were
much more successful with rule experimentation. Pregnant subjects
also did not believe that satisfaction was sufficiently
predictable to delay gratification, and demonstrated a lack of
belief in the trustworthiness of others. Results indicate that
total identity formation in pregnant adolescents is not as
healthy as in their non-pregnant peers.

433. Schneider, S.

    1982.   "Helping Adolescents Deal with Pregnancy: A
               Psychiatric Approach. ADOLESCENCE.
               17(summer):285-292.

    This study examines five issues in adolescent pregnancy:
(1)why the adolescent girl becomes pregnant, (2)how pregnancy
affects the adolescent's emotional development, (3)whether the
child will be at risk emotionally or physically, (4)what factors
are governing the adolescent's emotional make-up that may affect
the delivery process, and (5)how sex education can help
adolescents deal with the issue of pregnancy. The author
concludes that it should be the task of sex educators and mental

health professionals to help the adolescent learn more about "the self" and "the other" to foster more meaningful relationships and planned pregnancies.

434. Shaffer, D., A. Pettigrew, S. Wolkind, and E. Zajicek.

1978.   "Psychiatric Aspects of Pregnancy in Schoolgirls: A Review." PSYCHOLOGICAL MEDICINE. 8(Feb):119-130.

The author takes up the issue that illegitimate pregnancy in girls of school age is an indicator of underlying psychopathology and, in particular, that pregnancy or sexual activity provides a form of gratification for otherwise deprived young girls. There is a suggestion that younger pregnant teenagers come from unsatisfactory home backgrounds. Relatively few sexually-active teenagers use contraceptives. Girls who continue with their pregnancy when the choice of termination is available are more disadvantaged than girls who obtain a termination, although reasons for this association are not clear. The problem of schoolgirl pregnancy is compounded by interruption of schooling and early re-conception. Hence, social factors may play a larger role in problems of teenage pregnancy than the narrowly construed psychological aspects.

435. Smith, P.B. and D.M. Mumford. (eds.)

1980.   ADOLESCENT PREGNANCY: PERSPECTIVES FOR THE HEALTH PROFESSIONAL. Boston: G.K. Hall and Company.

Smith and Mumford's volume for practitioners provides basic information on adolescent pregnancy by offering creative approaches to the many health problems of teens who become pregnant. Some of the issues covered in these edited chapters include: adolescent psychosexual development, administrative concerns, psychiatric aspects of adolescent pregnancy, adolescent sexuality, pregnancy and childbearing, social implications of teenage childbearing, programs for sexually active teens, venereal disease and the adolescent, issues surrounding adolescent pregnancy terminations, parenting education, legal aspects of adolescent pregnancy, ethical issues of adolescent pregnancy, sex education, and sexual counseling for adolescents. In their preface the editors emphasize the need for diverse approaches by health and educational groups. In addition to the physician, other professionals, such as the nurse, social scientists and the committed lay worker all spend significant time and energy dealing with pregnant adolescents, often with inadequate information of the problem.

436. Tietze, C.

1978.   "Tennage Pregnancies: Looking Ahead to 1984."
         FAMILY PLANNING PERSPECTIVES. 10(4):205-207.

Statistics for 1976 and the Monthly Vital Statistics for
1978 are used in the estimation of pregnancy, birth, abortion,
and miscarriage experiences among 14-year-old girls. It is
estimated that by age 20 approximately 21 percent of all females
will have experienced at least one live birth. Fifteen percent
will have had at least one legal abortion and another six percent
will have had at least one miscarriage or stillbirth. These
estimates could be reduced if all young people used birth control
consistently. Sex education in junior high schools was also
suggested. However, limiting access to abortion through Medicaid
restrictions and requiring parental notification for minors'
could work to increase the number of unwanted births among
adolescents.

437. Wagner, C.A.

1980.   "Sexuality of American Adolescents."
         ADOLESCENCE. 15(59):567-580.

This article is a description of a research-based understanding of adolescent sexuality. Emerging trends resulting from
cultural change and altered life patterns in adolescence during
this period of human development are examined. Topics include
knowledge about sexuality, attitudes and values, masturbation,
homosexuality, heterosexual behaviors of petting and intercourse,
and the social context of sexual learning.

438. Wagner, H.

1978.   "Sexual Behavior of Adolescents." EDUCATION.
         99(1):44-47.

Adolescents are fascinated by sex as something for them to
look forward to in a world where, the author argues, they have
done just about everything they desire. The discussion of sexual
behavior is confined here to heterosexual activities. The writer
discusses peer relations, an aspect of the sex-role potential.
The adolescent search for a consistent sexual behavior code is
threatened by rapid changes in social conventions. Adolescents
must decide on an individual basis how far they will go sexually
before marriage. Reasons are cited for the apparent increase in
promiscuity among adolescents, and the role of sexuality in
gaining individuality. Factors influencing sexual behavior are
media images, religious values and the double standard.

439. Zelnik, M.

1979.   "Sex Education and Knowledge of Pregnancy
         Risk Among U.S. Teenage Women." FAMILY PLAN-
         NING PERSPECTIVES. 11(6):355-357.

This study examined data from a national survey of 1,899
females, aged 15-19, relating sex education to knowledge of
pregnancy risk. In this age group, 70 percent have had a sex
education course; almost 50 percent have been informed about
contraception, 60 percent about venereal disease, and 70 percent
about the details of the menstrual cycle. Of the women who had
studied the menstrual cycle, 60 percent claimed to know the time
of greatest pregnancy risk, but only 30 percent could correctly
identify it. This is important because many sexually active
teenagers rely on timing of sexual intercourse to avoid
pregnancy. For both whites and blacks, sex education is the most
common source of knowledge; parents are a distant second. Medical
personnel are the best source of pregnancy risk information, but
the one least sought out by teenagers. The least informed source
of information for both races are statements from friends.

440. Zelnik, M., J.F. Kantner, and K. Ford.

1981.   SEX AND PREGNANCY IN ADOLESCENCE. Beverly
         Hills: Sage Publications.

Melvin Zelnik and John F. Kantner are among the foremost
researchers in the area of adolescent sexual behavior. Along with
Kathleen Ford, they analyze the results of their two national
surveys, focusing on the sexual behavior of young women between
the ages of 15 and 19, and the choices that precede teenage
pregnancy and childbirth. Their analysis reveals significant
patterns of sexual activity, contraceptive use and nonuse,
pregnancy, abortion, and unwed motherhood. Factors that affected
female adolescent fertility and changes in attitudes and behavior
between the first survey in 1971 and the second in 1976 are also
examined. In a time when contraception, abortion and unwed
motherhood are major issues, SEX AND PREGNANCY IN ADOLESCENCE
should play a vital role in the formulation of social policy.
Researchers, policymakers, students, and human services
specialists concerned with teenage sexuality and family studies
will find this comprehensive work of special interest.

B. Contraception

441. Hansson, R., W.H. Jones and M.E. Charnovetz.

    1979.   "Contraceptive Knowledge: Antecedents and
             Implications." THE FAMILY COORDINATOR.
             Jan.:29-34.

    This article examines the relationship between both male and
female college undergraduates' contraceptive knowledge and their
sexual involvement, personal responsibility and perception of
options in the event of unwanted pregnancy. Utilizing written
questionnaires and the Bem Sex Role Inventory they discovered
that knowledge was not related to early sexual experience or
exposure to such material. Females were less reluctant to discuss
their contraceptive experiences and to consider abortion as an
option to unwanted pregnancy. Most undergraduates believed women
should assume financial responsibility for contraception. Females
were more knowledgeable about contraception than males, and
persons who identified themselves with nonconventional sex types
were more knowledgeable than their counterparts. The level of
knowledge was directly related to the expertise of the
undergraduates' information source.

442. Harari, H., T. Harari and K. Hosey.

    1979.   "Contraceptive Risk-Taking in White and Black
             Unwed Females." JOURNAL OF SEX RESEARCH.
             15(1):56-63.

    This study compares the contraceptive risk-taking
explanations of 28 black and 35 white unwed, sexually active, 14-
18 year old clinically-labeled female contraceptive rejectors
with those of a matched group of clinically nonlabeled subjects.
In addition, 90 college students were asked to predict the
subjects' explanations for risk-taking. The subjects' responses
were categorized by independent judges. Results indicated no
differences between the two groups. However, within groups,
clinically-oriented explanations tended to be more frequent than
political-economic explanations among the white subjects, while
the reverse held true for the black subjects. The college
students' responses indicated that clinically-oriented
explanations were common for white subjects; political-economic
rationales for rejecting contraception were expected among black
rejectors, and situational explanations when the race of the
subject was not mentioned.

443. Jorgensen, S.R.

1980.　　　"Contraceptive Attitude-Behavior Consistency in Adolescence." POPULATION AND ENVIRONMENT. Summer:174-194.

Adolescents experience a higher level of value-behavior inconsistency than individuals in other stages of the lifespan due to engaging in peer-oriented domains that are contrary to values shared with parental family. It is predicted that contraceptive attitude-behavior inconsistency would be greatest when parental and peer contraceptive attitudes are perceived to be incongruent. Analysis of questionnaire data from a sample of 167 sexually active adolescent females, aged 13-18, clients of Arizona Family Planning clinics in 1978 and 1979, indicates that general contraceptive attitudes are consistent with contraceptive use, whereas attitudes toward specific contraceptive methods are unrelated to contraceptive behavior.

444. Reichelt, P.A.

1979.　　　"Coital and Contraceptive Behavior of Female Adolescents." ARCHIVES OF SEXUAL BEHAVIOR. March:159-172.

In 1975, interviews were conducted with 532 females (ranging in age from 12-17, 70 percent white, 30 percent black) currently seeking contraceptive care at the Teen Center run by Planned Parenthood in a large midwestern city. Most of the subjects were from middle class or lower-middle class families. Over 40 percent did not live in the city where the clinic was located. Findings indicate that 92 percent were sexually experienced and 86 percent currently sexually active. In addition, over 60 percent of the subjects had their first sexual encounter at the age of either 15 or 16; previous contraceptive use was intermittent; methods used were nonprescription. Lack of birth control was attributed to fear of loss of sexual pleasure and contraceptive inaccessibility.

445. Reichelt, P.A.

1978.　　　"Changes in Sexual Behavior Among Unmarried Teenage Women Utilizing Oral Contraception." JOURNAL OF POPULATION. Spring:57-68.

A reason often cited for opposing contraception for adolescents is that it will result in greatly increased adolescent sexual activity. This assumption was examined, based on interviews with 213 females, both before and after receiving oral contraception from a Planned Parenthood clinic of a large midwestern city. The age range was 13 to 17 years. The majority of the subjects consistently used the pills throughout the year. Those who discontinued use of oral contraceptives for any time during the year, typically replaced it with either alternative birth control or sexual inactivity. The results, combined with other research, indicate that providing adolescents with effective contraception will not markedly affect their sexual behavior.

446. Zelnik, M. and J.F. Kantner.

    1979.   "Reasons for Nonuse of Contraception by Sexually Active Women Aged 15 to 19." FAMILY PLANNING PERSPECTIVES. 11(5):289-296.

Analysis of data from a 1976 national probability sample survey (approximately 700 subjects, aged 15 to 19 years) examines the reasons for nonuse of contraception by premaritally sexually-active females. Reasons for nonuse were elicited for the last reported intercourse, or in the case of pregnant subjects, for the time conception was believed to have occurred. Subjects were categorized according to those who: (1)had intercourse only once, (2)had intercourse more than once, and (3)were pregnant at the time of the interview. The results point to the inadequacy of current family planning, sex education programs and the need for new, more imaginative approaches.

447. Zelnik, M. and J.F. Kantner.

    1978.   "Contraceptive Patterns and Premarital Pregnancy Among Women Aged 15-19 in 1976." FAMILY PLANNING PERSECTIVES. 10(2):135-142.

Data are presented contradicting the argument that increasing the availability of contraceptives results in an increase in teenage pregnancy. Teenagers who take advantage of the increasing availability of contraceptives use methods effectively to prevent unwanted pregnancies, according to a national probability sample survey of ever-married and never-married females, 15-19, living in households in the continental United States. The sampling procedure utilized stratification by race to ensure a substantial number of interviews with blacks; the number of subjects was 2,193. The authors observed that back-up abortion services will continue to be needed by teenagers who have unintended pregnancies, but wish to avoid unintended births.

C. Education

448. Ambrose, L.

   1978.   "Misinforming Pregnant Teenagers." FAMILY
                PLANNING PERSPECTIVES. 10(1):51-57.

   Of all teenage pregnancies, 66 percent are unintended;
whereas of births resulting from teenage pregnancies, 50 percent
are unintended. The reason for these accidental pregnancies, the
author argues, is ignorance and misinformation about
reproduction, pregnancy and contraception. Informational
materials available to teenagers in many cases are not adequate
and rarely deal with such subjects as symptoms of pregnancy, the
pregnancy test, abortion, miscarriage, child care, educational
and career counseling, and financial aid. Most materials
published about pregnancy are written for older women and tend to
bypass teenage concerns. Many publications are aimed at married
couples and do not take into account the special problems of
young, unmarried teenagers. Commercial companies, goverment
agencies and charitable organizations need to review their
informational publications and revise them to represent the needs
of teenage mothers. New materials along with community
involvement in sex education would help provide teenagers with
the necessary information and services regarding sex,
reproduction, pregnancy, and contraception.

449. Chesler, J.S. and S.A. Davis.

   1980.   "Problem Pregnancy and Abortion Counseling
                With Teenagers." SOCIAL CASEWORK.
                61(March):173-179.

   A young woman who confronts a decision regarding the outcome
of an unplanned pregnancy may face difficulties when she and her
parents disagree about the best answer to the problem. Crisis-
counseling strategies that emphasize both client and parental
assertiveness, negotiation and the importance of compromise are
discussed. The objective for the counselor is to help the client
and her family find the option with the most merit and the fewest
disadvantages for the young woman. Case examples are provided.

450. Courtright, J.A. and S.J. Baran.

> 1980. "The Acquisition of Sexual Information by Young People: Peers and Media." JOURNALISM QUARTERLY. 57(Spring):107-114.

A study was conducted in response to the need to examine sexual-decision making among adolescents and the possible influence of peers, media and family. A total of 202 students from a Cleveland area public high school completed a questionnaire designed to measure the relative influence of three variables: peers (social comparison), family and mass media (television and film) on expectations and understandings of sex. In terms of the acquisition of sexual information among students who were virgins, family variables (which included religion, religious activity, ethnic background, and parents' presence) had no influence whatsoever. The media and peers were the significant influences. For those students who had coital experiences, their satisfaction, understanding and expectations of these experiences tended not to be influenced by their families.

451. Eggleston, A.P.

> 1981. "School-Based Sex Education: Recommendations for Reform." HUMAN ECOLOGY FORUM. 12(2):16-19.

Eight reasons are outlined which prevent school-based sex education programs from being effective. (1)Students take sex education classes for less than one percent of the time during their adolescence, and not at all before or after the teenage years. (2)Schools are only the fourth source of sexual information during adolescence. (3)Sex education courses are given to students too late in their developmental process. (4)The sexual behaviors of adolescents are strongly influenced by their emotional and sexual needs. (5)Sex education is required in only three states and Washington, D.C. (6) Many teachers who teach the subject lack formal training in sex education. (7)An extremely vocal minority in the U.S. is attempting to eliminate sex education from schools. (8)Teachers and administrators imagine greater resistance to sex education than actually exists. Solutions are discussed for each of these drawbacks.

452. Fox, G.L.

> 1981. "The Mother-Adolescent Daughter Relationship as a Sexual Socialization Structure: A Research Review." FAMILY RELATIONS. 29(1):21-28.

Fox reviews the research literature on the mother-daughter relationship as a transmission structure for sexual socialization. Although the literature indicates low levels of direct

communication about sex between mothers and daughters, the
influence of the mother on the daughter's social and
contraceptive behavior is apparent. Low levels of communication
between mothers and daughter have been attributed to the internal
dynamics of the family and to the interface between the family
and external socialization agents. The mother-daughter
relationship as a source of sexual socialization is under-
utilized by mothers and daughters and overlooked by social
service programs.

453. House Select Committee on Population Report.

1979. "Teenage Pregnancies Out of Control."
SCIENCE. 204(4393):597.

Despite a dramatic increase in the use of contraceptives in
this country, teenage pregnancies continue to be a serious
problem, the Report holds, affecting millions of lives and
costing the federal government billions of dollars a year in
subsidies. Recommendations include: easier access to birth
control, more pharmaceutical firms doing contraceptive research,
and less sex bias in Congress involving family planning clinics.

454. Jekel, J.F.

1977. "Primary or Secondary Prevention of
Adolescent Pregnancies." JOURNAL OF SCHOOL
HEALTH. 47(8):457-461.

This study discusses the theoretical, practical and
financial problems of primary-prevention-of-pregnancies-programs
for adolescents. The suitability of the medical-model description
of pregnancy is questioned, as are primary prevention techniques.
If teenage pregnancy is a symptom of underlying problems, primary
prevention may trigger symptom substitutions, such as suicide or
drug abuse. If, however, primary prevention is interpreted as
preventing the development of the underlying problem(s), no one
program would have noticable influence, particularly in the short
term. The article discusses cost-effectiveness issues and
presents a model for comparing cost-effectiveness factors.
Because primary prevention probably will not have any great
effect by itself, emphasis should be placed on easier access to
contraceptives and abortion services, and on intensive programs
for preventing pregnancies.

455. Kasun, J.

1979. "Turning Children into Sex Experts." THE
PUBLIC INTEREST. 55(Spring):3-14.

This survey includes the objectives, curricula and teaching
methods of contemporary sex education in public elementary and

high schools in the United States with special reference to California. "Model" curricular and teacher-training literature, as well as materials for students, are discussed. Kasun examines the ideology of the sex education movement, noting its emphasis on methods of "values clarification." This movement stresses the desirability of limiting family size and population growth, while encouraging acceptance of all forms of non-procreative sexual behavior. The article considers the approaches for instilling the desired ideological views, along with the progressive reinforcement which comes with these programs, especially when begun in grade school and continued on through high school.

456. Lang, S.F.

    1981.   "Q: Where Does Less Money Spent Mean More
             Money Spent? A: In the Teenage Pregnancy
             Prevention Program." HUMAN ECOLOGY FORUM.
             12(2):21-22.

    Federal reductions in services for teenage pregnancy prevention, as well as social and health programs for teenage parents, will cost tax-payers more in the long run, according to a report released October 13, 1981 by the New York City task force on adolescent pregnancy programs. For every dollar spent on family planning, the task force said, three dollars are saved in other human services programs by decreasing dependence in areas such as public assistance, food stamps and Medicaid. In 1980, $273 million was saved in health and social services to 16,215 teenage girls. A total of 2,027 teenagers will lose maternal and child health services. Under AFDC cuts in benefits to pregnant women (including teenagers), benefits will be prohibited until the last four months of pregnancy, thus eliminating prenatal care and denying food and rent allowances. The economics of health care for girls and women appears to lack advocates, the article infers.

457. Magrab, P.R. and J. Danielson-Murphy.

    1979.   "Adolescent Pregnancy: A Review." JOURNAL OF
             CLINICAL CHILD PSYCHOLOGY. 8(2):121-125.

    The effects of pregnancy on teenagers' health is profound, Magrab says. In addition, educational attainment, vocational opportunities and marriage status are negatively affected. There are also health risks and developmental consequences of infants born to teenage mothers. A review of intervention programs shows that adequate prenatal care for the pregnant adolescent reduces medical risk to both mother and child. Educational and psychosocial programs increase the teens' use of contraceptives in the future, result in more school years completed after delivery, and enhance her adjustment to the parenting role. Easily accessible, genuinely comprehensive services are needed to prevent both the unplanned pregnancy and subsequent social and health risks to the mother and child if the pregnancy is carried to term.

458. Rothenberg, P.B.

1980.   "Communication About Sex and Birth Control Between Mothers and Their Adolescent Children." POPULATION AND ENVIRONMENT. 3(1):35-50.

To explore the nature and extent of communication between parents and children about sexuality, interviews were held with 163 Cincinnati mothers and two of their children between the ages of 10 and 18. Of the mothers surveyed, 37 percent gave reading material about sex to their children, 45 percent explained intercourse and 57 percent discussed birth control. Mothers were more likely to talk to female (49 percent) than male children (30 percent) about contraception. Among the children, 67 percent discussed sexual relations with friends, 40 percent with their mothers and 20 percent with their fathers. Over two-thirds of the children discussed birth control with friends, nearly half with mothers, but less than one-fifth with fathers. For 83 percent of the children who had heard of birth control, most understood its correct meaning, and almost all could name a contraceptive method.

459. Stuart, I.R. and C.F. Wells.

1982.   PREGNANCY IN ADOLESCENCE (NEEDS, PROBLEMS AND MANAGEMENT). New York: Van Nostrand Reinholdt Co.

Among the many complex issues that seem to abound in the area of teenage pregnancy, none is more compelling than issues of how to diminish and possibly eliminate the costly consequences of an unwanted pregnancy. Taking an applied research and programs-planning perspective, the article focuses on material judged to be most useful to the professional working directly with teenagers.

460. Zellman, G.L.

1981.   THE RESPONSE OF THE SCHOOLS TO TEENAGE PREGNANCY AND PARENTHOOD. Santa Monica, Ca: Rand Corporation.

The passage of Title IX of the 1972 Education Amendment includes in its mandate equal rights for pregnant and parenting students. This study reports on the response of eleven school districts and twelve programs to this growing phenomenon. Some federal and state funding has been allocated for local programs, but there is a lack of leadership and support for innovative programs. The presence of a highly motivated administratior or faculty person seems to be a necessary condition for the success of school programs.

D. Law

461. Kenney, A.M., J. Forrest and A. Torres.

      1982.   "Storm Over Washington: The Parental Notification Proposal." FAMILY PLANNING PERSPECTIVES. 14(4):185.

On February 22, 1982, the United States Department of Health and Human Services (DHHS) proposed a regulation requiring family planning clinics funded under Title X of the Public Health Services Act to notify the parents of patients under 18 years of age when prescription contraceptives are provided. The main rationale for parental notification used by the department related to the health of the girls (the side effects of the pill). Some serious questions were raised about the constitutionality of the proposed regulation. The Supreme Court has recognized that minors, like adults, have a right to privacy in matters concerning procreation. The court, however, has never directly addressed the constitutionality of a parental consent or notification requirement for contraceptives.

462. Klassel, A. and A. Lewin.

      1978.   "Minors' Right to Abortion and Contraception: Prospects for Invalidating Less than Absolute Restrictions." WOMEN'S RIGHTS LAW REPORT. Spring:165-183.

The Supreme Court has ruled that minors have a right to contraception and abortion, but implied that certain restrictions may be placed on that right. This has led to legislative efforts to create restrictive laws. The application of the right to privacy of minors to these issues is considered. The inclusion of the right to abortion in the legal category of the right to privacy provides the basis for extending this right to minors. Such rules as parental notice and consultation and modified consent, or a distinction between the rights of married and unmarried minors, all lead to impairments of such constitutional rights. The impact of such rights on the interests of parents and doctors is considered.

463. Paul, E.W. and H.F. Pilpel.

      1979.   "Teenagers and Pregnancy: The Law in 1979." FAMILY PLANNING PERSPECTIVES. 11(5):297-302.

This article summarizes the Supreme Court decisions and

state policies and statutes since 1976 that affect the rights of minors to obtain abortions and other reproductive health services without parental consent or notification. Until recently, the Supreme Court addressed the issue of minors' rights only infrequently and inconclusively. In many states, minors were restricted from terminating unwanted pregnancies or obtaining contraceptive services without parental consent. However, three Supreme Court decisions--two dealing with abortion and one with contraception--have rendered obsolete many of these restrictions. In "Planned Parenthood of Central Missouri versus Danforth and Belloti versus Baird (1976)," the court established that mature minors have a right to an abortion on their own consent and that immature minors may be provided an alternative to parental involvement in abortion decisions. In "Carey versus Population Services International (1977)," the court determined that minors may not be restricted from purchasing non-prescription contraceptives. The effects these rulings have on various states' regulations and statutes are discussed. This is a very interesting article in light of the new "Squeal Law," wherein agencies must contact the parents when teens request birth control or abortion.

464. Torres, A.

    1978.   "Does Your Mother Know...?" FAMILY PLANNING PERSPECTIVES. 10(5):280-282.

    Laws and policies differ from state-to-state regarding parental consent to obtain contraceptive care. This pilot study was conducted to examine the effect that parental notification would have on the population of teenagers attending family planning clinics. Self-administered questionnaires were given to teenagers attending a geographically distributed non-random sample of 53 clinics. Subjects under the age of 20, numbered 2,054, those over 20 included 161. Only data from 1,442 subjects aged 17 and younger were used. Findings show that over 50 percent of the teenagers attending family planning clinics have informed their parents of their activities. This is in contrast to the widely-held opinion that minors will not inform their parents unless forced. It was also found that among those who attended clinics without their parents' knowledge, most would stop attending if their parents were informed. Many of those who would stop attendance indicated they would use non-medical methods of contraception. This study indicates that requiring parental notification will result in decreased sexual activity among teenagers, or contrariwise, lead to increased pregnancy rates.

XVI

The Older Woman

465. Derenski, A. and S.B. Landsburg.

    1981.   THE AGE TABOO: OLDER WOMEN-YOUNGER MEN RELATIONSHIPS. Boston: Little, Brown and Company.

Exploring the problems and satisfactions of 50 couples with long-term relationships who have challenged the age taboo of older women and younger men, the authors show great variation in age, with men being junior in age by six, eighteen and even fifty years. The book candidly presents significant issues: What psychological and cultural forces underlie the taboo against permanent liaisons between a woman and a younger man? How does the couple respond to family and friends' reactions of astonishment, doubt and disapproval when they announce their intention to live together or marry?

The book also deals with the older woman's private fears, as in the fear of losing the man to a younger woman, or becoming old and unattractive, and the man's fear that she will get bored, dominate him or leave him for an older, more successful man.

The authors cast light not only on how the older woman/younger man relationship can work, but on the fundamental nature of any successful emotional commitment between two people.

466. Fuchs, E.

    1978.   THE SECOND SEASON: LIFE, LOVE, AND SEX FOR WOMEN IN THE MIDDLE YEARS. Garden City: Anchor Press/Doubleday.

The purpose of this book is to present an informative view of women's experience with middle age and the fact of menopause. Some of the questions this book aims to answer are the following: Is the beauty industry a friend or enemy to the middle-aged? Do men go through menopause? How are homosexuals affected by the middle years? Does sexuality in women increase or decrease with menopause? Is there a change in social status for women in their middle years? Why do some societies regard menopause as stigmatizing? Why is the view of women as producers outside the home neglected? What are the significant threats to the relationship between mother and son, mother and son-in-law, mother and daughter, mother and daughter-in-law? When does menopause occur? Does the number of children affect the age when menopause begins? Is there a menopausal syndrome? Is depression normal in menopause? Are children born to women of later years

196

healthy? What are some new lifestyles older people can look forward to?
This is an excellent book, both scholarly and insightful. Especially noteworthy are the cultural comparisons (the author is a distinguished anthropologist). Perhaps the greatest single feature of the book is the author's forthrightness in confronting a taboo area.

467. Jacobs, R.H.

1976.   "A Typology of Older American Women." SOCIAL POLICY. 7(3):34-39.

An extensive typology of older women has long been needed to order and reshape the confusing and painful reality of growing old, a task undertaken by Ruth Jacobs, who develops relevant categories of older women. Whereas most typologies contain only four or five categories, this book includes thirteen categories: nurturers, unemployed nurturers, re-engaged nurturers, chum networkers and/or leisurists, careerists, retired careerists, seekers, advocates, faded beauties, doctorers, escapists, isolates, and assertive seniors. Jacobs displays an understanding of the roles of older women in assembling this typology, and in defining various role characteristics for each type.

468. Matthews, S.H.

1979.   THE SOCIAL WORLD OF OLDER WOMEN: MANAGEMENT OF SELF-IDENTITY. Beverly Hills: Sage Publications.

Matthews provides an insightful portrayal of the social world of old women by considering some critical issues associated with the aging process. Self-identity is not an isolated entity, she argues. Rather, it is related to the societal context in which old age, stigma, being an old woman, and relations in extended or nuclear families vary widely.
The author successfully raises issues about aging that relates this phenomenon to more general problems of isolation and poverty among women. Too often, the older woman experiences stigmatization and learned helplessness, which severely constrict her choices. While not a self-help book, the study points to some possible strategies for women coming to terms with the final stage of their life cycle.

469. Rubin, L.B.

1979.   WOMEN OF A CERTAIN AGE: THE MIDLIFE SEARCH FOR SELF. New York: Harper and Row.

In this study taken from interviews with 160 women, the empty-nest syndrome (as the alleged cause of mid-life crisis in

197

women) is reviewed and found wanting. Instead, the problem of middle-aged women's emptiness is more complex and hinges on the problems, obstacles, conflicts, and guilts of moving into the world as autonomous adults after a marital career as dependents. The book uses personal accounts to document the extent of perceived repression that women, as "master of the inner world," have, and the enormous strain of confronting and transcending those socialized limits. While written to appeal to a popular audience, the book includes an extensive bibliography and notes.

470. Schultz, C.M.

        1980.   "Age, Sex, and Death Anxiety in a Middle-
                    Class American Community." Pp.239-252 in C.L.
                    Fry and Contributors. AGING IN CULTURE AND
                    SOCIETY: COMPARATIVE VIEWPOINTS AND
                    STRATEGIES. New York: Praeger Publishers.

    In this research Carol Schultz combines two sociological issues, community and sex role differentiation to examine death anxiety. Death anxiety, as a response to the possibility of death, is investigated in a small homogeneous town in the Midwestern United States. Combining a dual research strategy of long-term observation with a survey instrument, the author discovers that the structuring of sex roles in her research community did not lead to healthy resolution of death anxiety on the part of older men. Older females are more accepting of death, inasmuch as women's styles of emotional expression, as well as activities, allow them to confront death. For example, their social usefulness remains high. Older men, who have repressed and denied death during their working years, are faced with an unresolved anxiety that surfaces following retirement. Cognitive and perceptual restructuring is required to reduce the negative effects of the death anxiety for older persons.

471. Shanas, E. (ed.)

        1970.   AGING IN CONTEMPORARY SOCIETY. Beverly Hills,
                    Calif.: Sage Publications, Inc.

    Ethel Shanas has gathered papers by ten authors, who are well known in the field of aging. The first paper by Neugarten discusses the roles of the aged in the present and the future. Streib follows with a paper that outlines the different family structures found in later life and makes some prognoses on which characteristics of older families will continue through the present century. The third paper by Lopata deals with one of the problem areas for which the elderly have no control--widowhood. She is followed by Rosow's paper on the changing environment of the aged. Papers five and six by Kreps and Sheppard, respectively, concern the work role of the older person and his/her overall economic status.
    Next, Huet's paper deals with a special aspect of aging in

France- the costs of the elderly to the society. Paper eight by Wedderburn is a discussion of the economic situation of the elderly in Britain and the extent to which they are integrated into British society. Weihl's paper, on the problems of aging in Israel, follows with the final paper written by Butler. This last article views American society and social change.

XVII

Treatment

A. General

472. Angrist, S., M. Lefton, S. Dinitz, and B. Pasamanick.

     1968.   WOMEN AFTER TREATMENT: A STUDY OF FORMER MENTAL PATIENTS AND THEIR FORMER NEIGHBORS. New York: Appleton-Century-Crofts.

     Immediate post-hospital success and failure provides the core theme, as mental patients are compared with their normal, or at least their never previously treated, women neighbors.

     This volume describes the changing patterns in psychiatric treatment, and traces the sudden transformation in these patterns since World War II. It contains a detailed description of the design, procedures, interviews, respondents, tests, and measures utilized to obtain data on post-hospital outcome. Findings on rehospitalization contrast the successful and readmission cases.

     WOMEN AFTER TREATMENT should be of interest to health professionals and social scientists concerned with the care, treatment and research in the field of mental illness.

473. Brodsky, A. and R. Hare-Mustin. (eds.)

     1980.   WOMEN AND PSYCHOTHERAPY: AN ASSESSMENT OF RESEARCH AND PRACTICE. New York: The Guilford Press.

     Already a classic compendium, WOMEN AND PSYCHOTHERAPY is comprised of fifteen background papers prepared for a conference focusing on the present status and future priorities of research on the treatment of women. This scholarly collection is divided into five parts: Part One deals with the influence of gender on research, and includes chapters on: "Gender and Psychotherapeutic Outcome," "Therapist Attitudes and Sex Role Stereotyping," and "Gender and the Process of Therapy;" in Part Two the issue revolves around disorders of high prevalence. Chapters focus on depression, anxieties such as agoraphobia and hysteria, eating disorders, such as obesity and anorexia, and marital and family conflicts. Part Three considers traditional and alternative approaches, and highlights such modalities as psychodynamic, behavioristic, feminist-consciousness raising, and self help. One chapter is specifically directed towards the needs of minority women. Part Four offers intervention in crises, such as those of reproduction, domestic violence, and marital transition. In Part

Five authors Brodsky and Hare-Mustin address the neglect of women's issues in psychotherapy in each of the topical areas covered.
The book concludes with a list of recommended priorities for research on women and psychotherapy. Extensive bibliographies follow the chapter for those who wish to do further research in a specific area.

474. Corea, G.

1977.   THE HIDDEN MALPRACTICE: HOW AMERICAN MEDICINE
         TREATS WOMEN AS PATIENTS AND PROFESSIONALS.
         New York: William Morrow and Co.

This expose of professional medicine directs the deviance label toward practitioners, examining the subtle and not-so-subtle manner in which medicine operates in highly unprofessional ways against women patients and women health professionals. The book summarizes the problems of medicine as inherently structural: sexual inequality, sex discrimination, client dependency, male power monopolies, and medical institutions as social control systems. These are among the medical practices that undermine women's health. The author compares institutional practices with the primarily reproductive-centered concerns specific to the feminist approach. This book offers a comprehensive review of the literature.

475. Deykin, E.Y., M.M. Weissman, and G.L. Klerman.

1972.   "Treatment of Depressed Women." BRITISH
         JOURNAL OF SOCIAL WORK. 1(3):277-291.

This treatment-centered article discusses case-work techniques useful in treating depressed female patients, whether in the hospital or in outpatient clinics. Depression specifically refers to the clinical syndrome consisting of a number of symptoms that sometimes appear singly and sometimes in multiple forms in the same patient. Examples of these symptoms include subjective feelings of despair, worthlessness, guilt, helplessness, and somatic symptomatology, such as urinary problems, headaches, chest tightness, and difficulty in breathing. Other features of the depressed state include anxiety, loss of appetite, fatigue, and insomnia.
Also discussed in this paper are the various issues arising from the casework treatment of hospitalized and outpatient depressed women. Two critical areas are the role casework plays in drug treatment and the influence of casework on the recovery phase and aftercare.

475. Franks, V. and V. Burtle (eds.)

1974.   WOMEN IN THERAPY: NEW PSYCHOTHERAPIES FOR A
          CHANGING SOCIETY. New York: Brunner/Mazel,
          Inc.

This collection of original essays by psychologists,
psychotherapists, and sociologists offers many far-reaching ideas
on therapy for women and a fuller realization of women's human
potential.
The volume offers such articles as: (1)An Historical View of
Therapy for Women; (2)Female Role Expectancies and Therapeutic
Goals;   (3)The Psychotherapist and the Female Patient;
(4)Cognitive Therapy with Depressed Women; (5)The Phobic Syndrome
in Women; (6)Women and Alcoholism; (7)New Viewpoints on the
Female Homosexual; (8)Women and Behavior Therapy; (9)The Therapy
of Women in the Light of a New View of Psychoanalytic Theory;
(10)A Gestalt Therapist's View of Women in Therapy; (11)Anna O.--
Patient or Therapist? (12)The Treatment of Sex and Love Problems
in Women; (13)Fight-Therapy for Divorcees; (14)Consciousness-
Raising Groups as Therapy for Women; (15)The Treatment of Women
in Prisons and Mental Hospitals; (16)Psychotherapy with Women and
Men of Lower Socioeconomic Groups; and (17)Constants and Change
in the Female Role.
In the foreword Charles G. Gross stresses: "Hopefully, this
book marks the beginning of a true psychology and sociology of
women and the end of the female in psychology as a slightly
degraded, slightly inverted, always derivative male."

475A.Friedman, S.S., L. Gams, N. Gottlieb, and C. Nesselson.

1979.   A WOMAN'S GUIDE TO THERAPY. Englewood Cliffs:
          Prentice-Hall, Inc.

This book aims to help a woman find a suitable therapist. It
offers guidance as to what a woman can expect from most therapy,
what she should look for in a therapist and what kind of therapy
she should avoid.
Topics covered include the woman who seeks therapy; the
potential for therapy; the decision to seek therapy; the power a
therapist can have over a patient's mind; sex roles and the
therapist; the therapist and female sexuality; on having orgasms;
psychological theory and the therapist; choosing one's therapist
in terms of sex, race, class, and sexual orientation; switching
therapists; policies and procedures in psychological service
institutions (including cost, eligibility, length of treatment,
kinds of therapy, tests, drugs, therapists, and staff); women and
mental institutions, including legal issues, drugs, seclusion,
lobotomy, and other kinds of psychosurgery.
This book should be very helpful to women who have been in
therapy, who are seeking therapy or who might seek therapy in the
future.

475B.Gottlieb, B.H.

1981.   SOCIAL NETWORKS AND SOCIAL SUPPORT IN
COMMUNITY MENTAL HEALTH. New York: Sage
Publications, Inc.

This volume of 17 essays examines how human attachments, in
the form of social-support networks, aid in the prevention and
cure of mental illness and other personal and social
difficulties. Such networks vary in structure, ranging from
mutual-help groups, neighborhood voluntary associations or family
ties, both biological and social. All networks share a common
task, however, that of providing support and help for the
individual in order to cope with stressful life events. Several
aspects of networks are discussed, including the aid in
individual coping, the functions in providing support and the
possibility of blending professional and informal care. This book
has special relevance for the community treatment of women.

476. Harmon, L., J. Birk, L. Fitzgerald, and M. Tanney (eds.)

1978.   COUNSELING WOMEN. Monterey, Calif.:
Brooks/Cole Publishing Company.

Based on two issues of THE COUNSELING PSYCHOLOGIST, titled
"Counseling Women" and "Counseling Women II," this book alerts
readers to both the present needs of women and the necessity to
develop new counseling approaches for these clients. Of
particular interest is section two which extends the premise of
section one; that is, that both the theory and practice of
counseling has been and remains inadequate to meet women's needs.
The book stresses a positive approach for many neglected female
subgroups, such as, counseling for the strengths of the black
women; psychotherapy and women's liberation; counseling "single-
again" (divorced and widowed women); and an intervention model
for rape and unwanted pregnancy. The bibliography is especially
useful for acquiring further information on counseling women.

477. Levin, B.S.

1980.   WOMEN AND MEDICINE. Metuchen, N.J.: The
Scarecrow Press, Inc.

Medicine resisted the acceptance of women as physicians and
scientists, a theme which is documented in this study of women
physicians. Exploring the biographies and achievements of women
who pioneered in nineteenth-century medicine the author presents:
Elizabeth Blackwell, Janet Travell, Mary Putnam Jacobi, Rosalyn
Yalow, Gerty Cori, and others, who tell the story of riots in
medical schools when women tried to enroll, of discrimination at
every level, of women overcoming obstacles to enjoy brilliant
medical careers and to make medical breakthroughs. Patients are
also featured, as Levin considers the influence of women patients

on physicians and hospitals, especially in the women-centered issues of abortion, child abuse, hysterectomies, and breast cancer.

478. Livson, F.B.

1980.   "Patterns of Personality Development in Middle-Aged Women: A Longitudinal Study." Pp. 344-350 in Martin Bloom (ed.), LIFE SPAN DEVELOPMENT: BASES FOR PREVENTATIVE AND INTERVENTIVE HELPING. New York: Macmillan Publishers Company.

This article focuses on a longitudinal study of the personality development of 24 women during their middle adult years (ages 40 to 50). Major tasks of this period include a growing awareness of death, a reevaluation of self, a reappraisal of earlier goals, children's departure and menopause. Findings indicate that role changes that occur in midlife affect women differently.

Dividing the women into two groups, the traditionals (extroverted, conforming women) and the independents (skeptical, unconventional women), Livson compares the development of each group as they progress from adolescence into middle age. Patterns of development that emerged reveal that the traditionals were conventional adolescents who tended to use repression as a tool to control anxiety. Independents, on the other hand, tended to value intellectual pursuits, and were more achievement oriented and introspective.

Each group pursued a different life path which converges at age 50 with an "evolved self," reflecting many earlier established patterns. Livson stresses that a key factor in the personality development during this critical transition in the life span is the compatibility of a woman's lifestyle and personality, i.e. roles that satisfy a traditional woman may be restrictive to an independent woman.

The theme thoughout this article echoes much of Gail Sheehy's PASSAGES with the message that middle age is a time that can be utilized for introspection coupled with expansion of individual boundaries and new opportunities for pursuing previously abandoned needs, goals and dreams.

479. Mander, A. and A. Rush.

1974.   FEMINISM AS THERAPY. New York: Random House.

This book examines the many facets of feminism that can be integrated into feminist therapy. This is a modality that favors group therapy due to its egalitarian concept. Rush labels herself a feminist therapist and contends that "one premise of feminism is that sexual oppression is the basis of all other repression." Critical of the post-Freudian psychoanalytic movement, she discusses the steps that feminism has taken to "eliminate some of the core causes of sexual repression."

480. Milio, N.

1975.   THE CARE OF HEALTH IN COMMUNITIES: ACCESS FOR
          OUTCASTS. New York: Macmillan.

This study is a sociological analysis of how health
resources and training are allocated and misallocated to
disadvantaged populations: the poor, women and minorities. The
data offer comparative analysis with an international
perspective.

481. Mitchell, J.

1975.   PSYCHOANALYSIS AND FEMINISM. New York: Random
          House.

"...Psychoanalysis is not a recommendation for patriarchal
society, but an analysis of one." With this quote, Mitchell
advocates Freudian ideas on feminism, as opposed to those of
Wilhelm Reich and R.D. Laing.
Presented here are Freud's theories of the unconscious,
narcissism, masculinity, femininity, bisexuality, the Oedipus
complex, and the marks of womanhood. In addition to explanations
of Freud's, Reich's and Laing's work, there is a critique of
other feminists--Simone de Beauvoir, Betty Friedan, Eva Figes,
Germaine Greer, Shulamith Firestone, and Kate Millett. The author
concludes with a section she calls "The Holy Family and
Feminists," in which she explores the patriarchal system and the
role of women as exchange objects. She also includes an appendix
on the status of psychoanalysis in Vienna at the turn of the
century.
One finds in this work a paradoxical desire to overthrow
patriarchy and at the same time, to defend Freud, whose work is
mired in the patriarchal context.

482. Scully, D.

1980.   MEN WHO CONTROL WOMEN'S HEALTH: THE
          MISEDUCATION OF OBSTETRICIAN-GYNECOLOGISTS.
          Boston: Houghton Mifflin Company.

Examining women's medicine and the male caretakers who
manage it, leads this author to conclude that both nineteenth-and
twentieth-century control practices have produced an "American
health un-care system." Scully documents this criticism by an
empirical examination of male domination over the women's health
care field. For instance, modern resident training in OB-GYN
emphasizes surgery, rather than primary care, a policy that
promotes the financial and professional interests of physicians.
"Aggressive surgical policies," in effect, transform women into

passive, dependent products of medical treatment, and deprive them of control over their own bodies. The author concludes that women's health knowledge and participation in health politics, which is, in part, directed against drug companies and unnecessary obstetrical intervention, can promote the effective use of women as health-care providers. Only this level of participation can effectively alter the current negative situation.

483. Silverman, P.R.

1981.   HELPING WOMEN COPE WITH GRIEF. Los Angeles: Sage Publications.

Grief involves a fracturing of one's identity as a wife or mother, a loss of self esteem, the distancing of friends and relatives, and the onus of a society that regards one as "damaged." These are commonly experienced by women who have suffered the loss of important attachments. Focusing on the plight of widows, women who have given up their children and battered women, Silverman examines the transition of bereaved women from grief to the creation of new lives and new relationships.

Illustrating her analysis with quotes from personal interviews, Silverman provides care givers with a clear framework for helping women who must reshape their lives following the severance of important relationships. Provocative questions lead to an understanding of the bereaved as they go through this reshaping, and pinpoint areas where agency policies may be inappropriate. Practitioners can maximize their assistance to bereaved persons by utilizing the recommended methods. Silverman also makes the case that bereaved women may benefit from association with others who have suffered similar losses -- person-to-person or in mutual-help groups -- in addition to professional care. In HELPING WOMEN COPE WITH GRIEF, human services workers, psychologists, counselors, physicians, researchers, and students in psychology, sociology and women's studies will find a much-needed guide to understanding and assisting bereaved women who must reorient their lives.

484. Smith, W., A. Burlew, M. Mosley, and W. Whitney.

1978.   MINORITY ISSUES IN MENTAL HEALTH. Reading, Massachusetts: Addison-Wesley Publishing Company.

In response to the dearth of research in the area of mental health among minority groups, the authors of this volume seek to enlighten care providers concerning the special problems and needs of minority groups. While the book focuses on problems often encountered by black women, many issues are pertinent to all ethnic women. The authors contend that black women bear the double stigma of being both black and female, as well as economically disadvantaged because of greater unemployment and underemployment, compared with white males, white females and black males. Stresses of professional black women are noted, but since few black women (only 12%) are professional, the authors are primarily concerned with women of lower economic status. The focus is thus multiple: economic discrimination, the matriarchy myth, strength versus dominance in male-female relationships, the shortage of black males, civil rights versus women's rights, black children's vulnerability, sharing pain with black men, the "loose" woman syndrome, defining beauty, and working with the social service system.

Four characteristics are identified as contributing to the resiliency of black women: inner strength, self-pride because of identifying with the black race, concern over femininity, and problem-solving skills.

485. Strouse, J. (ed.)

    1975.   WOMEN AND ANALYSIS: DIALOGUES ON PSYCHOANALYTIC VIEWS OF FEMININITY. New York: Dell Publishing Company, Inc.

Critiques of Freud's ideas about women began long before the current feminist debates. As early as 1926, Karen Horney pointed out that psychoanalysis was in many ways a male-centered psychology.

Is psychoanalysis really a masculine discipline? This book aims to explore this and other questions through a series of dialogues. Jean Strouse chose ten articles written about women by psychoanalysts and asked ten persons from various disciplines to write essays in response to the articles; each response to appear in "dialogue" with its subject.

The book opens with Freud's three theoretical pieces about women with responses by Juliet Mitchell, Elizabeth Janeway and Margaret Mead. Other pairs of essays include Robert Coles on Karen Horney, Marcia Cavell on Helene Deutsch, Barbara Gelpi on Emma Jung, Joel Kovel on Karl Abraham, Ruth Maulton on Clara Thompson and Ethel Person on Marie Bonaparte. In addition, Erik Erikson comments on himself, and Robert Stoller examines Freud's concept of bisexuality.

This volume is sufficiently controversial to promote lively debate.

486. Sturdivant, S.

    1980.   THERAPY WITH WOMEN: A FEMINIST PHILOSOPHY OF TREATMENT. New York: Springer Publishing Co.

Selecting the concept, "philosophy of treatment," as a starting point for a new approach to treating psychological distress in women, the author offers both a much-needed critique of the field and a new feminist theory. Psychotherapy has served as a major form of social control over women, Sturdivant asserts.

Traditional therapies drain power, competence and decision-making abilities from women through their use of expert, coercive and legitimate power. The new feminist therapy rejects "diagnostic labels or patronizing jargon..." nor does it "prescribe treatment." Instead, it is assumed that the therapist's opinions carry no greater weight than those of the client's. In turn, the client is responsible for being the "expert" on her wants and feelings, and for accurately reporting them to the therapist. The "double standard" of mental health, which places a double bind on women, fosters traditional sex roles, devalues women and encourages sexual abuse of the therapeutic relationship. The new feminist therapy, contrariwise, builds new strengths in women, enabling them to be choice-makers through an egalitarian relationship with their therapist.

This is a well-written book that contributes to the growing critical literature on feminist therapy.

487. Woodman, N. and H. Leena.

    1980.   COUNSELING WITH GAY MEN AND WOMEN: A GUIDE FOR FACILITATING POSITIVE LIFE-STYLES. San Francisco, Calif.: Jossey-Bass Publishers.

COUNSELING GAY MEN AND WOMEN explores the minority status of gays and the stigmatization they experience through an historical perspective. Terminology essential for an understanding of the gay experience is presented as a prelude to specific modes of treatment for gay clients. Woodman and Leena portray the struggle that gays experience while passing through the various stages of "coming out." Of special interest is a chapter concerning the problems of gay youth--a subject seldom explored in the professional literature.

The work features three additional themes: resolving individual sexual identity, maintaining a positive self-image and enhancing interpersonal relationships. A chapter on community stresses the resources available to lesbians and gay men, including the utilization of support groups, community centers and professional assistance.

B. Self Help

488. Davis, N.J. and B. Anderson.

1983.   "Beyond Disenchantment: Feminist Health
Movement as Commitment Organization." Pages
282-306 in SOCIAL CONTROL: THE PRODUCTION OF
DEVIANCE IN THE MODERN STATE. New York:
Irvington Publishers, Inc.

The feminist self-help movement, as an outgrowth of the
cultural revolution of the 1960s and 1970s, represented both a
reaction against professional medicine and an "alternative
system;" medicine by and for women. The self-help concept is the
term feminists use for their advocacy version of health care:
women helping women to take over their own bodies without the
dependencies of the standard service-delivery model. Based on
Davis' observations and interviews in 20 radical feminist health
centers in the San Francisco Bay area in 1979, self-help clinics
show distinct organizational strengths and weaknesses. For
example, the ideological commitment of sisterhood and holistic
medicine together with an egalitarian structure promote low-cost,
direct service health care to disadvantaged women and their
children. Such organizations have distinct problems. Lack of
formal boundaries around tasks, asymmetrical relationships with
professional and funding groups and high turnover in personnel,
weaken these organizations' capacity to impact effectively on the
medical environment.
This study documents the feminization of health care as a
broadly defined program to educate women in the anatomy and self
care of the reproductive and genital organs. The program has had
limited success (e.g. self-help breast care). Overall, though,
self-help remains a submerged or nonexistent value in the larger
health care system due to the current nature of monopolistic
medicine.

489. Dreifus, C. (ed.)

1978.   SEIZING OUR BODIES: THE POLITICS OF WOMEN'S
HEALTH. New York: Random House.

This collection of articles provides a feminist critique of
the health-care system and the problems for women that arise from
male control of the health institutions. For instance, the
gynecological surgery of the nineteenth century (e.g.
clitoridectomy and female castration), the dangers of oral
contraception, the scandal of the Dalkon Shield (an intrauterine
device which killed a number of women), the sterilization of poor
women, and the epidemic of unnecessary hysterectomies in the

United States, all raise questions about the safety of the medical care system. Feminist self-help is an uncompromising reaction to the current monopoly by gynecologists' who control women's reproductive health. This book misses little that is wrong with current medical domination. What is less apparent are proposals for revamping this outworn health structure.

490. Frankfort, E.

    1972.   VAGINAL POLITICS. New York: Bantam Books.

    This is a series of indictments of modern medicine and its sexist treatment of women. The author lists the most common abuses, including: general exploitation of women patients, exorbitant prices for pre-legal abortions, high price of drugs, unnecessary hysterectomies, radical mastectomies, and the general mystification and commercialization of American medicine. To counteract powerlessness, Frankfort endorses self-help groups-- women helping women to educate each other about their own bodies.

491. Gordon, L.

    1976.   WOMEN'S BODY, WOMEN'S RIGHT. New York: Viking.

    This history of the birth control movement, written from a feminist perspective, offers a lively and insightful analysis of the struggle to emancipate contraception from its negative label as immoral, and as associated with promiscuous women. The discussion of the sexist biases involved in restricting birth-control information and distribution clarifies how labels serve as significant barriers to a rational health program in human reproduction.

492. Kleiber, N. and L. Light.

    1977.   "Caring for Ourselves: An Alternative Structure for Health Care." REPORT OF THE VANCOUVER WOMEN'S HEALTH COLLECTIVE. University of British Columbia School of Nursing, Vancouver, B.C., Canada.

    This study entails a description and evaluation of the structure and services of a feminist health organization that provides health education and preventive care for women. The report deals extensively with the Collective's non-hierarchical work structure, feminist politics, the emphasis on self-help, and the participation of lay women in the delivery of health care.

210

493. Ruzek, S.B.

1978.   THE WOMEN'S HEALTH MOVEMENT: FEMINIST
          ALTERNATIVES TO MEDICAL CONTROL. New York:
          Praeger Publishers.

Based on fieldwork, formal interviews, informal
interviewing, and review of the feminist health literature, the
author identifies the key feminist issue: who controls women's
bodies?
The book covers a range of health-related issues, including,
conflict in the health-care system, abortion, mastectomy,
feminist body consciousness, sterilization, drugs, childbirth
practices, surgery, self-help gynecology, natural childbirth,
feminine and radical health politics, the social control function
of the physician, science and sexism in contemporary medicine,
sources of sexism in American medicine, male motivation in
obstetrics and health organizations, strategies to redefine the
boundaries of male medical authority, and alternative
institutions.
The author believes that the success of the women's health
movement is still difficult to assess, as with any social
movement that incorporates larger societal drifts. At this point
it is probably impossible to assign specific social changes to
movement activities. Nevertheless, the evidence suggests that the
women's health movement has been influential in supporting the
emerging direction of more control for women over their own
health care.

XVIII

Social Policy

494. Baxter, S. and M. Lansing.

    1980.   WOMEN AND POLITICS: THE INVISIBLE MAJORITY.
               Ann Arbor: The University of Michigan Press.

    Two developments signal the potential for significant social
change in American political behavior. One is the increase in the
number of women who vote and the other is the renaissance of a
women's movement, which aggressively seeks to obtain for women
the rights and responsibilities heretofore offered only to men.
Women now have the opportunity to become "co-signers of the
social contract," the authors say. The book documents the
political standing of American women in the last quarter century
and suggests that earlier studies that depict American women as
apathetic, and as leaving politics to the men in the family, may
require drastic revision. The question is, though, how many women
belong to the political elite and what factors account for their
ascendancy? If women do achieve more clout in political
decisions, is it a difference that makes a difference? The
current political and economic context may work against women
from becoming a visible political majority for some time to come,
unless institutionalized policy changes accomplish quietly and
routinely the goals of the women's movement.

495. Bernard, J.

    1971.   WOMEN AND THE PUBLIC INTEREST: AN ESSAY ON
               POLICY AND PROTEST. Chicago/New York: Aldine
               Atherton.

    Social policy is "constructive social action," which is
"advantageous" for the public interest. But "public interest" is
a difficult goal when "general welfare" has been defined and
programmed by men. Bernard emphasizes the newer policies of
protest based on "movement women" who challenge the status quo,
especially society's expectation that women specialize primarily
in childrearing. The "Women's Movement" revolution is the "most
universal, most humane and most human revolution of all," the
author believes, because it raises the fundamental question: How
can we be human? Social policy which aims at the public interest
may be violating the private well being of women and vice versa.
The family arena will continue to be an area of turmoil because
it appears impossible to reconcile equality and childrearing
under present conditions.

496. Cummings, B. and V. Schuck.

　　1979.　　WOMEN ORGANIZING. Metuchen, N.J.: The
　　　　Scarecrow Press, Inc.

Supporting diverse theories of women's political participation, this study emphasizes the need for women to organize in order to achieve full equality. The book has five sections: Part one explores theoretical alternatives to traditional patterns and attitudes about power. The second section considers women's alienation from society and the frustrations and struggles stemming from discrimination. Part three considers concrete women's organizations, while part four examines the economic problems that confront women who are not financially independent; those with low incomes or who are divorced, widowed or otherwise single. The fifth section includes a view of various aspects of political life, while the final section concludes with issues of discrimination, new occupational roles, inequality in the jury system, and an analysis of the Equal Rights Amendment.

497. Epstein, C.F. and R.L. Coser. (eds.)

　　1981.　　ACCESS TO POWER: CROSS-NATIONAL STUDIES OF
　　　　WOMEN AND ELITES. Boston: Allen and Unwin.

These papers are based on a conference on "Women in Decision-making Elites in Cross-National Perspective," held at Cambridge University in July 1976. They bring together data not easily accessible elsewhere on the structural and ideological factors that influence women's access to elite positions in goverment, business and the professions. The basic findings support Coser's statement: "The higher the rank, prestige or power within an occupation or profession, the smaller is the proportion of women." The reverse also holds true. Where the proportion of women is higher, rewards are substantially lower, as compared with those of men. Yet, there are variations among countries in the degree of change occurring in women's access to elite positions. According to Silver, a contributor to this collection, where women are most likely to attain managerial and executive positions is "in a context characterized by the use of universalistic employment criteria, a commitment to the pursuit of equality and an organizational setting that emphasizes rationality and efficiency without an excessive commitment to profit-making."

Three themes deserve special attention: One is the counterpoint between "feminist" policy initiatives by political elites and their perception of women's potential political influence. A second is the "ghettoization" of women elites into the traditional feminine sphere, such as health, consumer action and child care. Finally, there is the issue of what difference it makes if a few women advance into elite positions. Further research is needed to determine if successful women help to promote other women into the elite structure.

498. Giele, J.Z.

1981.   WOMEN AND THE FUTURE: CHANGING SEX ROLES IN
          MODERN AMERICA. New York: Free Press.

Giele defines, analyzes and evaluates the changes in the
status of women in various cultural spheres: government, work,
family, and community life. In offering a paradigm for reforms in
social organization, the author emphasizes that social justice
depends primarily on sexual justice, that is, for the equal
treatment of women. Policy implications of changing sex roles
implies, then, that changing individual attitudes through
education and socialization also require a massive attack on
deeply entrenched discrimination practices found in all of our
major institutions.

499. Githens, M. and L. Prestage.

1977.   A PORTRAIT OF MARGINALITY: THE POLITICAL
          BEHAVIOR OF THE AMERICAN WOMAN. New York:
          Longman.

Public policy in favor of women's needs and concerns has
been neglected because explicitly or implicitly, women have been
only marginal participants in the political process. These
political scientists assert that part of the problem resides in
female socialization in which learned attitudes, values and
behavior are perceived by women to be inconsistent with political
involvement. More important, though, are the structural hurdles
that prevent women at every step in the political process from
launching successful political careers. Subsequently, policy
outcomes reflect criteria devised for male officeholders. To
offset marginality, women need to develop new perspectives on
women's roles, as well as on politician's roles. Woman-centered
scholarship or action promotes increased political participation
that is also effective for reducing political marginality.

500. Glazer, N. and H.Y. Waehrer.

1977.   WOMEN IN A MAN MADE WORLD. Second Edition.
          New York: Houghton Mifflin.

Glazer and Waehrer's book approaches the study of women from
a Marxist perspective, stressing the economic issues involved in
women's position vis-a-vis men's. Part one of this book focuses
on general perspectives, including historical perspectives on
capitalism, as it has affected women's position in society. The
section also examines the ways in which feminist scholarship
offers a new perspective on history. Part two examines the
subjection of women in more detail from sociological and economic
perspectives. The book concludes with a section on methods for
creating sexual equality.

501. Goldstein, L.F.

    1979.   THE CONSTITUTIONAL RIGHTS OF WOMEN: CASES IN
                LAW AND SOCIAL CHANGE. New York/London:
                Longman.

The human rights issue invariably translates into legal rights. In the United States, due process and equal protection has served as the dual legal structure for promoting, upholding and extending women's legal rights. This book takes a constitutional law perspective to examine abstract legal terms, applying them to controversies of topical interest. Chapter 4, Sex as a Classification, and chapter 5, Women, Procreation and the Right of Privacy, are especially well developed chapters that examine normative and legal questions about women's rights. For instance, did the Supreme Court act as a body of non-accountable decision makers in the abortion case, acting purposely above political pressures because of their superior wisdom and power, as critics allege? How far can the Supreme Court distance itself from prevailing public opinion on highly-debated matters? Again, in the abortion case, women's rights are biological, rather than legal, the author contends. Because it is the woman who is more drastically effected by the denial or granting of the right to contraception and abortion (compared with men), the law must place prior emphasis on women's right to privacy.

This book opens up the women's rights issue as central to democratic social policy.

502. Gross, I., J. Downing, and A. D'Heurle. (eds.)

    1982.   SEX ROLE ATTITUDES AND CULTURAL CHANGE.
                Boston: Kluwer.

These articles address three themes: existing stereotypes limit the options for both females and males throughout the life cycle; social agents influence children's attitudes and behavior in all social settings; and, although the existing knowledge may be inadequate for understanding all the implications for attitude changes, a substantial body of information exists to provide clear direction for change. The book discusses a wide range of specific topics, including sexist language in school, female aspirations, sex-role stereotyping, mental-health standards, overemphasis on the mother role, and voluntary childlessness as a response to contemporary sex roles. The authors emphasize the mental-health problems inherent in traditional sex-role organization and recommend institutional changes.

503. Hutter, B. and G. Williams. (eds.)

    1981.   CONTROLLING WOMEN: THE NORMAL AND THE
                DEVIANT. London: Croom Helm, Ltd.

This edited volume developed out of a series of seminars

organized by Oxford University Women's Studies Committee in 1980.
It is a powerful book about the forms of moral regulation and
social control that are exercised over women. The study of
deviant women cannot be separated from the study of how all women
are defined and controlled, the authors propose. Contributors
examine motherhood, prostitution, abortion, alcoholism,
retirement, aging women, and legal control over sexuality in
Britain. The contributors stress that social control operates
because institutional arrangements are part of everyday routines.
They have, in effect, become part of the natural order of things.
The book identifies some of the ways in which women seek to
resist or circumvent these controls. This work offers a profound
rebuttal to the biological and, especially, sociobiological
interpretations of women's natural roles. We recommend the book
as a first-rate investigation of the central issues in women and
deviance. For policymakers and professionals concerned with the
counselling of women, whether in social, therapeutic or medical
fields, this book is required reading.

504. Jagger, A.M.

     1983.   FEMINIST POLITICS AND HUMAN NATURE. Totowa,
              N.J.: Rowman and Littlefield.

     In the tradition of normative political philosophy begun in
Plato and resuscitated in the last decade by John Rawls, this
unique contribution to feminist social science uses the method of
historical materialism in a more thorough, consistent way than
most Marxists writers to develop the new concept of socialist
feminism. This offers a systematic, philosophical framework that
analyzes the contemporary oppression of women, and indicates the
kinds of social change necessary for reform.
     Claiming that both traditional Marxism and radical feminism
treat the functions of sexuality, childbearing and childrearing
in a biologically determinist way, the author views all aspects
of human nature as dialectically related to human society. Within
the framework of socialist feminism, the author also endeavors to
show that only through such a conception of human nature can we
understand how the status of women has been influenced, but not
determined, by female biology. The book draws upon the radical
feminist critique of traditional political theory in holding that
both liberal and Marxist conceptions of equality, democracy and
freedom are inadequate, and shows that a necessary condition for
women's liberation is a rational restructuring of the "private"
area of life to which women have traditionally been relegated.
Unlike radical feminism, though, the concept of socialist
feminism is not limited by biologically determinist
presuppositions.
     This book is a valuable resource for sociologists, political
scientists, philosophers, and all those interested in the
changing status of women in society. Its intelligent discussion
of criteria for rational choice between competing political
theories suggests new answers to problems that women themselves
have identified in traditional theory.

505. Kelley, R.M. and M. Boutilier.

1978.   THE MAKING OF POLITICAL WOMEN: A STUDY OF
          SOCIALIZATION AND ROLE CONFLICT. Chicago:
          Nelson-Hall.

According to the authors, this study aims to reconceptualize
current thinking in popular literature and the social sciences
about female political socialization. Based on the humanistic
school of psychology (which assumes the equality of men and
women), Kelley and Boutilier examine 36 politically-active women
who have played specific policy-related roles. There is nothing
intrinsic in the political realm that militates against the
participation of women, the authors insist. Macro-level
developments, such as economic and technological growth, indicate
that the numbers of female political participants will continue
to multiply. Thus, political activism by women encourages the
development of an egalitarian sex-role ideology and the demise of
the traditional subordinate female status.

506. Kirkpatrick, J.

1974.   POLITICAL WOMAN. New York: Basic Books, Inc.

In this study of political participation, Kirkpatrick
studies legislative recruitment, socialization and role
performance of 46 women legislators, representing 28 states, who
are contrasted with 40 male legislators. Women are now a relevant
social group in whose name grievances are stated, political
claims are made and demands put forth. Women are also a symbol of
common identity as a result of the women's movement. This means
that women will increasingly be involved in the construction of
public policy. Presenting a profile of the "typical" woman
legislator reveals some surprises. Such women politicos tend to
be small- town persons with middle-class backgrounds who are
geographically stable and active in community service (as were
their parents). The author also discusses legislative
perspectives and roles, and offers an analytic typology of four
legislative styles among women: leaders, moralizers,
personalizers, and problem solvers.

507. Kohn, W.S.G.

1980.   WOMEN IN NATIONAL LEGISLATURES: A COMPARATIVE
          STUDY OF SIX COUNTRIES. New York: Praeger
          Publishers.

Kohn compares the role of women legislators in six Western
countries, discussing the history of women in their governing
bodies, election strategies used, the role played by their
husbands, and the length and impact of their service. He finds
that, although women are playing an increasingly important role
in the legislative process, the total number of women

participants is still quite small proportionate to the total number of women in the population. By examining three English-speaking countries, the United States, Britain and Canada, and three German-speaking countries, West Germany, Switzerland and Austria, Kohn offers a contrast of two distinct sets of electoral systems, in terms of their political impact on women. The book includes a bibliography of basic works.

508. Lapchick, R.E. and S. Urdang.

> 1982.   OPPRESSION AND RESISTANCE: THE STRUGGLE OF
>   WOMEN IN SOUTHERN AFRICA. Westport,
>   Connecticut: Greenwood Press.

South Africa's policy of apartheid (enforced racial separation and inequality) has been discussed, debated and condemned in virtually every corner of the world. South Africa's huge black majority, say the authors, suffers from the oppression of its inhumane system. Black South African women, discriminated against because of their sex, as well as their race, suffer the most. In fact, they may be the most oppressed group in the world today. Yet very little international attention has been paid to their special plight.

OPPRESSION AND RESISTANCE explores both the tragic position of black women in South Africa and their remarkable efforts to liberate themselves. The introduction traces the history and workings of the apartheid system, after which the authors examine the effects of apartheid on the social, economic and political status of black women in both urban and rural areas of South Africa and Namibia. Special attention is paid to discrimination against black women in education, health care, employment, and social security.

The book's second section is devoted to the role of women in the struggle for national liberation in Zimbabwe and South Africa. The authors find that women, despite their disadvantaged position, have been in the forefront of the liberation movements in both nations.

OPPRESSION AND RESISTANCE is a critically important addition to our understanding of the dangerous political situation in southern Africa and prospects for its resolution. International women's rights will be enhanced by the findings and insights.

509. Masi, D.A.

> 1981.   ORGANIZING FOR WOMEN: ISSUES, STRATEGIES AND
>   SERVICES. Lexington, Mass.: Lexington Books.

Masi provides a theoretical framework for community organization and applies it to women's groups and issues. She then extends this feminist-oriented analysis to the human services field, where most policies and programs are designed and administered by men for women clients. She goes on to suggest effective strategies for correcting deficiencies in the workplace and in government agencies. Case studies of community organizations applied to four women's programs illustrate this approach. Notable chapters include chapter 5, "Woman as Victim," and chapter 6, "Woman as Bureaucratic Object."

510. McCormack, M.

1977.   "A Feminist Perspective." SOCIAL POLICY.
          8(3):18-23.

After discussing social pressures on the consumer, Margaret McCormack demonstrates how a feminist consumer-education program would be a good asset for all women, rather than a select few. She discusses three major problem areas that plague women: transportation, housing and health care, and explains how a feminist consumer education program could transform each into a feminist economics program. Ms. McCormack states that such a program would take into consideration economics, ecology, politics, and all forms of discrimination: age, race, physical handicap, class, and sex. These programs would be aimed at coalition building for women, and at reducing the isolation of women. McCormack contends: "Only broadbased, strong political coalitions can bring about desired change."

511. O'Connor, K.

1980.   WOMEN'S ORGANIZATIONS' USE OF THE COURTS.
          Lexington, Mass.: Lexington Publishers.

The author states that an analysis of litigation from the latter part of the nineteenth century to the present time involves two concerns: one, the pursuit of women's rights and interests through court action. This involves an issue of intrinsic importance to the status of women; and two, the role of interest group litigation in the formulation of those issues and cases which are brought before the court. Three distinct modes of litigation activity are described: litigation for publicity, direct sponsorship of cases for desired policy outcomes and participation as friend of the court. The author discusses particular cases, and shows examples of "model litigants" who have worked at the fore of Supreme Court gender-based litigation. Strategies are shown to vary historically and situationally. The author emphasizes that, in some instances, interest groups have had to "wait out" the Court until a favorable social climate occurs. Sex discrimination and abortion cases are included as typical sources of court litigation.

512. Rossi, A.S.

1982.   FEMINISTS IN POLITICS: A PANEL ANALYSIS OF
            THE FIRST NATIONAL WOMEN'S CONFERENCE. New
            York: Academic Press.

This volume reports the results of the panel study of
participants in the first national women's conference in Houston
in 1977. Based on questionnaires administered before and after
the meeting, this work examines the impact of participation in
the conference on the political beliefs, activities and goals of
1300 feminist leaders who served as delegates, staff members or
commissioners. Substantive analytical topics cover an array of
themes, including: (1)belief and emotional structures that
differentiate members of elite political caucuses; (2)use of
political biographical data to test a model of women's political
development; (3)determination of aspirations for holding office
in mainstream and feminist politics; and (4)the impact of
participation in political network-building. This first-of-a-kind
study is significant because it examines the leadership of an
important contemporary socio-political movement by utilizing
quantitative methods rarely applied to similar social movements.
This is a rich data source, which should be useful to social
scientists.

513. Schur, E. M.

1984.   LABELING WOMEN DEVIANT: GENDER, STIGMA AND
            SOCIAL CONTROL. New York: Random House.

Feminist theory has recognized for some time that social
stigma is a key mechanism that backs up and enforces many of the
restrictions and limitations placed on women. Now, a
distinguished sociologist of deviance reasserts the link between
gender stereotyping, female devaluation and "the reproduction of
male dominance in everyday processes" that control female
behavior. "Between pervasive stigmatization, on the other hand,
and low status acquisition on the other, women are liable to lose
either way," Schur says. In this way, deviant women are socially
produced." To offset informal as well as formal deviance
labeling, policy studies should focus on the reaction process and
the official labelers (i.e., men in hierarchical positions. On
the more practical level, consciousness-raising groups,
assertiveness training and women's medical self-help programs all
work to help women to surmount devaluation. This is a highly
recommended treatment of the deviant-creating processes that
women universally experience in all societies and social
organizations.

514. Spiro, M.E.

    1980.   GENDER AND CULTURE. KIBBUTZ WOMEN REVISITED.
                New York: Schocken Books.

    Spiro takes a new look at social relations in the
contemporary kibbutz and asks to what extent and in what domains
can sex roles be changed by social and cultural engineering. He
discribes the counter-revolution that has occurred in
orientations to marriage, the family and work in the kibbutz
movement. A significant sequel to his pioneering KIBBUTZ: VENTURE
IN UTOPIA, social policies on women in Western societies can
benefit from this careful examination of women's issues in a
society geared for change.

514. Stewart, D.W.

    1980.   WOMEN IN LOCAL POLITICS. Metuchen, N.J.: The
                Scarecrow Press, Inc.

    This study documents the official participation of women in
legislative, judicial, executive, administrative, and political
party organizations. The book covers a wide range of concerns
from leadership selection to the enactment of official roles.
Using the established analytical paradigms of political science
and policy studies, the volume presents current data on women in
local politics. The empirical research for all ten articles was
completed under the sponsorship of the Center for the American
Woman and Politics and Eagleton Institute of Politics at Rutgers
University. This empirical study explores sex attitudes and
attributes as a growing political arena for American women.

516. Stimpson, C.R. (ed.)

    1979.   "Women and the American City." SIGNS: JOURNAL
                OF WOMEN IN CULTURE AND SOCIETY. 5(3):Special
                Issue.

    This special issue offers a collection of studies addressed
to the relationship between women and their adaptation in the
larger environment of the city. For example, Hurst and
Zambrana's examination of the health-care strategies of poor
Hispanic and black women in Harlem required women to study women
in this area of special concern. Many of the studies by women in
this issue deal with the community: the Community Action
Strategies To Stop Rape and an evaluation of a rape prevention
program for a grassroots feminist group. Other participant-
observation studies include analysis of a suburban women's self-
help network; a description of an ongoing investigation of the
role of urban and suburban organization of mothers in adopting
educational innovations; and other intensive research studies of
community participation by women.
    Jo Freeman's analysis of the implications of urban policy

for women deserves careful attention. On the whole, these articles indicate that, despite its disadvantages, the city offers more opportunity and freedom to women than does the suburb.

SUBJECT INDEX

Alcoholics Anonymous, 54, 57, 58
abortion, vii, viii, 3, 17, 28,
    43-51, 57, 121, 175-195, 204,
    210-211, 215-216, 219
adolescent, 41, 59, 67-69, 81-85
affective disorder, 161
agoraphobia, 200
Al-anon, 59
alcohol, vii, viii, 37, 52-61, 75,
    126, 128, 152, 169, 172, 202, 216
alienation, 17
ambisexual, 151
androgyny, 62
anorexia nervosa, 156, 157, 161, 163,
    164, 200
apartheid, 218

battering, ix, 72, 74-77, 206
beastiality, 88
Bem Sex Role Inventory, 185
Bible, 97
bibliography, iv, v, vi, 1, 11, 18,
    19, 89, 118, 171, 198, 202, 217
bipolar manic-depressive, 161
birth control, 27, 43-51, 125, 210
bisexuality, 62-63, 207
black women, 11, 17, 34, 39, 40, 54,
    55, 57, 59, 60, 86, 87, 106, 136,
    138, 142, 150, 160, 168, 170,
    171, 177, 178, 184-187, 200, 203,
    205-207, 218, 221
bondage, 88, 91
breast cancer, 204

Capitalism, 11, 17, 20, 28-30, 39-41,
    81, 90, 99, 112, 214
caste, 2
castration, 209
Cattell's 16-PF test, 147
censorship, 88, 94, 95, 106
child abuse, 75, 81-85, 176, 204
Chicano, 4
childcare, 17, 171, 178, 188

children, vii, ix, 14, 31, 37, 42, 43,
    49, 55, 56, 74, 81-85, 150, 153,
    158, 161, 164, 166, 176, 196,
    204, 206, 207, 137-139, 141, 146,
    148, 149, 209, 211, 212, 215, 216
class, 3, 5, 11, 17, 19, 20, 24, 26,
    31, 32, 40, 41, 46, 53, 56, 85,
    117, 133, 138, 145, 152, 167,
    186, 198, 202, 217
clitoredectomy, 22, 209
Commission on Obscenity and
    Pornography, 98, 103, 106, 107
Communism, 26
Consciousness raising, 220
Contagious Diseases Act, 134
contraception, 58, 175-195, 209,
    215
corsets, 32
corrections, 64-71
crime, viii, 27, 30, 43, 72-134
criminal justice system, 50, 64-71,
    77, 80, 86, 87, 111, 112,
    114-116, 118, 122, 123, 126
cross cultural, iv, v, vi, 4, 5, 9,
    13, 14, 22-42, 45, 113, 114,
    138, 217, 218
cruising, 144

Dalkon Shield, 209
Daughters of Bilitis, 154
death, 28, 198, 204
delinquency, 64, 113, 114, 120-124
depression, viii, xi, 53, 55, 60, 84,
    141, 156, 159, 161, 163, 165,
    166, 172-174, 200, 201
deviance, iv, vi, vii, x, xi, 10, 11,
    16, 17, 43, 55, 94, 100, 114,
    117, 120, 125-130, 133, 134,
    138, 146, 163, 164, 178, 213, 220
divorce, vii, 45, 55, 57, 85, 135-
    142, 169, 202, 203, 213
Draw-A-Person test, 154
drugs, vii, viii, 43, 52-61, 126,
    128, 130, 190, 201, 202, 206,
    210, 211
domestic violence, 72-87

self help, vii, 197, 200, 203, 206, 209-211, 220, 221
separation, 135-142
sex discrimination, 2, 3, 7, 8, 11, 19, 32, 59, 65, 66, 70, 84, 112, 122, 123, 149, 153, 162, 168, 169, 201, 203, 213, 214, 218, 219
sex differentiation, 5, 9, 10, 12, 14, 19, 38, 92, 93, 114, 116, 119, 124, 144, 158-160, 162, 174, 185, 192, 196, 198, 207
sex education, xi, 175-195
sexism, 2, 11, 13, 17, 37, 59, 99, 117-119, 162, 210, 211, 215
sex ratio, 6
sex roles, iv, v, viii, 2-15, 16, 25, 32, 34, 37, 39, 41, 42
sexual abuse, 81-85, 208
sexual harrassment, 8, 37, 76
sexual identity, 62
sexuality, vi, x, 2, 5, 6, 14, 17, 22, 24, 27, 97, 109, 110, 130, 133, 149, 153, 170, 175, 178, 182
sexual stratification, ii
singles, 169-171, 213
skid row, 57, 59, 168, 169
social change, viii, 14, 16, 24, 33, 42, 180, 199, 211, 212, 215
social control, iv, v, vi, vii, ix, xi, 6, 17, 21, 27, 84, 119, 123, 128, 159, 201, 209, 211, 215-216
socialism, 20, 26, 39, 41, 42, 216
socialization, 5, 12, 13, 14, 17, 42, 214, 217
social organization, 19
social security, 218
social structure, viii, 6, 13, 31, 39, 177
Standard Thematic Apperceptive Test, 7
sterilization, 209, 211
stigma, 45, 59, 62, 127, 150, 152, 169, 170, 196, 206, 208, 220
stress, 13, 53, 56, 166, 179, 180, 203
strikes, 66
sufferage, 25, 29

suicide, viii, 10, 53, 55, 60, 84, 141, 143, 152, 172-174, 190
symbolic-interactionist, 57

teenage pregnancy, vii, 48, 160, 161, 163-165, 169, 175-195
television, 14, 15, 189
temperance, 23
therapy, 10, 17, 53-56, 58, 60, 83, 85, 150, 151, 156, 157, 159-161, 163, 173, 180, 200-211
treatment, 46, 53, 57-60, 68, 80, 83, 85, 151, 155-158, 200-211

Urban and Rural Systems Associates, 132
U.S. Commission on Obscenity and Pornography, 106
U.S. Department of Labor, 71

venereal disease, 108, 128, 182, 184
voyeurism, 128

welfare, 167, 168
white slavery, 133
widowhood, vii, 45, 55, 135-142, 169, 174, 203, 206, 213
wife, 31, 35, 39, 40, 41, 53, 59, 135-142, 206
wife battering, 72, 73, 115
witch, 16, 17, 32
witchcraft, 14, 16, 27, 28, 37
women and change, 1
women's liberation, 17
women's movement, viii, x, 16, 21, 38, 212
women's studies, 22, 42
work, iv, 2, 8, 11, 13, 17, 20, 24, 26, 31, 32, 34, 35, 41, 42, 49, 53, 57, 59, 71, 112, 125-134, 138, 144, 151, 153, 158, 167-169, 191, 196, 198, 207, 210, 213, 214, 217, 218, 220

234